5.25
C

K/r
1/7,

D1535456

YSEULT BRIDGES

Two Studies in Crime

The Murder of Lord William Russell

The accused: François Benjamin Courvoisier

The Murder of Julia Wallace

The accused: William Herbert Wallace

HUTCHINSON OF LONDON

HUTCHINSON & CO. (*Publishers*) LTD
178–202 Great Portland Street, London, W.1

London Melbourne Sydney
Auckland Bombay Toronto
Johannesburg New York

First published 1959

*This book has been set in Baskerville type face. It has
been printed in Great Britain by The Anchor Press,
Ltd., in Tiptree, Essex, on Antique Wove paper and
bound by Taylor Garnett Evans & Co., Ltd., in
Watford, Herts*

Author's Note and Acknowledgements

No case in the calendar of our Courts is of more compelling interest, both criminological and social, than the murder of Lord William Russell in 1840; no case possessed so many unusual features, or had so dramatic and unique a climax; no case is better documented in contemporary literature, or has been so neglected since; and it would be hard to find in the ranks of criminals a more remarkable personality than the young assassin, François Benjamin Courvoisier.

Between life in the exclusive circle of Mayfair at the dawn of the Victorian age and life in a drab quarter of Liverpool ninety-one years later there is a whole world of difference, but murder knows no restrictions of time or space and its principal motives—sex, money and revenge—remain the same.

Money was the underlying cause of Lord William Russell's violent end; in that of Julia Wallace the motive was further to seek, and, it will be here suggested, was more subtle than any yet advanced. But the two cases are linked by that well-attested phenomenon, 'the drift of imitation in crime'.

I should like to acknowledge my indebtedness to the many who, ever since the publication of my first venture as an historian of crime, have been urging me to devote my attention to the Wallace case, sometimes accompanying their persuasions with gifts of literature on the subject. I sincerely trust that this, my response, will prove my appreciation.

To Mr Victor Bridges I wish to express my warm thanks for much kindness through many years, and for allowing me to have photographed the miniature of his great-great-grandfather, Lord William Russell, and Lord William's snuff-box, and to reproduce them here. My gratitude is also due to Mr John Stuffins, F.L.A., of Harrogate, for the valuable assistance he so generously gave me; and to the Librarian of the

AUTHOR'S NOTE AND ACKNOWLEDGEMENTS

Inner Temple for allowing me to consult the archives of that Inn. I should like to express to Mr Cherry Kearton, director of Hutchinson, my deep appreciation of the patience he has shewn over the length of time it has taken me to write this book, and finally I should like to take this opportunity of recording how greatly my husband has assisted with all my work.

CASE ONE

The Murder of
Lord William Russell

THE ACCUSED

François Benjamin Courvoisier

'No advocate in any circumstances should ever permit
himself to assert his own belief in the merits of the case
which he is arguing, or in the innocence of the prisoner
whom he is defending. The moment he does so he steps
outside his role of advocate.'

SIR JOHN SINGLETON

Contents

ILLUSTRATIONS

Background to Murder

'Man is his star, and the soul that can
Render an honest and a perfect man
Commands all light, all influence, all fate:
Nothing in him falls early, or too late.'[1]

I

IN 1840 Park Lane, its houses charming in their irregularity
and variety, and the network of little streets behind it
already formed one of London's most fashionable quarters.
Few of the houses in these little streets were particularly large—
indeed a number were quite small—and few had any pretensions to architectural distinction; yet all wore an air of dignity
and refinement, conferred upon them through occupation by
an aristocracy which still retained much of the eighteenth
century's elegance, as well as its scepticism and frivolity though
these were steadily being displaced by a new sense of decorum
evoked by the accession of the girl-queen and soon to percolate
throughout her Kingdom and ever-expanding Empire.

The area behind Park Lane constituted a serene little
backwater in the 'wealthiest city of the world', about which the
tide of noise and bustle, of vice and violence, might ebb and
flow, but by which it was never swamped—until that morning
of 6th May 1840 when it swamped Norfolk Street lying in its
very heart.

The houses were still drowsing in the early sunshine and
within them the servants, scarcely astir, had not yet folded back
the window shutters, when suddenly the front door of No. 14
was flung wide and a distracted housemaid rushed down the

[1] John Fletcher, 1579–1625.

steps and across the street to tug frantically at the bell of a house opposite. Getting no immediate response she ran back again to tug at that of No. 22, and even as she did so a footman opened the door of the house where first she had rung. Turning, she called to him in a voice of panic:

'Go fetch the police, Young! Go quickly! His lordship's in bed and there's blood all over the pillow, like he's been murdered!'

As Young obediently set off at a run, she besought the servant who had now appeared at No. 22 to hurry to Cleveland Row and summon the surgeon, Mr John Nursey. Then back she sped and closed the door of No. 14 behind her.

How swiftly the sense of catastrophe will spread! In a matter of moments window shutters were being folded back and eyes were peering from behind curtains. How quickly word of it will speed from lip to lip! Within the briefest space of time footsteps were echoing along the pavement and converging on No. 14. A brougham drove up, and the whisper went about: 'The doctor!' A trap drawn by a fast-trotting horse clattered up: there was no mistaking that vehicle, or the two men who sprang from it almost before it had stopped: 'The Metropolitan Police!'

And so the muddy waters of crime eddied into Norfolk Street and overflowed from it in all directions; and since it was easier to believe almost anything of that exclusive little thoroughfare than that one of its residents had been murdered in his bed, the rumour spread that Lord William Russell, uncle of the Duke of Bedford and of Lord John Russell, Secretary of State for the Colonies,[1] had committed suicide. By noon it had reached Buckingham Palace, and gravely Prince Albert informed the Queen. She was shocked, and ordered a messenger to be sent forthwith to make inquiries at Lord John's residence.

Lord John responded in person and was immediately granted an audience. White-faced and shaken, he told Her Majesty that his uncle had not taken his own life: he had been murdered while he slept.

---

[1] Later three times Prime Minister. Created first Earl Russell (1861). Great-grandfather of Bertrand Russell.

LORD WILLIAM RUSSELL

(From a miniature in the possession of Victor Bridges, Esq.)

The life which had been closed by a treacherous act of violence in the small hours of that May morning had opened seventy-three years earlier, also under the shadow of tragedy. Shortly before Lord William's birth his father, the Marquess of Tavistock—the Duke of Bedford's heir—had met his death as the result of an accident in the hunting-field, and his mother had died while he was still an infant.

For a short while he had occupied a seat in Parliament, but a delicate constitution and a preference for scholarship and the arts combined to prevent him from taking an active part in public life. His two brothers succeeded in turn as fifth and sixth Dukes of Bedford, and he found an outlet for his considerable talents in advising and assisting the latter[1] to acquire those famous pieces of sculpture which still adorn the gallery at Woburn.

The happiest years of his life were spent at Geneva with his wife and their family of seven children.[2] Her death in 1808 was a blow from which he never fully recovered. With a sensitivity which today would be regarded as morbid he always carried on his person a gold locket containing a curl of her hair, and kept on his bedside table her miniature painted on ivory, while the bed itself he always had made up with the two pillows side by side as it had been when she had been alive to share it with him.

In 1825 he suffered another bereavement in the death of his eldest son, Captain George Russell, R.N., but in spite of these losses, in spite of increasing deafness and the curtailment of his activities by a severe rupture which necessitated his wearing a truss day and night, he retained a vital interest in art, scholarship and the world of affairs.

With his daughters married and his sons settled in life, he had found in 14 Norfolk Street a house large enough to take his books, his collections of fine porcelain and rare prints, and

[1] The 6th Duke of Bedford had died the previous November—1839.
[2] He married, in 1789, Lady Charlotte Villiers, daughter of the 4th Earl of Jersey, and had four sons and three daughters.

yet small enough to be run by a staff of two women servants and a butler-valet and still afford him that life of comfortable simplicity and smooth routine which both his tastes and his health demanded.

It was a typical London house of its size and period. Steps led down from the pavement to the basement, where a door opened into a passage giving access, in turn, to the kitchen, the scullery and the butler's pantry, and, passing the foot of the service-stairs, ended at another door opening into a small paved backyard enclosed on its other three sides by high, whitewashed walls.

On the ground-floor the front door opened into a similar passage, off which was the dining-room, a cloak-room and water-closet, the head of the service-stairs and the foot of the staircase to the upper storeys; and it, too, ended at a door, glass-panelled on this floor, outside which a flight of steps led down into the backyard.

The three storeys above each consisted of a large front-room communicating with a smaller one behind it, forming, on the first-floor, a drawing-room and writing-room, and, on the second, Lord William's bedroom and an unused dressing-room. The bedroom was entered from the landing by a baize-covered door which closed silently on a spring-hinge. Across the landing another door shut off the stairs to the top storey. Here the front-room—the one above Lord William's bedroom—was shared by Sarah Mancer, the housemaid who had given the alarm, and Mary Hannel the cook. Both were verging on middle-age and had entered Lord William's service three years' previously with 'unexceptionable characters'. The back-room was occupied by the butler-valet, who, until five weeks before the crime, had been one James Ellis. He had been in Lord William's service even longer than the two maidservants, but had then left to 'better himself' in the employment of the Earl of Mansfield.

From among those who had applied for the situation as his successor Lord William had selected a young Swiss named François Benjamin Courvoisier, who was furnished with the highest testimonials from those who had previously employed him during the four years he had been in England.

When the police took their first statements from the

servants on that May morning, Mary Hannel and Sarah Mancer both told them that they and Courvoisier were on good terms. This may have been broadly true, but it was presently to emerge that the harmony and efficiency with which the domestic wheels had revolved in James Ellis' day had departed with him. It seemed that the young Swiss had often irritated the two women servants by his flippancy and irresponsibility, and had been causing their master increasing annoyance by a growing carelessness and forgetfulness in the performance of his duties. Nevertheless he had always contrived to reinstate himself in the good graces of them all by the exercise of a peculiarly ingratiating manner. Whether the cook was less susceptible to this than the rest of the household, or whether she had some other reason to mistrust or dislike the valet is unknown, but on 1st May—five days before Lord William's murder—she gave her employer a month's notice, saying no more than that she 'desired a change'.

3

Courvoisier provides an outstanding example of the cynical young man who, with everything in his favour, deliberately chooses to follow the path of crime.

Born near Geneva—where his victim had formerly resided so happily—his eminently respectable parents had given him an excellent education which befitted him to occupy a position as secure as their own. His mind was quick; French was his native tongue, but he quickly learned to read English, and to speak it grammatically and colloquially. His body was strong, agile and graceful, and soon he became an accomplished dancer. He was a skilful carver and executed intricate designs in wood, bone and ivory. He also became an expert juggler able to perform feats of *legerdemain* with ambidextrous adroitness. He could adapt his manner to suit any company in which he found himself, meeting his elders and social superiors with a suave blending of deference and confidence; mingling with those of a lower station with a free-and-easy cordiality. Few could resist his charm.

From an early age, however, he had shewn an incurable propensity towards falsehood and deceit. This increased as he grew up and, along with it, went a liking for the society of undesirable acquaintances, and a dislike of any settled occupation. At the age of nineteen he absconded from home and made his way to London. His money at an end, he took the first job he could get, as bar-boy and bottle-washer at a small hotel in Soho. But in a month's time he was taken on as a waiter at the Hotel Bristol, Jermyn Street, whence he entered private service, winning the golden opinion of each of his employers. Always proud of his talents, he took every occasion to display them—except his gift for *legerdemain* which caution prompted him to conceal, but of which he was to make considerable use when suspicion fastened on him after the crime, as we shall see.

The impression he created in the minds of those who knew him finds ample expression in a paragraph which appeared in the *Dumfries Courier* after his arrest and was widely quoted in London journals.

'Courvoisier, when in the service of Mr Fector, M.P., resided on the banks of the Cairn and was well known in the surrounding district. He was remarked by all to be a most attentive servant, not only to his immediate employers, but to any of their friends and visitors, and always conducted himself in such a manner as to appear a trustworthy person. He once figured at a wedding at Thornhill, when his dancing powers were much admired, and we were shewn a ring which he presented to his partner on this festive occasion. This trinket, which appeared to be of bone, curiously ornamented, was of his own manufacture, and did great credit to his ingenuity and neatness of hand.'

He kept himself extremely well-groomed, and, in spite of a low, narrow and receding brow, which bulged curiously at either side, gave the impression of being good-looking; but in profile his head was so flat at the back as to appear almost wedge-shaped. His complexion was habitually pale; his abundant hair was straw-coloured, smooth and sleek. His voice, too, was smooth and sleek—indeed everything about him was smooth and sleek, and his movements so sinuous and soundless as to suggest the feline.

As a junior manservant in the large establishments where he had previously worked he had been subjected to rigorous discipline at the hands of a first footman and butler, and he had been kept fully occupied; but as the sole manservant at 14 Norfolk Street he was independent of everyone but his master, and took precedence 'below stairs', while his duties were light— too light, for there were long hours when he had nothing whatever to do. Many of these he spent shut up in his pantry— the manservant's special preserve—reading an assortment of books and periodicals dealing with the careers and exploits of notorious criminals, and he was later to confess how he longed to emulate them, how he planned his own crime, and how careful were the steps he took towards putting it into execution.

Such, then, was the background against which this crime was committed; such, briefly, are the life-stories of murderer and victim.

Thomas Campbell's proverbial lines that 'coming events cast their shadows before' are particularly apposite in cases of domestic murder, but all too often the shadow passes unnoticed by those athwart whom it falls until after the event which cast it has occurred.

We will now follow the course of events in that small household on the day preceding the crime, and watch the gathering of the shadows which were to herald the event.

2

14 Norfolk Street

'The desire of money is the root of all evil, and they that
lust after it pierce themselves with many arrows.'[1]

O N THAT morning Sarah Mancer got up at six o'clock
as usual to begin her day's work. Since Courvoisier was
apt to be lazy and unpunctual she had made a habit of
knocking on his door as she went downstairs, and to keep on
knocking until she got a response.

She had a great deal to do—re-laying the fires, sweeping and
dusting—and had been at work about half an hour when Mary
Hannel came down to re-kindle the kitchen range and to put on
the kettles for Lord William's hot water, which the valet would
carry up to his bedroom at eight o'clock. Then the servants had
their breakfast, and at nine o'clock Lord William would appear
in the dining-room for his. As soon as he had finished he would
go up to the writing-room on the floor above to scan the daily
paper and attend to his correspondence, for, like most of his
generation, he exchanged long, discursive letters with a large
circle of relatives and friends. This done, he would ring for the
valet and give him his orders for the day. On this particular
Tuesday he did so at about 12.30. Telling him that he would
be lunching out, Lord William gave him some letters to post
and various verbal messages to deliver. Among the latter was
one to his coachman York, who lived over the mews belonging
to the house, and another to an upholsterer to request him to
come and tighten the bell-wire in his bedroom. Ten minutes

[1] I Timothy x, 6.

18

later, the day being mild and sunny, Lord William left the house on foot, walking with the aid of a stick.

Up to this moment Sarah Mancer had noticed nothing unusual in Courvoisier's manner. The first hint of anything amiss came when he, she and the cook sat down to their dinner in the kitchen at 12.45. The valet grumbled that his lordship had given him 'five messages to deliver'.

'I'm afraid I shall forget some of them,' he said. 'One is to tell York to call for him at Brooks's with the phaeton at five o'clock.' Then he asked: 'What is Brooks's?'

'It's a club,' Sarah Mancer informed him.

That was all, but much was to develop out of it.

Dinner over, Courvoisier went out. When he returned at about 4.30 the upholsterer's man was waiting to be told what to do. The valet took him upstairs and shewed him. While he was thus engaged a friend and former fellow-servant in the Park Lane establishment of Mr Fector, Member of Parliament for Dover, named Henry Carr, looked in to see him. The kitchen table was laid for tea and Courvoisier invited him to join them, taking the seat at its head with his back to the window. Thus it was that when York came down the area steps the former did not see him until he had entered the door. Glancing first at York and next at the clock, the hands of which stood at 5.15, the valet exclaimed:

'Oh! You ought to be at Brooks's now, but I forgot to tell you! I'm afraid his lordship will be angry—he said five o'clock.' Then he added with a shrug: 'I shall tell him I understood him to say half past five.'

As York hurried away to harness his horses Sarah Mancer said severely:

'You had better tell his lordship the truth.'

'I shall tell him he said half past five,' retorted the valet. 'He is very forgetful sometimes, and must pay for his forgetfulness.' Then, pushing back his chair, he invited Henry Carr into his pantry, shutting the door behind them both.

Since the pantry was to be the scene of several of the forthcoming events it merits some description. The window overlooked the walled backyard and beneath it was a sink with a water supply. Against one wall stood a large press, its upper half fitted with baize-lined shelves and drawers for plate, its lower part fitted as a cellarette, with racks for tumblers and wineglasses. The keys of the press, like those of the pantry itself, were in Courvoisier's custody. Behind the door stood a table and a couple of chairs. Upon these last the valet and his friend now seated themselves. Whether they partook of any of the wines and spirits in the cellarette is not recorded, but the valet was to confess that he had sometimes done so and was to do so again at ever shorter intervals during the course of that evening and night. However they were soon interrupted by an indignant peal on the front-door bell which announced the return of Lord William by hackney-cab.

Mary Hannel, who corroborated Sarah Mancer's evidence as to the events just related, stated that they both heard the valet admit Lord William, and heard them go into the dining-room directly above the kitchen, and, although they could not hear what was being said, they got the impression that his lordship was taking Courvoisier severely to task for his failure to carry out his orders. Shortly afterwards the former went upstairs and the latter returned to the kitchen, where he told the two women, and Henry Carr, that 'his lordship was angry at first, but good-tempered afterwards,' adding suavely: 'I soon persuaded him that the mistake had been entirely his own.'

In the written confession in which he was later to acknowledge his guilt he admits that this was not the truth, and that when the writing-room bell summoned him thither about a quarter of an hour later Lord William handed him two letters with the words: 'I have been compelled to write these owing to your incompetence. You are to take them to the mews for York to deliver by hand, and you will bring back the dog with you.' But the valet said nothing of this when he and his friend subsequently left the house together; he took the letters to the mews and returned promptly with the dog, which was kennelled there, and which Lord William now took for a run in the Park.

The time was then about six o'clock. Courvoisier had gone back to his pantry whence he was called by Sarah Mancer and asked to carry the step-ladder, which the upholsterer's man had been using, out into the yard.

At 7 p.m. Lord William sat down to dinner, and as usual

he was waited upon by Courvoisier; and as usual he afterwards went up to the drawing-room where Sarah Mancer had closed the shutters, drawn the curtains and placed his reading-lamp on the table beside his armchair near the fire. As usual, too, York called to fetch the dog at nine o'clock, and as usual Lord William rang for his China tea at ten o'clock.

As soon as she had served Lord William's dinner Mary Hannel announced her intention of going out, and took herself off, leaving Sarah Mancer to have supper *tête-à-tête* with the valet, who, the latter stated in evidence, seemed 'out of temper'. He began by referring to the cook's absence and went on to say that she had been right to give notice; he could not imagine, he said, why either she or Sarah Mancer herself had stayed so long in his lordship's service. For his part he wished he had never entered it. 'I shall not remain in it long,' he declared. 'His lordship is too fussy.' He went on to say that at Easter— which Lord William had spent at the Castle Hotel, Richmond —his lordship had been 'cross and peevish, and had changed his room three times'. While there—and it was the first Sarah Mancer had heard of it—'his lordship had lost a gold locket and had made a great deal of fuss over it'.

Brought up in the best traditions of domestic service she doubtless regarded the valet's references to their employer as devoid of that respect which was due to him on account of his age as well as his rank, and no doubt consoled herself with the reflection that he was a foreigner, so knew no better. But his next remark completely scandalized her: 'Billy is a rum old chap,' he said. 'If I had half his money, I wouldn't remain long in England.'

As Courvoisier was coming downstairs after taking up Lord William's tea at ten o'clock the front-door bell rang and he found the cook awaiting admittance. Why she should have conferred upon herself the privilege of entering this way, instead of through the area, was never explained, but at least it allowed her to testify that she heard Courvoisier lock and bolt the door, and put up the chain, as she went along the passage to the service-stairs, down which he followed her.

Two incidents then took place which deserve attention. The valet, in a sudden access of affability, volunteered to go out and fetch the cook some beer to drink with her belated supper. He had never made such an offer before, but he promptly went out to fulfil it, leaving and returning by the area door. When he returned he locked the door behind him, and instead of leaving the key in the lock, as was usual, he brought it into the kitchen and put it on the table. He then filled a tankard for the cook, while Sarah Mancer accepted 'a small glass'. Replying to a question about that beer she was to state: 'I think something had been put into it. Soon after drinking it I began to feel drowsy.'

That Courvoisier drugged the beer in order to ensure that the two women should fall asleep quickly, and sleep too heavily to be disturbed by any sounds emanating from below, seems a fair inference.

It was now about 10.15. The evening had turned chilly, and Sarah Mancer, on her way upstairs to prepare Lord William's bedroom for the night, looked in at the drawing-room to ask him if she should light the fire there. He was sitting in his armchair reading, and, glancing up over his spectacles, signified assent. This, she testified, was the last time she saw him alive. Then, lighting her way with a tallow candle, she went up to his bedroom and entered it by the baize-covered door from the landing.

Like the rest of the house this room was elegantly furnished, and practically every object she could behold within it—and some she could not—were to propound both a puzzle and a paradox to the police rather less than twelve hours later. To appreciate this, we must follow her closely as she moves about the room.

To her right as she entered stood a curtained four-poster, near the wall but with ample space to allow passage between the two. Its head was towards the door, but, owing to its curtains, it was impossible to see whether it was occupied or not without going round to the side. The foot was towards the first of three windows which overlooked Norfolk Street.

She set down her tallow candle, crossed to the fireplace at the far end of the room and lit the fire. In the recess of one side of the chimney-breast stood a dressing-table, on which were arranged the gold-mounted fittings of Lord William's dressing-case and a leather case containing a pair of ivory-handled razors. All these articles were engraved with the Russell crest—a goat *statant*. Several rings, some pearl studs and a couple of pairs of jewelled cuff-links were in a silver trinket-box.

In the opposite recess was the washing-stand, beneath which was a *bidet* and slop-pail. The jug stood in the basin with a towel folded on top of it. Other towels hung upon the towel-horse. All these articles were clean and orderly, as she had left them when she had tidied the room earlier in the evening after Lord William had changed for dinner.

She next closed and latched the window shutters, then went to the bed and turned down the bedclothes, disclosing the two pillows placed side by side. She drew the bed-curtains closely together on the side nearest the wall, but on the other side she adjusted them so as to leave a gap next the night-table. This table had a drawer which was always kept locked, the key being attached to the bunch which Lord William kept on his person in the daytime. On the table stood a watch-stand, a miniature of his late wife, a round snuff-box, and a fresh rush-light in a holder. Lighting the latter Sarah Mancer picked up her tallow candle and, after a final glance about her, mounted the stairs to her room above.

'I was very quickly in bed,' she told the Court. 'The cook came in a few minutes afterwards. I was awake then, but did not long remain awake. The cook fell asleep and was snoring at once. I slept soundly all night. When I awoke next morning at six o'clock, which was my time for getting up, the cook was still sleeping heavily and did not stir. I knocked on the valet's door to let him know the time. Often I had to knock several times before he answered: that morning he answered at once.'

Vaguely surprised at this unusually prompt response she descended the stairs to begin the measured routine of the day's work on that Wednesday, 6th May.

3

The Discovery of the Crime:
Wednesday, 6th May

'I formed an idea that would enable me to travel from city to
city for six or seven months. . . . I would go to a town, take a
lodging, and, after remaining five or six days, I would depart
without making payment. I thought £10 or £12 would suffice for
this excursion, but then I thought that was not enough. I began to
premeditate taking what this venerable victim had with him in
gold and bank-notes, and his watch. But even that did not satisfy
me. . . . It was not enough only to rob my master.'[1]

'APLACE for all things and everything in its place,' was
a maxim on which Sarah Mancer, like other domestic
servants, had been trained, and she consequently gave
an exclamation of annoyance when, tripping over something
lying outside Lord William's bedroom door, she saw that it was
the warming-pan which the valet had left lying there after
warming his lordship's bed the night before instead of returning
it to its proper place in the kitchen.

On the floor below she clucked her tongue at what she
thought was another example of his carelessness: the door into
the writing-room was wide open, and it was his duty to see that
all the doors on the two lower floors were locked at night.
Next moment, however, she was standing agape on its threshold
for the room was in a condition in which her scrupulously tidy
employer could never have left it. His Davenport writing-
table had been turned completely round, and from every
drawer protruded a welter of letters and documents, while on

[1] Courvoisier's confession.

24

the hearthrug, among the scatterings of more correspondence, lay the bunch of keys which never left his keeping.

Staring uncomprehendingly at this disorder her eye was caught by a screw-driver lying on the seat of a chair: it looked remarkably like one which was normally kept in the pantry.

Uncertain and bewildered, she continued downstairs, where once again she halted. Near the front door was heaped a strange assortment of articles: piled on top of what she recognized as Lord William's evening cloak were his silver trinket-box, his gold-mounted opera glasses, one of his gold pencils, and, of all things, a silver thimble, while a damask table-napkin was knotted about some bulkier object. Her startled eyes passed from these to the door itself, and, though it was shut, she saw with dismay that the chain was down and the bolts withdrawn. The door of the dining-room stood ajar: in trepidation she looked in to behold a scene of chaos. A couple of chairs had been overturned; the candelabra lay beneath the table, while on the table itself, on the sideboard and scattered about the floor were forks and spoons and other silver. With thudding heart Sarah Mancer fled upstairs and burst in upon the still heavily sleeping cook.

'I had to shake the cook to wake her,' she told the Court. 'She was hard to wake. I told her what I had seen and to get up and dress. Then I knocked on the valet's door. He opened it at once. He was fully dressed except for his coat. . . . Usually it was half an hour, and sometimes an hour, after I had called him before he was ready to come downstairs. I told him: "I have found all the silver lying about in the dining-room. Do you know anything of what happened last night?" He looked very pale, but he made me no answer. He pulled on his coat and came out of his room. I followed him downstairs.'

As they went she spoke of the state of the writing-room, but without the slightest indication that he had heard what she was saying—without even a glance at the room in question—he continued on his way. Disregarding the things near the front door he went into the dining-room, glanced quickly round it, then, pushing past Sarah Mancer, made his way to the service-stairs and went straight down to his pantry.

Here the chaos was even greater. The press had been

pulled away from the wall; the doors of its upper portion had been wrenched open, and the contents of the baize-lined drawers were strewn about the room—salvers, coffee-pots and tea-pots, spoons and forks. 'It looked,' as Inspector Tedman, who was subsequently in charge of the investigations, was to testify, 'as though they had been gathered up in handfuls and flung about.'

Then, at long last, Courvoisier spoke.

'My God!' he exclaimed. 'Someone has been robbing us!'

Until then Sarah Mancer's mental state had been one of stunned incredulity. The valet's words aroused her to a sense of reality, and her critical faculties began to assert themselves. She became aware of the strangeness of his behaviour, of something about him which she could not describe; a dark sense of foreboding descended upon her and she cried out:

'For God's sake let's go and see where his lordship is!'

To a Court as silent as that house had been she described how the valet went 'into his lordship's room *without knocking*'; how, instead of going to the side of the bed where the curtains were parted to inform Lord William of what they had found, he went round between the bed and the wall, and, merely ejaculating with a gesture, 'There he is,' moved towards the windows.

Instinctively she went to the other side of the bed in order to look through the gap in the bed-curtains and awake her master. With the shutters closed the room was dark, and all she could discern was the mere outline of Lord William's body lying on its right side. 'I said loudly to wake him, because he was deaf: "My lord! My lord!" '

At that moment Courvoisier opened the shutters of the middle window and daylight streamed into the room. In an instant she saw that a towel, clotted with blood, was spread over her master's face, and a blood-saturated pillow was thrust behind his head. All the fashionable world of London who had managed to crowd themselves into the Old Bailey, including the Queen's uncle, the Duke of Sussex, listened with excited attention as she continued:

'On seeing the blood I screamed and ran out of the room. My first intention was to alarm the cook, and then I thought I would give the alarm in the street. I went to Mr Latham's house, which is nearly opposite. I rang the bell and, finding the servants didn't come, I went to No. 22. I rang that bell, and the servant came out. Mr Latham's servant came out while I was standing at that other door. I asked him to fetch the police, and the servant at No. 22 to summon his lordship's medical gentleman from Cleveland Row . . . I then returned to the house.'

And, having returned to the house, she beheld the man-servant whose responsibility it was to take control, sitting abstractedly at the dining-room table, in the midst of the chaos, with a pen in his hand and a sheet of note-paper in front of him. Years of genteel restraint snapped like a thread and furiously Sarah Mancer demanded:

'What the devil do you sit there for? Why don't you *do* something—or get a doctor?'

'I must write to Mr Russell,'[1] Courvoisier replied, but she noticed that 'he had only written about three words'.

As to how he had spent the time while the housemaid was giving the alarm there is no positive evidence. He would appear to have re-closed the window shutters which he had opened with such dramatic effect. But the Prosecution was to suggest that he had also made certain additions and alterations to the objects on the bedside table.

Now, as Sarah Mancer, hot with indignation, left him, he thrust aside the writing materials in that disordered room and immured himself in the even more disordered pantry.

---

[1] Lord William's eldest surviving son who lived in Chesham Place.

4

The Investigations: Wednesday, 6th May

'I read a book containing the history of thieves and murderers,
and I did not think it would be a great sin to place myself among
them. I was particularly struck with the history of a young man,
born of respectable parents, who spent his property on gaming
and debauchery, and I admired his cunning instead of feeling
horrified by it. . . . I had the idea that by killing my master the
robbery would be better concealed, and that I should have done
with him all at once. . . .'[1]

I

MEANWHILE Daniel Young—Mr Latham's footman—
had carried out Sarah Mancer's request and informed
John Baldwin, the parish constable of St George's,
Hanover Square, that something was seriously wrong at 14
Norfolk Street. Baldwin undertook to pass the information on
to the Metropolitan Police and come himself to the house as
soon as possible. On his way back Young met York, and,
having apprised him of the course of events, the two men
hastened to No. 14.

Entering the kitchen they found the cook and housemaid sitting together in stricken silence. Learning that the valet was in
his pantry they went there, and discovered him 'seated behind
the door with his elbows on the table and his face in his hands'.

He did not speak, or even look up, when they entered. He
did not reply when they exclaimed at the disorder, or even
when York observed that 'someone should be in charge
upstairs'. Only when he repeated more sharply: 'Someone

---

[1] Courvoisier's confession. It is suggested that the 'history of the young man'
to which he alludes was Defoe's account of the career of Jack Sheppard, which
the latter himself gave Defoe in his cell at Newgate.

Photo. Adams, Rye

LORD WILLIAM RUSSELL'S SNUFF-BOX

'There was a little box near the pillow under his head.'
(Note the bloodstains on the underside)

(By courtesy of Victor Bridges, Esq.)

should be there; you had better take us upstairs,' did Courvoisier at last find his voice.

'Oh my God,' he moaned, 'what shall I do? I shall never get another situation.'

So far as York knew the manner of Lord William's death had not yet been ascertained, or even if he were dead at all. But he had no authority indoors: that lay with the valet until he was superseded by one that was higher. So he and Young stood helplessly in the passage while Courvoisier continued to sit at the table with his face in his hands. And so the minutes ticked by until at last the sound of a heavy footfall announced the arrival of John Baldwin, the parish constable.

'I found the valet sitting behind the pantry door,' he was to state, 'I asked him why he did not get up and assist, but he gave me no answer, although I repeated the same thing several times. . . . I then requested the two women servants and the valet to accompany me upstairs and shew me where the body lay.'

The coachman and Young went with them. In his report Baldwin stated that all the window shutters in the bedroom were closed, and the bed-curtains still drawn.

'I opened the shutters, and saw by the gap in the curtains that the deceased lay on his right side with a towel covering his face. I removed that and pulled down the bedclothes and found a great quantity of blood. It came from a large gash in the throat. There was a little box near the pillow which was under the head. . . . When I lifted the towel off the face the valet exclaimed loudly: "My God, what shall I do? They will think I did it. I shall never get a place again!" And he fell back into a chair.'

Baldwin sent York to fetch the nearest doctor, a Mr Elsgood of Park Place, who arrived within a few minutes, but on learning that Mr Nursey, the deceased's own medical attendant, had already been summoned, he confined himself to making a superficial examination only, in order not to disturb the position of the body or the bedclothes.

While he was thus engaged a clatter of hooves proclaimed the arrival of Mr Richard Mayne,[1] Commissioner of the

_____
[1] Later Sir Richard Mayne.

Metropolitan Police, and Inspector Tedman. Hard on their heels came Mr John Nursey, and the Commissioner, having requested the two medical men to make 'a thorough examination of the body', ordered the servants to leave the room. All gathered in the kitchen, with the exception of Courvoisier, who, without exchanging a syllable with anyone, again shut himself in the pantry.

Therein lay his cunning: from the moment Sarah Mancer had summoned him from his room he had uttered no word which could be used in evidence against him and had abstained from any action which might direct suspicion towards himself. The impression he was obviously intending to create was that of one dazed by shock. That he might be overacting the part does not seem to have occurred to him until the following exchange took place. Baldwin, coming downstairs with Inspector Tedman, remarked to the valet:

'This is a shocking job.'

'I shall lose my place and lose my character,' he wailed.

'I think you've made a damned pretty mess of it,' retorted Baldwin.

If this somewhat cryptic observation was intended to startle Courvoisier into some unguarded protest or admission, it failed in its purpose; but it revealed that his former attitude had been assumed, for he suddenly ceased to bewail his lot and, getting to his feet, was galvanized into a sudden eagerness to render assistance.

'We have been robbed,' he said. 'Here's where they came in.' And leading the way to the door into the backyard he pointed to some bruises on the woodwork and to the top bolt, which was hanging loose, being held by only one screw.

In his evidence Inspector Tedman was to say:

'I saw some bruises on it which appeared to have been made by some blunt instrument. The door-post was bruised in a similar manner. The marks did not exactly correspond, the door being bruised in one place and the post in another. . . . The bolt at the bottom appeared very rusty and could not be fastened. The screws of the top bolt were rusty and a good push would have torn them loose. The bolt was hanging down. I saw a ladder[1] upright against a party wall on the other side of which was an outhouse. The wall could have been scaled from the roof of the outhouse, and down into the backyard by the ladder. The wall was newly whitewashed, and I could find no marks on it of anyone having come over, which I should have expected to see if anyone had entered that way.'

It struck this experienced officer that any thief who knew his business would have made his entry, not by this basement door, but through the glass-panelled one up the steps on the floor above. But that door shewed no signs of having been tampered with. Nor, on examination, did the area door or the front door.

The inspector next scrutinized the heterogeneous collection of articles which had been deposited near the latter. The object tied up in the table-napkin proved to be a silver dish-cover, and the officer noticed the exact neatness with which the cloak had been folded. All, stated the valet, were Lord William's property, except the silver thimble 'for which he could not account'.

No professional thief, Inspector Tedman decided, would have 'scattered articles about as had been done in the pantry and the dining-room'. Asked if anything were missing from these rooms Courvoisier replied that 'he had not checked the inventory, but he thought some pieces of silver had disappeared'.

They then proceeded up to the next floor. In contrast to the disorder in the writing-room, the drawing-room had been undisturbed. Lord William's chair stood beside the fireplace; on the table beside it was a book with an embroidered bookmarker between its pages. It conveyed the impression of having been laid there by Lord William when he had risen to go to bed the previous night. Glancing around the room Inspector Tedman noticed that it contained many valuable *objets d'art* of no great size, and it struck him as odd that the thief should have wasted time and trouble ransacking the drawers of the desk in the adjoining room when he could have slipped so many of these articles into his pockets. Taking possession of the bunch of keys from the hearthrug in the writing-room he

[1] The step-ladder which the upholsterer's man had been using the day before.

asked the valet if he knew anything about the screw-driver which was lying on the chair.

'It is my own,' Courvoisier replied, 'I keep it in a tool-box in the pantry, and it was there when I went to bed last night.'

They now went upstairs to the bedroom. After the medical examination had been concluded the towel had been replaced over the face of the corpse and the bed-curtains re-arranged as they had been when the crime was discovered.

Inspector Tedman, without appearing to do so, was watching the valet very closely. He shewed no reluctance to enter the room, no particular emotion, no curiosity. His face was mask-like and impassive, and he stood as a well-trained manservant stands when awaiting orders, in an attitude of detached attentiveness. What followed next was thus described by the inspector in his evidence:

'On the table by the bed was a miniature of a lady. There was a book with a pair of spectacles on it, and I asked the valet how it came there. He said he had left his lordship reading it when he went to bed the night before. There was an empty purse and a watch-stand, with no watch hanging on it. I asked the valet if the watch had been there when his lordship went to bed the night before. The valet answered: "Yes, it was." He said the purse was the one in which his lordship kept the coin he carried on him. There was a rushlight on the table which was burned but little, and a wax candle which had burned down to the socket of the candlestick.'

But later that day in questioning the housemaid he learned that never before had she seen either a book or a candle on Lord William's bedside table. After carefully marking their respective positions, Tedman took away both the candle and rushlight in order to carry out a test at Scotland Yard, and they, together with the book and the spectacles, were to furnish useful clues. Now, however, he turned his attention to a Russian-leather box lying on an adjacent table. This was an article specially designed for gentlemen to keep their money in when travelling. It was fitted with a tray divided into six little compartments, each fitted with a leather case, known as a *rouleau*, made to contain gold coin. Altogether these *rouleaux* would hold about £200. Beneath the tray was a space for bank-notes. Both space and *rouleaux* were empty, but the latter shewed signs of having been removed from their compartments and hastily replaced.

Tedman learned from the valet that this box was kept in the drawer of the bedside table, and when he applied for money for household purposes Lord William would unlock the drawer, take out the box, unlock that, and give him what was required. The keys of the drawer, and box, were on Lord William's bunch. Here was a strange incongruity: the drawer was locked; so the thief had painstakingly relocked it after taking the box out of it, then unlocked the box, and, having presumably helped himself to its contents, thrust the *rouleaux* hurriedly back again and thrown the box aside. Forming yet another incongruity was a writing-case which had been prised open at the hinges, although its key was also on the bunch. The inspector wondered if two persons had been involved: one committing the murder with remarkable dexterity, the other committing the burglary with astonishing stupidity.

Followed by the valet the inspector now went over to the dressing-table. Earlier he had wondered why the thief had failed to take any of the valuable articles openly displayed upon it. In particular he had noticed a tie-pin with a large pearl.

'I picked up the tie-pin,' he stated, 'and shewed it to the valet. He said: "His lordship wore that yesterday." I asked if his lordship had other articles of jewellery. He said: "Three or four rings are missing." I saw four walking-sticks in a stand, two mounted in gold. I observed to the valet that it must have been a very curious thief to have left all that valuable property behind.'

Previously he and Baldwin, together with the two doctors, had closely examined the pair of razors in the case on the dressing-table, and four others in a wall-cupboard above the washstand. All were clean and bright, and their delicate edges shewed no signs of having been used to sever cartilaginous tissue such as occurs in the human throat. If the crime had been committed by someone from outside, then the probability was that he had taken the weapon away with him; if it were an 'inside job', and the murderer had an accomplice, then the latter might have carried off the weapon; but if he had had no accomplice, then the weapon must be somewhere on the premises. It was not present in the room. The doctors took the view that the wound could have been inflicted with a sharp carving-knife as readily as with a razor.

When Tedman expressed a wish to look at Courvoisier's hands and forearms, the latter unhesitatingly took off his coat and exposed them, revealing no suspicious marks or stains of any sort. Nor was there the slightest trace of blood upon his clothing. After some routine questions, and a warning that he must not leave the premises or hold communication with any-one from outside, Tedman dismissed him, telling him to send up Sarah Mancer. Before she entered he drew the bed-curtains together so as to conceal the body on the bed.

He asked her where and when she had last seen her master alive, the time at which he usually went to bed, and to describe the bed as she had left it before he had retired the previous night.

Although still suffering from shock, she replied to all his questions composedly and convincingly: she had last seen Lord William alive in the drawing-room at 10.15 the previous night; he usually rang at eleven o'clock for the valet to light him upstairs with the lamp; she had turned down the bed-clothes—the pillows had been side by side in the customary manner; and in the customary manner she had drawn the curtains of the bed. She had then gone up to her own room, been in bed by 10.30, and had slept without waking until six o'clock.

Tedman then asked her what objects there had been on the bedside table. The rushlight, the snuff-box, the watch-stand and the miniature, she told him: she had lighted the rushlight as usual just before leaving the room. To other questions she replied that when his lordship was in bed the valet always took the lamp downstairs; she had not noticed whether there was a candle on the bedside table when she entered the room with the valet next morning—a candle might have been there without her seeing it because the room was in darkness until the valet had opened the shutters, and then she had seen the blood and run from the room. The valet had opened the shutters of the middle window only. She was emphatic that she had never found a candle on the bedside table in the morning, nor had she ever known his lordship to read in bed at night.

He had been reading a book in the drawing-room when she last saw him alive. She could not say what the book was. She, the cook and the valet were on good terms; she had never seen or heard of him before he entered his lordship's service, but understood he had last been employed as second footman to Mr Fector, M.P., in Park Lane. To enter Lord William's service as butler-valet would be an advancement.

'On which side of the bed did his lordship sleep?' asked Tedman.

'On this side—furthest from the wall,' she replied.

She continued: when she had run from the house to give the alarm the front door was only on the latch; she had not noticed the condition of the back door and had not known there was anything the matter with it.

After a few more routine questions Tedman warned her, as he had warned the valet, and was about to warn the cook, that she must not leave the premises or hold communication with anyone from outside, and that no sweeping or dusting was to be done. He then dismissed her with the instruction to send the cook to him.

There was little to be extracted from Mary Hannel. She had nothing to do with the housework. She had gone out immediately after serving Lord William's dinner. She returned at ten o'clock and the valet had let her in. She heard him bolt and lock the front door behind her. She had gone to bed at about 10.30 and had slept until Sarah Mancer had awoke her with the news of the disorder downstairs. The valet was responsible for locking up the house.[1]

2

From the position of the body it would appear that Lord William had been asleep when the attack had been made. The

---

[1] Courvoisier himself volunteered the information that he had gone out to fetch the beer, though not until next day, at the inquest.

carotid artery had been severed, which meant that, the instant this was done, the blood would have spurted out in a strong jet and sprayed everything within range—the bed-curtains, for instance, to say nothing of the hand, forearm and torso of the assassin. But except on the pillow, the towel covering the face, and in the bed beneath the body, nowhere in the room, nowhere in the entire house, was there a smear or drop of blood.

It seemed safe, therefore, to deduce that the murderer had stemmed the spraying of the blood by clamping that extra pillow down upon his victim's face. Thus the hand holding the pillow might not have received stains; the other, and the weapon, had evidently been wiped upon the towel.

But blood must have penetrated into the pores and creases of the hand which held the weapon, and though it may have been wiped upon the towel, enough would have been retained—until it was washed—to leave imprints on anything it touched. Yet there were no such imprints on the Russian-leather box or the writing-case, both of which had obviously been handled. And the murderer had certainly not washed in that room. Everything on or about the washstand was free from any trace of blood. The towels had not even been unfolded, and there was no bloodstained water anywhere. And not the least extraordinary aspect of the crime was that the murderer, who had so callously and deliberately taken the life of a defence-less old man while he slept, should have made that apparently reverent gesture, of covering his victim's face.

Again arose the question: were two concerned—the remorseless, skilful killer, and the troubled accomplice? And if so which, if either, was an inmate of the house? Or were both? Already Tedman had come to one conclusion: the condition of the back door had been contrived to give the impression that it had been forced from outside; that the unlocking of the front door, and the piling of the objects just within it, had been done to suggest that the robber had been alarmed and hastily taken his flight. That robbery had been the motive for the crime might be deduced from the fact that not a penny-piece remained of whatever money Lord William had had in his possession.

Locking the bedroom door behind him and slipping the key into his pocket, Tedman went downstairs to find two constables awaiting to report their arrival. One he posted outside the house to see that no unauthorized person gained admittance; the other he despatched to find, and take a statement from, Henry Carr. Then, entering the dining-room, he opened the three drawers of the sideboard. In a baize-lined compartment of the centre one he found four carving-knives. Closely he examined each in turn: on one, just where the damascene blade joined the ivory handle, he perceived a small, rust-coloured stain. Carefully wrapping the knife in his handkerchief he put it in the inside pocket of his coat.

At that moment a brougham drove up, from which stepped Lord John Russell, followed by the dead man's son and Mr Wing, the family solicitor. Almost simultaneously the Commissioner—who had departed soon after the medical men—returned accompanied by another inspector named Pearce.

5

The Inquest: Thursday, 7th May

'On Tuesday night when his lordship went to bed—he had been rather cross with me before about the carriage—he rang and I took the warming-pan up with coals in it. . . . He began to grumble because I did not go up to see what he wanted instead of taking up the warming-pan. . . . He told me, rather crossly, that I should take more notice of what I was doing, and of what he was telling me. I did not answer, as I was very cross. . . . I went downstairs and put everything in the state it was found in the morning. . . .'[1]

I

PARTLY to scotch the rumour that Lord William had committed suicide, partly to permit his son to have the body removed to his own house, and partly to enable the police to proceed with their investigations without any further delay, it was arranged that the Coroner, Mr G. R. Dawson, should open the inquest on the premises next morning, Thursday, 7th May.[2]

He and the twelve jurors viewed the body and made a complete tour of the house, beholding every room in practically the same state as it had been when the police had arrived on the scene twenty-four hours earlier. Even in the drawing-room, where the proceedings took place, Lord William's chair, the table beside it with the book upon it just as he had placed it before going up to bed for the last time, had been left undisturbed.

Having formally opened the proceedings the Coroner called the first witness. This was Mr Elsgood, surgeon, of Park

[1] Courvoisier's confession.
[2] The Press was not represented, but the Coroner's notes of the proceedings, from which the following account is taken, were distributed for publication.

Place, who testified that he had been sent for at 7.30 the previous morning and had immediately responded. He had not attended the deceased before. 'I found him lying partially inclined on his right side. He was in his nightdress, and had been dead about three or four hours.'

The Coroner: 'Do you think he might have been dead seven hours?'

Witness: 'No, not more than three or four.[1] I found a wound extending from the shoulder on the left side down to the *trachea*. It was four to five inches deep, and about seven inches long, dividing the vessels and the *trachea*, which must have caused instant death. It was inflicted by some sharp instrument and must have been done from the left.'

To other questions from the Coroner witness replied:

'The edges of the wound were not jagged. There was a towel over the face when I went in. I did not see any cut on the thumb. The carotid artery was wounded, so was the jugular vein. The blood had not spurted out. . . . I saw no appearance of any contusion.'

Mr Nursey, surgeon of Cleveland Row, was then called and stated that he had been the deceased's medical attendant for some time. He had come to the premises as soon as he could, arriving about eight o'clock.

The Coroner: 'When you examined the body did you observe that one hand was wounded?'

'Yes; I observed that the ball of the right thumb was cut off and hanging from it.'

'Can you account in any way for the cut on the thumb?'

'I should say it was inflicted in his endeavours to prevent the action of the instrument by which his throat was cut.'

In reply to other questions witness said:

'I am quite satisfied deceased could not have committed the act himself for three reasons: first, that he could not have placed the towel over his face himself; secondly, from the extent of the wound; and thirdly, from the nature of the wound, which extended from the cervical vertebrae to the shoulder. Also

---

[1] This was mainly guesswork. As will be seen, Mr Nursey did not quite agree with this estimate, while other evidence, including Courvoisier's own confession, indicates that the murder had been committed by 1 a.m. at the latest. That Mr Elsgood was not a very exact observer will presently become still more apparent.

because, with the last witness, I examined the bed and the room to see if there was any instrument present with which the wound had been inflicted, but could find none.'

Asked to account for the presence of the pillow behind the deceased's head, witness said:

'Unless something such as the pillow had been used to stem the blood when the wound in the throat was inflicted—and had nearly severed the head from the body—the blood would have spurted, which was not the case.'

Concluding his evidence witness said:

'From the position of the body, from the position of the truss which the deceased wore, and from the cut on the thumb, I believe that Lord William had been lying on his right side when the attack took place, and that he made some slight struggle. . . . I consider that death had taken place not less than four or five hours before I saw the body at eight o'clock yesterday morning.'

John Baldwin, parish constable, part of whose evidence has already been quoted, was questioned concerning the position of the bruises on the back door and the condition of its fastenings. He stated that the bolt at the top could have been torn away had it received 'a good push from the outside' and that there were no marks to indicate that the backyard wall had been scaled 'such as I would expect to see had that been done'. He continued that 'at the servants' own request a search had been made of their rooms and boxes on the previous evening. Nothing bearing any suspicious stains, or any of the articles believed to be missing, had been discovered therein. But a purse containing a £5-note and also six sovereigns had been found in the valet's box.'

The Coroner: 'Is the bank-note marked in any way?'

'Yes, it is marked on the back.[1] I asked the valet where he got the note from. He said he gave five sovereigns to Lord William for it some time ago in exchange. I asked him if Lord William was in the habit of having much money about him. He said: "I saw a £5-note and a £10-note in his possession yesterday, in the usual place in a box in a drawer close to the head of the bed". . . .'

[1] It had been initialled at the bank.

In reply to a question from the jury as to the servants' demeanour, witness replied: 'The manservant seemed very much concerned all day, and kept running and drinking water.'

François Benjamin Courvoisier, the next witness, 'being of foreign nationality . . . was especially cautioned by the Coroner against saying anything that might implicate him, and was advised that he need not take the oath unless he wished to do so. He took the oath voluntarily.'

In reply to questions from the Coroner he stated that he had come to England about four years previously. He had been a waiter at the Hotel Bristol, Jermyn Street, for nearly a year and had left of his own accord to enter private service. He had first gone as second footman to Lady Julia Lockwood, and then, after nine months, to Mr Fector, M.P., also as second footman, and in that capacity had frequently acted as valet to Mr Fector's guests in Dumfriesshire. After two years, desiring to 'better himself', he had applied for the post of butler-valet with Lord William Russell.

Asked to account for his actions on the day preceding the crime—Tuesday, 5th—witness said that after his dinner at midday he had gone out to deliver some messages for his lordship. He returned about four o'clock, and Henry Carr, who had been Mr Fector's coachman when witness was employed there, had called to see him. Witness had invited him to tea, Mary Hannel and Sarah Mancer also being present. About 6.30 p.m.[1] witness had gone to the mews to fetch the dog for his lordship to take out, as was his custom. Henry Carr had walked as far as the end of Norfolk Street with him, and there they had parted. Witness had gone straight down the mews, which ran parallel with the backs of the houses, and had come straight back with the dog. After his return he had not left the house except for a few minutes at about 10 p.m. to get some beer for the cook's supper.

In reply to questions about locking up the house witness said that immediately after admitting the cook, about 10 p.m. he had locked and bolted the front door, and put up the chain. He had locked the area door when he returned with the beer,

[1] He apparently said nothing about the *contretemps* over the carriage.

and, bringing the key into the kitchen, had put it on the table. The cook and housemaid were both present at the time. 'I did not leave the house again that night, and I have not left it since,' witness said in answer to a question from the jury.

Continuing, he said that on Tuesday night he had attended his lordship to bed in the usual way. He had left him reading in bed by the light of a candle on the bedside table. At about 11.30 he had locked and bolted the back door. The glass-panelled door above it on the ground-floor was never unlocked as no one used it. He had fastened all the windows, closed and latched the shutters, and turned the keys in the doors of the various rooms as usual. There was a key on the inside of his lordship's door, but, so far as he knew, his lordship never turned it. He had gone to bed, fallen asleep almost at once, and had not been disturbed by any sounds during the night. Next morning Sarah Mancer had informed him of the disorder in the house and on going down to the pantry he had noticed that the back door was ajar and the bolt hanging down. He had then said to the housemaid: 'We have been robbed.' She had replied that they had better tell his lordship, and had accompanied him upstairs for this purpose. They had found his lordship lying dead in bed with blood on the pillow, and the housemaid had screamed and rushed out of the room. He knew she had gone to give the alarm in the street, so he had started to write a letter to Mr Russell, his lordship's son. He had been greatly affected and upset: he had only been five weeks in his lord-ship's service and felt that suspicion might fall upon him.

Courvoisier had given his evidence with composure and his manner had created a good impression. The Coroner thereupon informed the jury that 'his former employer, Mr Fector, Member of Parliament for Dover, had given him an excellent character before the opening of the proceedings'.

Sarah Mancer, the last witness to be called, was only briefly interrogated. She stated that she had not left the premises at all on the day preceding the crime, and had not left them since. She had last seen his lordship alive at about 10.15 when she had gone to the drawing-room to inquire if she should light the fire in his bedroom. She had slept undisturbed throughout the night. When she had seen the confusion next morning on going downstairs she had first informed the cook and then the valet.

In reply to the jury she said: 'When I went down to the pantry with the valet I did not notice the back door. The valet said nothing to me about it, but he said: "We have been robbed." ' On seeing the blood on his lordship's pillow she had screamed and rushed out of the house to give the alarm.

As the door closed behind her the Coroner asked the foreman of the jury if he desired any other witnesses to be called, or the inquest adjourned. After a whispered consultation with his colleagues the latter replied that they saw no reason to call any other witnesses, and 'they unanimously preferred returning an immediate verdict of Wilful Murder against Some Person or Persons Unknown, and he observed that by this course they were most likely to allay popular excitement and throw discredit upon any false report as to the cause of Lord William Russell's death'.

2

The verdict of the Coroner's jury certainly discredited any false reports as to the cause of Lord William's death, but at the same time the medical evidence given at the inquest had presented the public with the facts of a crime committed in so mysterious and treacherous a manner as to provide a fertile field for speculation and debate.

The Times commented as follows:

'Not a single drop of blood was observed in the room or about the bed, except within about eight or ten inches of the spot on which his lordship's head was lying, hence it is inferred that the assassin must have placed the pillow over the deceased's head and face whilst he inflicted the fatal wound, and, by that means, prevented the blood from spurting about, which must otherwise have been the case to a very great extent. It is also a remarkable fact that not the slightest trace of bloody finger-marks could be discovered on any doors, or upon any of the articles in the room. . . .

'The bloodstained assassin had negotiated the stairs from Lord William's bedroom on the second floor without leaving a single indication of his passage. Where had he washed? With what had he wiped his hands? There were smudges as of dirty hands where the area door[1] had been forced, but nothing was even faintly tinged with blood.'

Indeed, from the servants' rooms right down to the basement no damp towels or cloths had been found, which would have suggested that they had been used for such a purpose and afterwards washed free from stains. In fact it quickly became apparent that the murder had been carefully planned, and that the murderer had taken every precaution to leave no clue which would lead to his identity.

'London [*wrote Mr Serjeant Ballantine*[2]] was in a state of excitement. The age of the nobleman, his great historic name, and position in Society, all combined to exaggerate the horror naturally excited by such an event.'

The public expected—nay, it demanded—miracles from its 'new police', to the formation of which it had been so bitterly opposed; and as early as Friday, 8th May, *The Times*, in the course of a leading article, deplored the disbanding of the old Bow Street Runners and the 'thief-takers' and lamented the inefficiency of their supplanters. 'At the end of the second day after a barbarous murder,' it impatiently complained, 'it appears that the police are without a clue.'

All the jealous fears of Government interference with the liberty of the subject had been aroused when Sir Robert Peel created his uniformed police, and not even the most emphatic assurances that the force would be equipped only with truncheons, similar to the cudgels of the Bow Street Runners, could allay the general suspicion that this was the first step

---

[1] The back door.

[2] *Some Experiences of a Barrister's Life*, by William Ballantine, Serjeant-at-Law (1812–1887). His father, also William Ballantine, barrister, had, as magistrate of the Thames Magistrate's Court, control over the river police from 1821 to 1848. The son enjoyed the reputation of having 'defended more criminals than any barrister of his time'. Among them was Arthur Orton, the Tichborne claimant. He is generally credited with being the original of 'Chaffanbrass' in Anthony Trollope's *Orley Farm*.

towards the formation of an armed *gendarmerie* on the Continental model. Thus the early 'Peelers' were more hated by the honest citizen than they were feared by the criminal.

They were to be severely castigated—not without some justification—both in Court and out of it, for their handling of this sensational crime. Nevertheless, on the very day on which *The Times* published its criticism Inspector Tedman was already applying for a warrant for the arrest of François Benjamin Courvoisier.

But meanwhile, in Mayfair's innermost circle, a whisper was circulating, told in such close confidence that, though its substance finally seeped out, the names of those whom it concerned have never done so to this day. It was to the effect that, on the night of Tuesday, 5th May, a 'young nobleman' had been paying a clandestine visit to a lady in the house opposite that of Lord William Russell. On taking his departure some time after midnight he had beheld therein, through an uncurtained window, a strange apparition. After learning the result of the inquest he had recognized the possible significance of what he had seen, and, in some perturbation since the lady's honour was involved, he consulted his solicitor as to what he ought to do. He was advised to do nothing for the present.

It was probably a garbled form of this very whisper which inspired the following rather cryptic paragraph in *The Times*:

'We have heard it stated that the servants living in the house opposite, No. 23, observed some circumstances on the evening preceding the murder which has since struck them as wearing a suspicious appearance, but we understand that at present they decline stating what it was that attracted their attention, and the reason they give for withholding this information arises from the fear that they might implicate some party against whom no previous suspicion attached. The police will, of course, see that the ends of justice are not retarded by any false delicacy on the part of the servants in question.'

Leaving these matters in abeyance for the present, we must return to the events taking place within the walls of 14 Norfolk

Street. They possess a degree of fascination which is special and unique, for through the evidence of the police on the one hand, and the written confessions which Courvoisier was to make[1] on the other, one is able to watch a grim, fantastic game of move and counter-move played out between the hunters and the hunted as the former drew their net closer and closer about their quarry through three long days and nights—and all within the narrow confines of that little house.

But first of all we must note the stage which the investigations had reached when the inquest closed.

---

[1] Courvoisier made three separate confessions, which will be considered in due course.

6

The Investigations Proceed

'I went into the dining-room and took a knife from the side-board. . . . I then went upstairs. I opened the bedroom door and heard him snoring in his sleep. There was a rushlight in the room at the time. I went near the bed, by the window side, and then I murdered him. He just moved his arm a little and never spoke a word.'[1]

I

A T NO time, would it appear, did the police harbour much, if any, suspicion that the two women servants were involved in either the murder or the robbery. But they did at first entertain suspicions concerning Henry Carr. After some difficulty his whereabouts were traced, for he had left the service of Mr Fector and was out of employment. He was very closely questioned and though his account of his movements on the night of the crime did not immediately convince them that he might not have been implicated in it, further inquiries served to establish his innocence and to satisfy the officers that no one from outside was involved, but that the valet, and the valet alone, was the guilty party.

Through information supplied by the family, and by James Ellis, the former valet, they were able to confirm that five rings, a pair of cuff-links, and Lord William's fob-watch, with a couple of gold seals attached to it by a corded ribbon, were missing. On re-checking the inventory of table-silver—which had been proved correct only five weeks previously when James Ellis had handed over to his successor—it was disclosed that fourteen spoons and forks, all engraved with the Russell crest,

[1] Courvoisier's confession.

were unaccounted for. It was also learned that a couple of days before his death Lord William had drawn £20 from his bank in the form of one £10-note, one £5-note and five sovereigns; that it was his habit to keep the greater part of his money in the Russian-leather box, carrying in his purse only two or three sovereigns and his small change. The empty box and the empty purse pointed to the probability that the murderer had seized their contents, as well as the missing articles; but how could a stranger know that that box was kept in the drawer of the bedside table? If that murderer were Courvoisier, he *would* know. In that case these things were probably still somewhere on the premises.

Lord William's family supported Sarah Mancer's contention that he had never been known to read in bed. As to her further assertion that she had always found the rushlight completely burned out of a morning and never seen the remains of a candle on the bedside table, it would indeed have been a strange coincidence if a man so rooted in habit as Lord William should have happened to change it on that night of all nights—and stranger still that he should have extinguished the rushlight and left the candle to gutter itself out. But strangest of all was the fact that, from the position of the candle, it was obvious that no one lying in the bed could possibly have read by its light.

Experiments at Scotland Yard with a similar rushlight shewed that it would burn for seven hours, and that the one in question had burned for only two and a half hours before it had been extinguished. Since Sarah Mancer stated that she had lighted it at about 10.30 p.m., then it must have been put out not later than 1 a.m. It seemed likely, therefore, that that was the hour at which the murder had taken place.

Courvoisier had stated that when he had finished 'attending his lordship to bed' he had carried away the lamp as usual and left Lord William reading by candlelight. The police, however, had now come to the conclusion that these had been placed where they were found for the sole purpose of confirming that statement.

Tallow candles—not wax candles, such as that found by the bedside—were provided for the use of the servants. Two tallow candles had been found in the maidservants' room on the morning the crime was discovered, but no candle at all, tallow or wax, was in the valet's room: yet he, like they, would have had to light his way upstairs the previous night.

And if the murderer were an intruder, so too would he —and not only upstairs, but down again. It also seemed likely that he would leave the remains of his candle behind him when he took his departure. But no such remains were found.

The conclusions arrived at from all this were that the valet, after removing the lamp and leaving his master settled down for the night with the rushlight burning beside his bed, had filled in the time until the latter might be trusted to have fallen asleep by faking the forcing of the back door and disordering the various rooms; then, taking a knife from the sideboard drawer, had lighted his way upstairs with one of the wax candles from the dining-room; quietly opening the door of Lord William's bedroom, and hearing from his breathing that he was sound asleep, he had put down the candle on a table just inside the room, and crept forward and murdered him, accidentally extinguishing the rushlight in the course of that proceeding. Having wiped the knife and his bloodstained right hand on the towel, he had opened the door with his clean left hand, which had been protected from blood by the pillow, held it open with his foot, picked up the candlestick in the same hand and gone down to the basement where he had washed all traces of the crime from his person and, as he believed, from the knife, afterwards destroying the cloth or towel with which he had dried himself in the kitchen range.[1] Returning the knife to the drawer he had gone up to the bedroom again to possess himself of his master's money and those other trinkets which had captivated his fancy, and after concealing these somewhere on the premises, had lighted himself up to his own room with the same candle.

It was only next morning, the police thought, when Sarah Mancer had fled from the room, leaving him alone in it, that he had noticed the unburned rushlight, and with the pressure

---

[1] No tinder was found there because the cook had cleaned out and rekindled the range before the investigations began.

of guilt upon him, had realized that the presence of a *wax* candle in his bedroom might involve him in awkward explanations. His cunning mind promptly conceived the idea of placing the candle, the book and the spectacles on the bedside table, and of saying that when he left his master the previous night he had been reading in bed.

The carving-knife had also been submitted to careful scrutiny at Scotland Yard, but in 1840 there was none of the tests which a century later would have revealed the nature of the stain upon it beyond the shadow of doubt. It had therefore to remain conjectural. Mr Richard Mayne believed it to be a bloodstain, and Mr Hobler, the Crown Attorney, to whom he forwarded the knife, 'concurred in the opinion that it was the very instrument by which the murder was effected'.

2

From the first Courvoisier sensed that the police suspected him, for he seemed able to read their thoughts and intentions while these were still half formed, so he was able for the present to keep a lap or two ahead of them, making prompt and effective use of their weaknesses and blunders. Nor did he shew the least sign of chagrin or anxiety at the increasing restraints which they put upon him.

In the Russian-leather box, besides the £10- and the £5-notes, he had found a Waterloo medal and nine or ten double-Napoleons—beautiful gold coins which Lord William had collected. The purse had yielded a surprise, too, in the shape of another £10-note, as well as two or three sovereigns. All these, the rings, and the watch with its two seals and keys, he had tied up in a piece of rag and hidden, on the night of the crime, among a number of dirty cloths in a basket in the scullery. There they remained concealed all day Wednesday and Thursday, for by the time the inquest was over it was too late for the police to begin a systematic search for the articles they knew to be missing —knowledge which did not include either the double-Napoleons or Lord William's gold locket.

Officers of the police force, at this early stage in its development, were for the most part insufficiently trained, indifferently educated, and sometimes untrustworthy; and in this instance they were suddenly confronted with the task of bringing to justice the perpetrator of a crime which had affected a member of the exclusive governing class, shocked Society, and aroused the indignation of those in authority. Consequently the case was given official priority and pressure was put upon the police to bring about a speedy arrest.

As we have seen they had good grounds for suspecting Courvoisier, but no one could have looked less like a murderer thant his young Swiss with his genteel deportment. He was an enigma to them, and it is scarcely surprising that some of them, at this stage in the investigations, fell to some degree under his spell; for so had his employers in the past; so in the near future were the prison chaplains, sheriffs and gaolers to do, the brilliant barrister who defended him, and the Chief Justice whose eyes filled with tears as he passed sentence of death upon him; so, finally, did Thackeray, who, beholding him on the scaffold, was so moved by compassion, and so ashamed of his own presence in that vast concourse which had gathered to see this man hanged, that he averted his eyes from the last act of all and went home to brood and reproach himself, and ultimately to write an article[1] in which he did not say a word too much to condemn the barbarous practice of public execution, but in which he indulged in sentimental imaginings concerning what he supposed must have been the feelings, during his last hours, of this callous and deliberate criminal.

Even though his confessions were composed when his doom was sealed, the exultance Courvoisier had felt in tricking those clumsy, heavy-footed English police rings through the sentences in which he describes the bizarre game he played against them, beginning that Thursday night, when he gave the slip to the two officers posted in the house to keep him under observation, and continuing until he was committed for trial. He thus records the first incident:

> 'On Wednesday, when the police had searched a little everywhere, I perceived that they watched me more

[1] 'Going to See a Man Hanged' (*Fraser's Magazine*, August 1840).

attentively than the other servants. . . . Next night, when the two policemen were not observing me, I crept into the scullery and seized the parcel I had put there during the night before, and put it in my pocket.'

He next describes how on going up to bed he tore the seals from the corded ribbon, and, when dressing next morning, distributed the various articles in his pockets, intending, as opportunity offered, to conceal them in certain nooks and crannies of which he knew and where he felt sure they would escape the notice of the police during their search. He had already stowed away between the stair-carpet and one of the risers, just below the second-floor landing, a pair of Lord Willam's cuff-links, a couple of sovereigns and a pair of gold-rimmed spectacles, and he was confident that they would be safe there for the present.

On coming downstairs, however, he was disconcerted to find an officer waiting to conduct him to the kitchen, who stood nearby while he ate his breakfast, and afterwards escorted him to the dining-room where he told him to remain until further orders. But Courvoisier shewed no trace of his feelings and quietly acquiesced.

He and the two women servants had invited a search of their respective rooms and belongings on the previous day: then, too, the police had examined his clothes for bloodstains, so now he began to wonder if they intended to make another search of his person. If they did so before he could rid himself of the articles in his pockets his fate would be sealed; to do this, therefore, as expeditiously as possible, was a compelling necessity.

While he lingered in solitude all through the long hours of that morning, not knowing from minute to minute what the next move of the police might be, he may have sought distraction from his preoccupations by gazing out of the window. If so, the first thing he would have seen would have been the removal of his victim's body, and subsequently the arrival of Mr Mayne, one or two members of the Russell family, and their solicitor, Mr Wing. He would then have heard the murmur of their voices as they conferred in the drawing-room overhead, and later on seen them all depart after they had reached a decision to offer a reward of £400—half to be contributed by the Authorities, and half by the family—for information which would lead to the apprehension and conviction of the criminal, another £50 for the discovery of the missing property, and to have bills advertising these rewards printed and displayed in prominent places all over London.

He would also have heard, during his enforced seclusion, such recognizable sounds as a sweep's brush being thrust up various chimneys, and sundry tappings and hammerings; for the searchers were being exceedingly thorough. Bricks at the backs of fireplaces were being examined and any loose ones removed to make sure that nothing was hidden behind them; upholstery was being prodded, carpets taken up and floor-boards examined; the contents of drawers were being removed, and the drawers themselves carefully scrutinized.

The police had been confident that no difficulty would be experienced in finding such bulky articles as the missing forks and spoons, yet at 12.45, when an officer told Courvoisier that his dinner was ready, they had not been discovered.

Preceding the officer down the service-stairs with unhurried gait Courvoisier turned into his pantry to wash his hands at the sink. While the officer stood at the door paying little heed to his movements he reached for the towel and began to dry his hands, contriving as he did so to 'palm' the bank-notes which he had wrapped about the sovereigns and the Waterloo medal. Then, as though by accident, he dropped the towel, and, stooping to pick it up, slipped the little package into a crevice of which he knew between the skirting-board and the wall. He dared not at that moment run any further risk, but fortune favoured him before he was again conducted upstairs, and he managed to get into the pantry for a moment.

'Nobody being there,' he was to write, 'I placed the watch and the rings where they were [ultimately] found.'

This was in an aperture where the zinc casing of the sink had been cut away to admit the waste-pipe. He endeavoured to put the seals there as well, but found they were too large, and before he could force them in he was interrupted. How-ever, he felt confident that he would be able to do so when

53

allowed to wash his hands before tea, but when the time arrived he found the parish constable in the pantry. There ensued an incident which, except for his presence of mind, and the constable's stupidity, might then and there have proved fatal to him.

'I bent down to look at something the officer was doing and the locket fell out of my breast pocket. I pretended not to notice it. I was just going to put my foot on it, when he picked it up. "What's this?" he said. "Oh, that's a locket—it's mine," I said. I took it out of his hand and put it back in my pocket.'

Such *sang-froid* was evidently outside the scope of Constable Baldwin's experience; he tamely acquiesced.

3

The shadows lengthened in Norfolk Street; twilight gathered; the search of the house continued, and Courvoisier knew that only with the descent of darkness would it end.

'I hoped the things I had hidden would not be discovered. I was kept in the dining-room the whole day, excepting when my room was searched.'

As the law required, this was done in his presence. He stood looking on with the incriminating seals, watch-keys, fragment of black ribbon and the double-Napoleons still upon him, and wondering whether the search would now be extended to himself. It was not. And as he stood there he heard two officers below discussing as to whether or not they should take up the stair-carpet. They decided it was unnecessary, so his *cache* beneath it was never discovered until the house itself was dismantled and he had already died a felon's death.

With the tide of luck still flowing in his favour he was returned to the dining-room. But the first sign of its ebb quickly followed. Inspector Pearce and Constable Baldwin entered and triumphantly confronted him with the bank-notes, sovereigns and Waterloo medal. The former demanded:

'Can you look me in the face and say you know nothing of these things?'

'I know nothing about them,' he answered smoothly, lifting his heavy lids to look the policeman in the face. 'I am innocent and my conscience is clear. I never saw them before.'[1]

They had, of course, no proof that Courvoisier had put them where they had found them. Nevertheless the latter had received a shock, and he received another when, on passing the scullery on his way to supper, he beheld a couple of brick-layers dismantling the sink and realized that it would next be the turn of the sink in the pantry. But he betrayed no sign of emotion, merely resolving to use all his ingenuity to rid himself of the seals, watch-keys and ribbon. He determined to cling to the double-Napoleons as long as possible, and thought out a ruse for concealing them from the police.

'I went into the kitchen and burned the watch-ribbon.[2] I did not know what to do with the seals and watch-keys. . . . While they were not looking I put the large seal under the boiler, at the same time dropping the smaller one on the floor. . . . I put my foot on it in order to bend it.[3] Stooping as if to look under the boiler I picked it up . . . leaned against the wall, and when the inspector and the two masons were occupied and not watching me, I placed the seal behind the pipe. I broke the watch-keys in pieces and put them in the fire.'

He broke them, he adds, between the fingers and thumb of one hand while they were in his trousers pocket; then, pretending to catch his foot in the hearthrug, he bent down to pull it straight and, while doing so, pushed the locket down a crevice between two of the hearth-stones.

He had accomplished all this with the police within a few

[1] Evidence of Inspector Pearce.
[2] Under pretence of warming his hands at the fire.
[3] i.e. flatten it.

feet of him. Now he was rid of everything but the double-Napoleons, to which he sometimes refers by their proper name, but more often as the 'gold pieces', or even as the 'sovereigns' as below:

> 'On the next morning, Friday 8th, I wrapped the sovereigns, separately, in some paper and concealed them in my stockings.'

That day he was again confined to the dining-room and the search went on as actively as before. It was extended to the water-closet, and the drains were opened in the hope of finding the forks and spoons. While this was being done a police sergeant noticed a scratch on the pantry windowsill, and another scratch on the wall outside, just beneath it. The position and character of both suggested that they had been made by the heel of a boot worn by someone who had hoisted himself over the sink and out through the window into the yard. This was to form another link in the lengthening chain of suspicion against Courvoisier, and in his confession he was to write:

> 'I made the marks on the door on the outside for the purpose of having it believed that thieves had broken in. . . . I got out of the pantry window and broke in at the door.'

The bricklayers had now turned their attention to the pantry sink and soon brought to light the watch and the rings. This discovery was not revealed to Courvoisier, and the sink was replaced before he was allowed down to dinner; but those sleepy-looking eyes of his were quick to notice traces of their work and he was forewarned. In the course of the morning, too, the police had found the seals and the locket, but the whereabouts of those largest and bulkiest objects of all—the fourteen forks and spoons—still eluded them. However, even without them, Inspector Tedman decided that he now had enough evidence against the valet to justify him in applying for a warrant of arrest.

During his hours of enforced seclusion that afternoon Courvoisier had much wherewith to occupy his thoughts. He knew that the net was closing about him. He could feel the double-Napoleons pressing into the sole of his foot—all that was left to him of the fruits of his crime. Not thirty pieces of silver, but a few pieces of gold, remained as the reward of his treachery.

As he sat there, waiting, waiting, in tedium and anxiety, a couple of officers entered and ordered him upstairs.

'Two policemen took me to my room and searched me. They made me take off my boots, but not my stockings.'

Once more his luck had held, and as soon as their backs were turned he drew an extra stocking over the foot against the sole of which the gold pieces lay. But he must have sensed that the end was very near for, except for removing his coat, he lay down on his bed fully clad.

'A few minutes later they came up, made me raise, and led me to prison.'

He wasted neither time nor energy in useless protestations. Without a glance about him he descended the stairs of 14 Norfolk Street for the last time, preceded by two policemen and followed by a third—yesterday had joined yesteryear, and tomorrow was unborn. His whole mind was occupied with the subterfuges and sleights of hand he must employ to prevent his captors discovering the gold coins; the dissimulations he must practice to win the goodwill of his gaolers. Nor must one assume that this attitude was the result of courage, or stoical fortitude; it not infrequently arises from a pathological indifference which is incapable of any sensation other than physical pain.

'In Tothill Fields prison they searched me very carefully. I feigned to be very cold and shivery, as a person who has the trembling fever [ague] thinking they would let me keep my stockings on.'

But they were not so obliging; nevertheless he succeeded in outwitting them.

> 'I took off first the stocking which was alone, then one of the others. While they were examining my clothes . . . I took off my under-stocking. Keeping the gold pieces under the thumb of my hand I placed them under the bed. The following morning they made me take a bath, when I had a good opportunity of hiding them on my person.'

Thereupon he was conveyed to Bow Street, formally charged and remanded in custody. On Tuesday, 12th, he again appeared, and was remanded for a week. On that same day the body of his victim was interred in the family mausoleum at Chenies, Buckinghamshire, the funeral service being conducted by the rector, the Reverend Lord Wriothesley Russell, who was not only Lord William's nephew, but also one of his sons-in-law. On that day, too, the police were informed through the medium of General Orders of the two rewards of £400 and £50 respectively which were being offered, and the bills advertising them were issued and distributed over a wide area.

4

No. 14 Norfolk Street, with everything in the locked death-chamber unaltered save for the absence of the body, and with the two women servants still in residence, continued to be under police supervision day and night. It had become clear that the missing table-silver was nowhere in the house. Visits to pawnbrokers and metal-merchants had been made without success; it was as though those fourteen forks and spoons, each engraved with the distinctive Russell crest of a goat *statant*, which had been solidly in existence when James Ellis and Courvoisier had checked and signed the inventory only five weeks previously, had vanished into thin air. Not only was there nothing to shew *where* they had gone, or at what *date* they had gone, but *nothing to shew that the valet was responsible for their disappearance*.

So far as that went, there was no proof that the valet had concealed the other articles in the places where they were found by the police, though it was highly suspicious that most of them should have been discovered in his pantry. But the fact which baffled the police and weakened the case against the prisoner more than anything else, was that no trace of blood had been discovered upon his person or any of his possessions.

Two searches had been made of his room; the first at his own request soon after the discovery of the crime; the second almost immediately before his arrest. On this last occasion Inspector Tedman and two officers, in the presence of the prisoner and of Inspector Pearce, had taken every article out of his box and laid each separately on the bed without coming upon anything which was the least incriminating. Everything was then repacked in the box, the key of which was given into Tedman's keeping.

On Tuesday, 12th, after the valet had been remanded at Bow Street, he asked for a change of linen and Tedman went to Norfolk Street to fetch what was required. Upstairs he went, dragged the box from under the bed, and, as he was to testify at the trial: 'I was astonished to find that the prisoner's box was unlocked.' He was more astonished still when, on taking out a shirt, he found between its folds a pair of white gloves such as footmen wore with their livery, which 'were slightly stained with blood'. He seized upon them, but apparently, in the excitement of the moment, he not only failed further to investigate the contents of the box, but forgot to lock it before pushing it back under the bed. Returning next day to remedy these omissions he came upon a silk handkerchief and a 'dickey', or false shirt-front, each bearing a few spots of blood.

Counsel for the Defence was to contend that the police—with or without the connivance of the women servants—had themselves placed these articles in Courvoisier's box in order to incriminate him and 'share the reward of £400 over his coffin'. Naturally there was no evidence to associate anyone in particular with such a plot, and the general feeling was that Tedman was unlikely to be implicated in it, for he candidly admitted that it would have been impossible for the articles to have escaped his notice had they been in the box when he searched it on the previous Friday evening. But he undoubtedly contributed to it by his negligence, and after the trial was over he received a severe reprimand and was temporarily suspended from duty. Two constables were dismissed.

5

On being informed of her son's arrest Courvoisier's widowed mother made contact with the Reverend Mr Baup, who held a Swiss chaplaincy in London, and begged him to do what he could for her son. Mr Baup consequently obtained permission to visit the prisoner, and went daily to Tothill Fields prison to render him spiritual and material comfort, and to report on his state to the distracted widow.

She must have found Mr Baup's letters consoling, for he was immensely impressed by Courvoisier's demeanour, which struck him as combining in a remarkable degree Christian fortitude and resignation, filial affection and a grateful appreciation of the pastor's own kindness.

Although Mr Baup's kindness never once failed up to the moment when he gave Courvoisier his final blessing on the scaffold, truth compelled him to admit that, while initially he had been convinced of the young man's guilt, after being in his company for a while he 'entirely altered his opinion in consequence of the ingenious acting of the prisoner', who had, however, eventually 'acknowledged to him that, from his earliest youth, he had had an unconquerable propensity for lying', and confessed his guilt.

Courvoisier made an equally favourable impression upon all with whom he came in contact at Tothill Fields. He had meanwhile contrived to retain possession of the double-Napoleons, but when on May 19th, having appeared at Bow Street and been committed for trial, he was placed in a cell to await transfer to Newgate, caution at last prevailed.

'I thought I should be examined there more closely and if the money was found on me, it would be sufficient to condemn me to death. I placed one gold piece behind the post of a bench in the cell at Bow Street, . . . three on the top [*lintel*] of the door, one in the window, and four or five in the pit of the water-closet.'

One can imagine the scramble there must have been to find them when this confession was published in the Press.

7

The Public

'I took a towel which was on the back of the chair, and wiped
my hands and the knife. After that I took his key and opened the
Russian-leather box . . . and I took all the things that were found
downstairs. The towel I put over his face.'[1]

I

DURING the six weeks which ensued between the murder
of Lord William Russell and the opening of
Courvoisier's trial at the Old Bailey on 18th June the
latter became the most talked-of man in London. Thackeray
tells us that the case was the chief topic of conversation in the
clubs, and betting ran high on the outcome of the trial. It was
debated with equal intensity in drawing-rooms and servants'-
halls, in fashionable places of entertainment and in thieves'
dens.

The aristocratic Lady Julia Lockwood declared her willing-
ness to give evidence on behalf of 'this harmless young man of
gentle and inoffensive habits'. To his fellow-members of the
House of Commons and to his guests at his Park Lane house
the wealthy Mr Fector expressed similar sentiments. Mr
Peter Jellings, proprietor of the Hotel Bristol in Jermyn Street,
indulged in an even warmer eulogy. He had known 'the
unfortunate young man ever since his arrival in London', and
not only had he found him a most trustworthy employee, but a
state of friendship had existed between them after he had left
him for private service. The views of the employers were
amply corroborated by the employed, in the form of Lady
Julia's butler and Mr Jellings' head waiter.

[1] Courvoisier's confession.

To all these excellent people Courvoisier had seemed a model of propriety, and none of them had the smallest inkling that much of his time off duty was spent as the boon companion of criminals in the various haunts of vice which made up the London underworld, and not even Mr Jellings, who regarded himself as Courvoisier's intimate friend, had any idea that his hotel was not the first place at which the prisoner had worked on his arrival from Switzerland—that was a fact to be revealed in dramatic circumstances, and with dramatic results, on the third, and last, day of his trial.

2

The news that Mr Charles Phillips[1] had been briefed to defend the accused was hailed with satisfaction by the latter's friends and by all who had any misgivings as to his guilt, for none could doubt that, if there was any flaw in the evidence against him, this brilliant advocate would find it and add yet another triumph to the long list of those he had already gained. It would have appeared incredible that he would emerge from the trial with his reputation tarnished and his professional conduct the subject of a controversy which is argued in legal circles to this day.

Mr Serjeant Ballantine, who knew him well, tells us[2] that he had 'well-formed, expressive features and a musical voice', added to which he possessed ardour, eloquence and great personal charm. But he was also impulsive and quick-tempered, and had twice challenged acquaintances to duels. Since duelling was already illegal in England his honour could only be satisfied by a trip across the Channel and an exchange of ineffectual shots upon the sands of Calais.

---

[1] *Charles Phillips* (1787–1859). Born at Sligo and educated at Trinity College, Dublin. Called to the Irish Bar, 1812; to the English Bar, 1821. Was junior Counsel for the Defence of Probert at the trial of Thurtell, Hunt and Probert for the murder of William Weare (1823). Appointed Commissioner of the Bankruptcy Court, Liverpool (1840), and Commissioner of the Insolvent Debtors' Court, London (1846). Author of *Recollections of Curran*, described by Lord Brougham as one of the most delightful pieces of biography in the language; also (1856) of a pamphlet entitled *Vacation Thoughts on Capital Punishment*.

[2] *Op. cit.*

One of these reluctant adversaries was none other than Mr John Adolphus,[1] who, as Counsel for the Crown, was also to be ranged against him at the trial of Courvoisier. No two men could have been more dissimilar. Where Mr Phillips' volatile genius and *élan* had swept him irresistibly forward to the position he was now enjoying as a leader of his profession and a favourite of Society, Mr Adolphus, nineteen years the elder, had won his way step by step through sheer hard work, ability and integrity to become the *doyen* of the Criminal Bar; an achievement all the more outstanding at a period when criminal practice was apt to attract only the less scrupulous members of the legal fraternity and the term 'Old Bailey lawyer' was one of opprobrium.

John Adolphus, one of the several children of an impecunious German father and an English mother, had been adopted by the latter's wealthy brother, who gave him a roof over his head and paid for his education, but kept him short of pocket-money and saw as little of him as possible. At the age of nineteen or twenty the young Adolphus had been sent out by his uncle to one of the smaller West Indian islands where the latter owned estates. A life of loneliness and monotony, interspersed with frequent attacks of fever, had undermined his health and a return to England became imperative. He had then begged his uncle to allow him, belatedly, to study law and, after being called to the Bar at an age which was in consequence somewhat more advanced than usual, had embarked upon a career of unremitting, but contented, toil. Imbued with the deepest veneration for the House of Hanover he was particularly proud of his friendship with the Duke of Sussex, uncle of the Queen, and was transported with delight at Her Majesty's recognition of a poem written in her honour by his daughter. The hardships of his youth, tropical illness and years of arduous toil, had undermined his health, so that by 1840 physical exhaustion and failing eyesight had compelled him to abandon much of his practice. When he and his former

---

[1] *John Adolphus* (1768–1845). Called to the Bar 1807 and specialized in criminal law. Defended the Cato Street conspirators, 1820. In 1840 was leader of the Bar at the Central Criminal Court. Wrote a number of historical works, of which the best known is *The History of England from the Accession of George III down to the Year 1803.*

antagonist on the sands of Calais confronted each other at the trial of Courvoisier, Charles Phillips had another twenty years of life ahead of him, John Adolphus only five.

Through the writings of some of Mr Phillips' contemporaries we learn that he 'believed most firmly' in his client's innocence; through the entries which he made in his diary[1] we shall see that Mr Adolphus believed no less firmly in in his guilt:

'*8th June 1840.* Lord William Russell, brother of the Duke of Bedford,[2] having at the age of 72 been most inhumanly and mysteriously murdered in his bed, and his Swiss valet, Courvoisier, being committed under strong circumstances of suspicion, I am retained by the Prosecution and this day attended a consultation on the spot with Bodkin and Chambers.

'The house, No. 14 Norfolk Street, is small and unpretentious, but was adequate for his lordship's wants, and beautifully adorned with pictures and china. I saw the bed on which he was murdered, just as it was, the pillow saturated with blood and the furniture in disorder. I viewed the pantry and all places where property had been found.

'I have not the slightest doubt of the wretch's guilt, but many are of the opinion that the Jury will not convict on circumstantial evidence, and I am far from being sure that they are mistaken.

'*13th June 1840.* I have been much, and, I may say, continuously, engaged in the case of Courvoisier. On this day another consultation on the spot, and afterwards at my Chambers. The brief consisted of much paper, but chiefly depositions before the Coroner and at Bow Street. I had, therefore, considerable difficulty in arranging and digesting the matter in such order as to obtain an outline of a clear and connected narrative.'

At the end of the week Mr Adolphus recorded:

[1] This was edited by his daughter and published after his death under the title, *The Life of John Adolphus.*
[2] Actually uncle: *vide* page 13.

'On this task I spent the whole day—17th—from half-past eleven in the morning to the same hour at night. The next day the trial began before Tindale (Chief Justice)[1] and Parke (Baron).[2]'

3

The opening scene of this memorable trial presents the social historian with an illuminating glimpse of contemporary men and manners, and our interest in it is enhanced because we may view it from three different angles: from that of Mr Adolphus, who dearly loved a lord; from that of Serjeant Ballantine whose professional *amour-propre* was affronted by the spectacle; and from that of the special correspondent of *The Times* whose reactions were purely objective. Let us begin with Mr Adolphus.

'*18th June 1840.* The Court was crowded with nobility and persons of distinction, and a larger assemblage of the Bar than I ever witnessed in the Court. The Duke of Sussex was on the Bench. . . . Among the distinguished foreigners were the Marquis Saldanha, Portuguese Ambassador, and the Secretary of the Dutch Embassy. The opening took somewhat less than two hours. My two juniors were Bodkin and Chambers. Against me Phillips and Clarkson. I was heard with great attention and the case proceeded until 7 o'clock. My witnesses stood cross-

[1] *Sir Nicholas Conygham Tindale (1776–1846)*: a man of vast legal learning who numbered Lord Brougham and Baron Parke (Associate Judge in the Courvoisier case) among his pupils. Called to the Bar, 1809; appeared with Brougham as Counsel for Queen Caroline, 1820; M.P., 1824; Solicitor-General, 1826; Chief Justice of the Common Pleas, 1829. Famous cases tried by him include that of Daniel M'Naghten, 1843, a mental defective whose name is perpetuated in the 'M'Naghten Rules'.

[2] *Sir James Parke (1782–1868)*. Called to the Bar, 1813; appeared as Junior Counsel in support of the Bill of Pains & Penalties against Queen Caroline, 1820; raised to the King's Bench, 1828; Privy Counsellor and member of Judicial Committee, 1833; transferred to Court of Exchequer, 1834; raised to peerage as Lord Wensleydale, 1856. Was presiding Judge at the trial of Thurtell, Hunt and Probert, in which case Charles Phillips appeared for the Defence of Probert. Assiduously cultivated a reputed resemblance to George III. Among his grandchildren were the 1st Viscount Ridley, the 1st Viscount Ullswater (Mr Speaker Lowther) and the 9th Earl of Carlisle.

examination perfectly well, but I am still apprehensive of the result. . . . I dined upstairs with the Duke of Sussex, the Judges etc. . . .'

Mr Serjeant Ballantine, justly indignant of anything which impinged upon the dignity of the Court, is caustic in his comments:

'The occasion might, from the appearance of the Old Bailey, have been one of the most festive character. The Court was crowded with ladies dressed up to the eyes, and furnished with lorgnettes, fans and bouquets; the sheriffs and under-sheriffs, excited and perspiring, were rushing here and there offering what they deemed to be delicate attentions. A Royal Duke honoured the exhibition with his presence, and upon the occasion of a witness giving a particular answer to a question from Counsel, shewed his approval by an ejaculation of "Hear, hear!" Sir Nicholas Tindale, the presiding Judge, was so hemmed in by the extensive draperies of the surrounding ladies that he had scarcely room to move, and looked disgusted at the indecency of the spectacle. . . .'

The professional zeal of *The Times* correspondent was tempered somewhat by indignation at the Press being denied the facilities so lavishly accorded to the privileged members of Society.

'On Thursday, 18th June, and the two following days, François Benjamin Courvoisier was tried for the murder of his master, Lord William Russell. The Court was from an early hour besieged by a number of ladies and gentlemen who had been fortunate enough to obtain cards of admission from the Under-Sheriffs, and no one who had not obtained such a card was allowed under any pretext to enter the precincts of the Court—not even the regular reporters of the newspapers.

'This stringent regulation had been previously ordered to prevent persons, not having business, from crowding the

Court to inconvenience, which is often the case at trials of great public interest. By 9 o'clock many of the best seats in the Court were occupied by ladies, and on the Bench were the Earl of Cavan; Lord Arthur Lennox, Lady Arthur Lennox; the Hon. Mrs Villiers; Sir Montagu Chapman; the Sheriffs, Under-Sheriffs; Alderman Harmer; Sir Matthew Wood, and Alderman Humphrey. Shortly afterwards Mr D. W. Harvey, Lady Granville Somerset, the Earl of Mansfield, the Earl of Sheffield, and other noblemen, gentlemen and ladies, entered the Court. . . .'

Bows, nods and chatter ceased, and silence descended, eyeglasses and lorgnettes were raised, as the prisoner was placed at the Bar. Clad in black that was unrelieved except for the glimmer of a white shirt-front, his face pale but composed, his figure erect, he bowed ceremoniously to the Bench, then stood in rigid stillness. In a voice that was low and tense he pleaded Not Guilty of the crime of which he was accused, and—to a ripple of approval from the spectators—repeated the wish he had already expressed; to be tried by a jury of Englishmen, rather than by one composed as to one half of his fellow-countrymen.

8

The Trial: Thursday, 18th June

'I took the jewellery after I had committed the deed. . . .
I went to bed about 2 o'clock. I burned nothing. I did not wash
my hands or the knife in the *bidet* in his lordship's room. I am
the only person who is guilty.'[1]

I

ON Mr Adolphus' opening speech the *Annual Register*
was to comment:

'He went into a minute, elaborate and very able
statement of all the circumstances connected with the
murder, presenting a mass of circumstantial evidence
against the prisoner. . . . One part of that evidence on
which much stress had been laid Mr Adolphus made
slight account of—the discovery of the blood-stained gloves
and linen in the prisoner's portmanteau.'

Indeed, in regard to those discoveries, Mr Adolphus was
only too well aware that the police witnesses would be exposed
to a relentless cross-examination, and that, so far as the Prosecution was concerned, the less said about them the better. He
also knew that, though the chain of circumstantial evidence
against the prisoner was strong, it lacked one vital link—those
still-missing pieces of table silver. Moreover, in Mr Phillips he
was facing a formidable adversary, who would pluck his arguments to pieces and quickly turn any flaw in them to his own
advantage.

[1] Courvoisier's confession.

The whole nature of the murder was unusual, and Mr Adolphus decided to adopt the unusual course of rebutting in his opening speech the arguments which the Defence were most likely to produce. Legal opinion was to question his wisdom in doing so. It was also to contend that he carried at least one of his observations beyond those bounds of propriety required of Counsel for the Crown, thereby presenting Mr Phillips with a weapon he was quick to turn to his own advantage. In all other respects his speech was a masterly one, without over-emphasis, and stamped throughout with that quality which arises from the speaker's conviction that his arguments are true.

After describing the discovery of the murder, and the peculiarities surrounding it, Mr Adolphus declared that it was impossible that it could have been committed by a burglar or burglars. 'It would be shown,' he said, 'that there were marks on the backyard door and its doorpost, and that the position of these marks demonstrated that they had not been made from outside the house, but from within it. A high wall enclosed the backyard into which there was no entrance save through this back door. Against one wall a step-ladder had been propped, and on its other side was an outhouse. The wall had been newly whitewashed, and it would be shewn that there were no marks upon it such as a person clambering over it would be likely to make. It would also be shewn that no strangers had gone into the house next door on that day.

'The front door, which there was evidence to shew had been locked and bolted soon after 10 p.m., was found unlocked and unbolted, and the manner in which various articles of property had been disposed immediately within it suggested an attempt to create the impression that a burglar had entered at the back, taken alarm, and gone out by the front door.'

Counsel asked the jury to consider the conduct of the prisoner upon being summoned by the housemaid, upon being shewn the disorder in the house, and upon entering his master's bedroom. 'Was it consonant with innocence? Would an innocent man, believing his master's house to have been burgled, and entering his bedroom to inform him of the fact, have gone past the bed whereon his master lay, and to the window to open the shutters, trusting to the clamour of a maidservant to awake his deaf and ageing master? Would he not have gone himself to the bedside, spoken to him and attempted to allay his alarm?'

It was true, he observed, that no stolen articles had been found in the prisoner's box, 'but no man possessed of even moderate cunning would have placed stolen articles in a repository liable to immediate search. On the other hand articles belonging to deceased had been found in a place to which the prisoner had peculiar access—in his own pantry. From almost the moment the murder had been discovered the house had been in the possession of the police, and it was impossible that any other person could have concealed those articles in the place where they were found. As to the subsequent discoveries in the prisoner's box, the Prosecution attached no importance to them, although he, Counsel, was in no doubt that the Defence intended to suggest that those things had been placed where they were discovered by the housemaid for the purpose of fixing guilt upon the prisoner, or by the police themselves in the hope of claiming the £400 reward.

'I am aware that an attempt will be made by the Defence to shew that Sarah Mancer is not a trustworthy person, but I defy them to damage her character.'

Having thus forestalled this line of attack, Mr Adolphus proceeded to his next argument. It would be shewn, he said, that the valet had been discontented with his situation and was desirous of returning to his own country. The two maids had been with Lord William nearly three years, and their characters were unexceptionable; the valet had come into his service only five weeks before. 'He came with an honourable character from persons who would not have given it unless he had deserved it. He came from a service of wealth into a service of distinction. . . . A man who is on trial for his life ought to have the full benefit of his character; it is the crime, and the crime alone, on which it is my duty to address the Court.'

Counsel then narrated in detail the events of Tuesday, 5th May. In regard to the affair of the carriage he said: 'There is no evidence of what occurred between the master and the valet, or whether he received a scolding or not.' The cook, Counsel continued, had gone out after serving his lordship's dinner, and he described how the valet, after admitting her by the front door, had 'good-naturedly' offered to go out and get her some beer for her supper. 'When they heard the house-maid's evidence the Court might think that something had been put into the beer.'

Lord William went to bed at about 11.30. There was a key to his bedroom door, but it was not his custom to lock it. At about 10.30, the housemaid had lighted a fire in that room and had also lighted a rushlight.[1] 'That rushlight had been extin-guished.' Counsel paused, glancing from Bench to jury in order to fix particular attention upon his next point:

'Experiments proved that the rushlight had not been burning for more than an hour and a half; consequently the crime must have been committed an hour and a half after the maid had lighted it.'

A wax candle had been placed at the bedside to give the impression that Lord William had been reading by its light; a book and his spectacles were also on the table. But it was well known that he never read in bed, and, had he done so, the angle at which the candle was set would have made it impos-sible to read by its light. The candle had burned down to its socket.

'The inference is,' said Counsel, 'that the rushlight had been put out either before or after the crime, the candle having been used by the prisoner to light his way about the house, and then to leave it in such a position as to indicate that Lord William had been reading in bed.' Perhaps with the disappearance of the table-silver in mind Counsel added: 'It is regrettable that the prisoner was not charged at once. But the police kept him under strict *surveillance* to prevent communica-tion between himself and the female servants, and with anyone from outside.'

After touching upon the watch and the pieces of jewellery which had been taken from Lord William's bedroom, and

---

[1] Lord Russell of Liverpool in *Though the Heavens Fall* states that the rushlight was in *the valet's* bedroom. Not only does the evidence make it clear that it was in Lord William's, but it is difficult to see what significance it could have had, if it had been in Courvoisier's.

describing the Russian-leather box with its tray and *rouleaux* which 'were found empty, and there was evidence that they had been searched', Counsel went on to consider the large press in the pantry.

'This had been moved, and one door forced open with the aid of a chisel, or a blunt instrument. The window was unfastened, and on being asked if he had left it latched the previous night the prisoner said, "Yes". There were no scratches on the backyard wall, but there was a scratch on that window-sill.'

Enumerating the articles found by the police in the pantry, and describing their places of concealment, Counsel declared:

'Had a *thief* entered—had a thief *entered*—he would have *taken these things away*. But observe the fact that they were found in the place where the valet had peculiar access!'

Evidence would be produced to shew that the £10-note found behind the pantry skirting-board had been traced to Lord William's possession, and one of his relations would identify the gold locket which the prisoner had had in his possession *before* the murder.

Having commented upon the prisoner's strange behaviour in failing to render any assistance after the discovery of the crime, upon his peculiar agitation, and upon the fact that he had been fully dressed that morning, except for his coat, nearly an hour before his usual time, Mr Adolphus then gave vent to that observation already referred to, which, as Sir Harry Poland, K.C., was later to write,[1] gave Mr Phillips 'a fine topic in his speech to the jury'.

'The prisoner,' said Counsel, 'was a foreigner. Foreigners believed that English noblemen carried vast sums of gold about with them, and with foreigners murder was only too common a prelude to robbery, for they imagined that if they destroyed the life of the person they robbed, there would exist no testimony against them.'

When it came to Mr Phillips' turn to address the jury he construed this as meaning, 'This man is a foreigner, and foreigners always murder where they rob', and he manifested

[1]*Report on the Trial of Courvoisier for the Murder of Lord William Russell, with an Introduction by Sir Harry Poland and an Appendix by J. E. Latton Pickering,* printed for private circulation at the request of the 11th Duke of Bedford.

much moral indignation. But reference to the quotation from Courvoisier's confession which appears as the heading to Chapter 4 indicates that Mr Adolphus had exactly interpreted Courvoisier's sentiments.

2

Sarah Mancer was the first witness. The greater part of her evidence has already been incorporated in the narrative, and it is only necessary to consider that portion of it which furnished Mr Phillips with material for his cross-examination, the character of which aroused some adverse comment.[1]

Under examination she testified that the relations between herself and the prisoner had been friendly. At first he appeared contented with his post, but had latterly complained that his lordship was 'fussy' and hard to please. He had twice remarked to witness that if he had 'half old Billy's money, he would not remain long in England'.

On more than one occasion she had observed the valet 'looking into his lordship's property—not in one room, but all over the house'. When the valet had said in his pantry, 'My God, someone has been robbing us', witness had answered, 'For God's sake let us go and see where his lordship is'. Witness knew nothing about any articles being found in the valet's box until after his arrest.

Witness then described how, after drinking 'a small glass' of the beer which the valet had fetched, she had felt very drowsy, and went on to describe the difficulty she had had next morning in arousing the cook who had drunk considerably more. She believed 'something must have been put in the beer'.

Mr Phillips began his cross-examination by asking the witness if she had not already been questioned several times. Upon her acknowledging that she had, he asked her if this were

[1] That eminently fair commentator, Serjeant Ballantine, who was present throughout the trial observes: 'There is not, I think, any ground for saying that he endeavoured to fix guilt by unworthy means upon a servant girl. It may be said that in every case where it is acknowledged that an offence has been committed, the defence of the client must be founded on the assumption that someone else is guilty.'

not the first time she had said anything about the valet 'looking into his lordship's property'. She had to admit that this was so.

When giving the alarm in the street, Mr Phillips next inquired, had she not used the phrase that his lordship was 'murdered'? Witness hesitated, as though desirous of qualifying any answer she gave, but upon Mr Phillips repeating the question she replied in the affirmative.

'Then why,' demanded Counsel, 'did you only tell the Coroner that you said there was "blood on the pillow"?'

Had she been given the opportunity she might have explained that in her alarm she had not unnaturally associated the sight of her master's blood-soaked pillows with the thought of murder, and that she had not used the word 'murder' at the inquest, because the possibility of suicide had meanwhile arisen. But no such opportunity was afforded her and Mr Phillips proceeded to press her 'as to her motives' for saying to the valet, 'Let us go and see where his lordship is', when the 'obvious phrase' would have been, 'Let us go and tell his lordship that the house has been robbed.' Witness could only reply that she had no 'motives' for saying what she had said, and readily admitted that it was at her request that the valet had carried the step-ladder into the backyard.

'By means of which,' suggested Counsel, 'anyone could have got over into it from the adjoining one?'

Again witness could only agree.

After eliciting from her a description of the marks on the back door in words which suggested she had noticed them before the arrival of the police, Counsel induced her to agree that she had not looked at them until *after* the police had entered the house—an admission which furnished him with ammunition for later use against those officers.

But though the Defence had scored certain points, the main body of Sarah Mancer's evidence remained unshaken.

Mary Hannel, the cook, in reply to Counsel for the Crown, corroborated Sarah Mancer's evidence on all points within her knowledge; she had not actually seen the prisoner secure the front door after admitting her to the house on the night of 5th May, as she was going along the passage when he did so; but she had distinctly heard him shoot the bolts. She had drunk the beer he had fetched; he had never offered to fetch beer for her, or any other form of refreshment, until that night. She had felt very tired and sleepy, and on going to bed had fallen asleep at once. Usually she heard the housemaid get up at six o'clock, but that morning she had slept on, and had still been asleep when the housemaid had come up to tell her of the confusion below.

Mr Phillips scored two points by eliciting from her that 'the beer had seemed like any other beer' when she drank it; and, repeating a question he had put to Sarah Mancer, obtained a similar reply: namely that the missing table silver could have been carried off by anyone who had had access to the house at any time between the date on which the inventory had been checked and that on which the crime had been committed.

William York and *Daniel Young* gave evidence as to the events of that fatal morning, and the prisoner's strange demeanour, but concurred in Mr Phillips' suggestion that 'the sight of his master weltering in blood was enough to affect the nerves of the stoutest and strongest man'.

Doctors Elsgood and *Nursey* repeated the evidence they had given at the inquest.

Thomas Selway, footman at the house next door to No. 14, stated that while it would be possible for anyone to have climbed on to the roof of the outhouse in his master's yard and thence down the step-ladder into the backyard of No. 14, no strangers had been on his master's premises that day. He next shewed himself more observant than the police by pointing out that recently there had been no rain; as a result a coating of dust had formed along the top of the wall, which would have been disturbed, or shewn imprints, had anyone climbed over it, and this was not the case. The only point in favour of the Defence which Mr Phillips was able to gain was witness' statement that he had seen all the servants after the discovery of the crime and 'the maidservants had seemed just as agitated as the valet'.

Counsel on both sides generally manoeuvre to leave their case 'high' at the close of the day's proceedings, so that the jury may still be under the influence of its strength when the hearing is resumed next morning. It was a tactical error on the part of the Prosecution to put up *Constable Baldwin* as the last witness before the Court adjourned that day, for in his cross-examination of him Mr Phillips 'fell upon Baldwin and tossed and gored him',[1] thus leaving the case for the Crown in the doldrums.

John Baldwin, after describing how he had been summoned to the house, stated that he had found the prisoner 'sitting behind the pantry door with his hands to his face, refusing to get up and render assistance'. He then described the scene in Lord William's bedroom and his subsequent investigation of the premises. There was no sign that anyone had climbed over the wall, and he was positive that the back door had been forced from the inside in order to create the impression that someone, having come over the wall, had entered the house by it.

Counsel for the Crown had hardly seated himself when Counsel for the Defence was on his feet demanding to know why witness had stated at the inquest that the door had been forced from the *outside*, and now stated that an appearance of forcing had been *faked* from the *inside*. Witness replied that at first he believed that the door had been forced from the outside, but later had come to the conclusion he had made a mistake.

Mr Phillips: 'Might not mistakes be made intentionally?'

'I am not liable to make mistakes intentionally.'

'Do you know that such a thing amounts to misinformation?'

'I know that if a man does a thing intentionally, it is misrepresentation and not a mistake. I did at first think that someone had broken in, but afterwards I found that that was a mistake.'

Counsel then asked the witness if by then he had heard of the reward of £400 for information which would lead to the arrest and conviction of the murderer? Witness denied that he had heard of the reward. Had he not, persisted Counsel, seen the bills advertising it? Witness replied that he was much too busy a man to stop and read public notices. Had he not, Counsel demanded inexorably, *heard* the information read out aloud to all police officers in General Orders? Under the compelling eyes and minatory tone of his inquisitor the wretched

[1] *Famous Trials of the Century*—J. B. Atlay.

man was gradually and reluctantly forced to retract his denials
and confess that he had been present when the information had
been read out in General Orders; that he had seen and read
the bills advertising the rewards, and that he regarded the sum
of £400 as a great deal of money. Then, limp and discredited,
he made an ignominious exit from the witness-box.

'The Prosecution,' it was declared that evening, 'has no
case beyond suspicion and they cannot carry it further.'

In the London clubs that night the betting was heavily in
favour of Courvoisier's acquittal.

9

The Trial: Friday, 19th June

'For murder, though it have no tongue, will speak
With most miraculous organ.'[1]

I

THROUGHOUT the first day's proceedings no flicker of
expression had indicated what the accused man's
thoughts might have been, while every line of his body
had proclaimed the faintly ceremonious air of the well-trained
manservant. Next day, Friday, 19th June, he re-entered the
dock in the same deferential manner and maintained the same
demeanour. Again the Court was crowded with prominent
members of Society; again it was honoured by the presence of
the Duke of Sussex, wearing the little round black cap he
always affected; again a considerable crowd had assembled
outside its doors.

Although the English are a law-abiding people, they take
a peculiar pleasure in the discomfiture of Authority and are
wisely resentful of any suggestion of official corruption. The
exposure of Constable Baldwin the previous day had therefore
increased the feeling of hostility against the police, and this still
permeated the atmosphere when *Inspector John Tedman* entered
the witness-box. When he left it, however, he had succeeded in
dispelling some, at least, of the antipathy.

In reply to Mr Adolphus he described in detail his arrival
at the scene of the crime, the condition of the murdered man's
bedroom, and the disorder which had been created in other
parts of the house. The valet had appeared 'much concerned',

[1] *Hamlet*, Act II, Scene 2.

79

yet he did not then shew that disposition to render the assistance which might have been expected of him.

From the position and character of the bruises on the back door it seemed to witness that some had been made from the inside and others from the outside, and after describing these he said that neither they nor the confusion in the various rooms suggested the work of burglars, but rather that all had been deliberately contrived to create the impression that the house had been entered and burgled.

Next he described the search which had been made for the missing articles, and where and when the watch, seals, rings and the gold locket had been found. All these were proved to have been the property of the deceased, and all, except the locket, had been in deceased's possession at the time of his murder. Furthermore there was proof that, until Easter, the locket had also been in his possession and had disappeared while he was at Richmond and the prisoner had been in attendance upon him. There were witnesses to prove that a £10-note had been handed to deceased shortly before his death, and that note had been found hidden in the prisoner's pantry.

Mr Phillips, in cross-examining, was mainly concerned to try and expose a police plot against the prisoner.

'Are there not,' he asked, 'a number of bruises on the back door which were not there when you first examined it?'

'Yes, sir.'

'Did you give orders for those marks to be made?'

'I did not, sir.'

After a number of other questions to all of which he received equally unequivocal replies, Mr Phillips asked:

'Did you examine the prisoner's hands, forearms and clothing soon after you reached the scene?'

'Yes, sir.'

'Did the prisoner shew any reluctance towards this examination of his person?'

'No, sir.'

'He shewed no reluctance, no disinclination, no confusion?'

'No, sir; none.'

Turning to the gloves, handkerchief and 'dickey' found in the prisoner's box after his arrest, Counsel asked if these could have been overlooked by witness when he had previously searched it.

'I took each article out of the box and placed it separately on the bed, and I found nothing the least incriminating.'

'Then the articles mentioned could not have been in the box without your observing them?'

'No, sir; not without my observing them.'

'You believe them to have been placed there subsequently?'

'They could have been placed there subsequently.'

'The box was left unlocked and the police had access to it?'

'Yes, sir.'

Having thus suggested a conspiracy on the part of the police to 'frame' a case against the accused, Mr Phillips went on:

'I am given to understand that several articles of table silver are alleged to be missing?'

'Yes, sir; fourteen table forks and spoons. They were included on the inventory, which was checked and signed by the prisoner when he took charge from the former valet.'

Mr Phillips: 'You made an extensive search of the whole premises, had the carpets up, the drains up, and sweeps to search every chimney—from attic to basement the search was made?'

'Yes, sir.'

'The prisoner did not leave the premises after ten o'clock on the night before the crime; he was segregated from the other servants and not permitted to hold any communication with anyone from outside the premises—yet no piece of those missing forks and spoons has been found?'

'No, sir.'

'Nor heard of?'

'No, sir.'

Witness went on to admit that if the fourteen spoons and forks had been anywhere on the premises they must inevitably have been found.

Inspector Tedman was followed into the witness-box by a succession of officers, of whom it fell to the lot of *Inspector Pearce* to solve the riddle as to how the additional marks on the back door came to be made. 'I made them,' he stated, 'in the course of carrying out some experiments.' Mr Phillips handled him somewhat roughly for having said to the prisoner when shewing him the articles discovered behind the pantry skirting-board: 'Can you look me in the face and say you know nothing about these things?' This, Counsel suggested to the Court, had been done with the object of forcing an admission from the accused, and so staking a claim to any reward that might be proffered. The witness, while admitting the words, denied the motive attributed to him.

Sergeant Collier, another police witness, was treated by Counsel for the Defence in the same peremptory fashion. He stated that he had been present when Inspector Tedman had searched the prisoner's box on the day of his arrest, and Mr Phillips elicited from him the admission that 'it would have been practically impossible for the bloodstained things to escape notice if they had been there'.

Mr Phillips: 'They must have been seen?'

'If they had been there, no one with eyes could have failed to see them.'

Counsel also extracted from witness the further admission that the police, and the women servants as well, had had at all times unimpeded access to the valet's room, and that the former had been aware, on the Monday following that search and the prisoner's arrest, of the proffered reward and regarded £400 as a handsome sum.

The advantage which had hitherto accrued to the Defence was to some extent offset by the testimony of the last two witnesses called by the Prosecution. The Defence did not cross-examine.

Thomas Wing, the Russell family solicitor, identified the £10-note found in the pantry by the initials on its back as one which he had drawn in a cheque for £200 on behalf of his client, Lady de Clifford, who before her present marriage had been the widow of Lord William's son, Captain George Russell, R.N. His client had handed it to the deceased who was to have passed it on to his sister-in-law, Lady Janet Bailey, for the benefit of charity.

Lady Janet Bailey stated that Lady de Clifford subscribed to various charities in which she, witness, was interested. She had been expecting a visit from Lord William at the time of his death. He came frequently to see her in her apartments at Hampton Court Palace, and had done so at Easter while staying at the Castle Hotel, Richmond. He had attended Service in the private chapel with her on Easter Sunday. Before doing so he had taken out his pocket-book to shew her a letter and a gold locket had dropped out with it. 'I gave it to him. He laid it on the table. . . . When we returned from Service I saw him put it in the breast pocket of his coat. He had a great regard for it and was very distressed by its loss. There was a curl of hair in the locket; the hair was tied with blue ribbon. I cannot swear whose hair it was.' Having examined the locket, which was handed to her witness said: 'The locket now shewn me is that locket, and the hair in it is the hair I saw, tied in that particular way with the blue ribbon. . . .'

That closed the case for the Prosecution.

2

Lady Julia Lockwood was the first witness called by the Defence. Her evidence was brief and uncontested by the Prosecution. The prisoner, she stated, had been in her employment as second footman for nine months; she had been entirely satisfied with him and considered him a quiet, harmless and inoffensive young man. She had never had any reason to suspect him of dishonesty, and he had left her service for a situation in a larger establishment.

Mr Fector, M.P., stated that the prisoner had come to him from the service of the last witness, and had remained with him nearly two years. Throughout that time he had been obliging, efficient and respectful, and on good terms with everyone. He had left witness' service of his own accord to enter that of Lord William Russell.

Peter Jellings, proprietor of the Hotel Bristol, Jermyn Street, testified that the prisoner had been a waiter in his employment 'from the time of his arrival in England' until he had left to enter private service. He had worked well and had been well liked, and witness 'had been impressed with the kindness and humanity of his disposition'. Since then he had made a habit of coming to see witness in a friendly way, and witness had always been pleased to see him.

James Noble, waiter at the same establishment, corroborated his employer's evidence. The prisoner 'was the most humane young man, the most quiet and respectable young man, he had ever known'.

Henry Pritchard, butler, stated that he had known the prisoner 'ever since he had come to this country four years ago'. He and witness had been in the service of Lady Julia Lockwood at the same time, and witness had seen him often since. He was a young man of 'great good feeling'.

The general impression abroad in London that evening was that, although with the evidence of Mr Wing and Lady Janet Bailey the case against the prisoner was strong enough to convict him had he been charged with theft, it was not strong enough to convict him of the charge in the indictment. So long as those missing pieces of silver were undiscovered the possibility remained that a second person had been involved in the crime, and therefore that he, and not Courvoisier, might have been the actual murderer. So long as that possibility existed no jury was likely to return a verdict against him, and in consequence the intensity of public excitement was that night somewhat abated. Nevertheless a large section of Society was eagerly looking forward to the next day's proceedings, which would open with Mr Phillips' address to the jury. This would undoubtedly be a *tour-de-force*; the cadence of his golden voice, his histrionic powers, his elegant good looks, would all be exercised to the full on behalf of his client; and everyone who could contrive to squeeze themselves into the Court intended to be present.

While the last of the witnesses for the Defence were giving their evidence Mr Adolphus had been summoned from Court to a consultation with the Attorney-General over the arraignment of a mulatto named Edward Oxford on a charge of High Treason. The events leading up to this charge had shocked the loyal Mr Adolphus, as they had shocked the whole country—indeed, all Europe. In February London had been *en fête* for the marriage of the Queen to Prince Albert of Saxe-Coburg-

Gotha, and there was general satisfaction when, about the time she celebrated her twenty-first birthday in May, it began to be rumoured that she was *enceinte*. Even in these days, case-hardened though we be to atrocities, it is not difficult to imagine the sense of horror which ensued when, as the royal couple were driving up Constitution Hill at a quarter past six on the evening of Wednesday, 10th June, Edward Oxford stepped out from among the spectators on the pavement, drew two pistols and fired them both in succession at Her Majesty, fortunately without effect.[1]

3

While Mr Adolphus was in consultation over this grave case, while Courvoisier, from the dock, was listening to the witnesses who were testifying to his humanity and other good qualities, and while Mr Phillips was, perhaps, turning over in his mind some telling phrases for use on the morrow, a man named Joseph Vincent was idly scanning the pages of a French news-paper in the saloon of a small and rather dingy commercial hotel off Leicester Square.

There were several small hotels of varying degrees of dingi-ness in that particular neighbourhood and most of them bore unsavoury reputations, but the reputation of the Hotel Dieppe had so far been preserved unblemished. Joseph Vincent was its part-proprietor with a Frenchman named Louis Piolaine, who was married to Vincent's cousin Charlotte. And Charlotte was the manageress of the hotel.

As Joseph Vincent's glance strayed up and down the columns of that newspaper, the fate of the man in the dock hung in the balance, for whether he should 'die a death of shame on a day of dark disgrace', or whether he should go free,

---

[1] 'It would be difficult,' says the *Annual Register*, 'to describe the state of loyal excitement into which the metropolis has been thrown by this event. At the different theatres, and at places where public dinners were held, as soon as the news transpired on Wednesday evening "God save the Queen" was sung with loyal fervour.'

Edward Oxford was eventually found guilty of High Treason and sentenced to death but reprieved on grounds of insanity. Queen Victoria herself made frequent inquiries concerning him and kept him supplied with reading matter.

depended upon whether Joseph Vincent's eye was caught and held by a certain paragraph, or whether it passed on.

It was caught and held, and he read—though without paying much attention, for he knew it already—that a young Swiss of the name of François Benjamin Courvoisier, who had been employed in domestic service in London for the past four years, was being brought to trial on Thursday, 18th June, on the accusation of having murdered his master, Lord William Russell. It was the next portion of the paragraph which aroused Joseph Vincent's interest, and sealed the fate of Courvoiser; this was to the effect that, since the English police had failed to find certain articles of value which had disappeared from the murdered man's residence about the time of the crime, it might be worth their while, if they had not already done so, to search the known resorts of foreigners in London, such as Soho.

It did not appear likely to Joseph Vincent that, at this late stage in the proceedings, the police would adopt this advice, but since the *clientele* of the Hotel Dieppe was almost exclusively foreign he took the paper up to his cousin's room and shewed her the paragraph. She read it and put the paper aside, for she was busy; but while the name 'Courvoisier' conveyed nothing to her, the wording of the paragraph awoke an echo in her memory. The accused was Swiss; he was young, and had come to London about four years previously; the articles had been missing since the crime was committed, which was six weeks ago. And six weeks ago there had occurred a little incident at the Hotel Dieppe to which Madame Piolaine had not given a second thought, but which now recurred vividly to her mind.

Going to a cupboard she unlocked it and took out a parcel. About eighteen inches long and rather less in breadth it was very neatly wrapped up in strong brown paper of good quality, with every knot of the string carefully sealed. She noticed, too, that it was curiously heavy for its size.

She shewed it to her cousin. Her husband was absent in France and after some discussion she and Joseph Vincent decided to ask the advice of a friend of theirs, Louis Gardi, as to what they should do, with the result that shortly afterwards the two men set out for the City to consult a solicitor of their acquaintance, Mr Richard Cumming.

Thus it was that, as the Court was on the point of rising that Friday evening, Mr Cumming was travelling as fast as a hackney-cab could carry him from Marlborough Street police station, where he had made a deposition, to the Old Bailey with the object of obtaining an interview with Counsel for the Prosecution. He was received by Mr Adolphus' juniors, who, in their turn, were soon hastening to acquaint their leader with a new development. *For that parcel contained the missing plate.*

Thus it was that, under that date, *Friday, 19th June,* Mr Adolphus recorded in his diary: '*On this evening a new line of facts was disclosed.*'[1]

Smarting from their handling by Mr Phillips, and spurred on by the knowledge that the attack he would launch against them the next day would be virulent indeed, the police, all through that livelong night, worked with feverish energy to discover the whereabouts of those fresh witnesses who would be needed to establish this 'new line of facts' and so deprive Mr Phillips of his ultimate triumph.

4

That great criminal lawyer, Sir Harry Poland, was to write in years to come that he could not recall a single other instance in the history of our Courts where evidence of a conclusive nature was, as in this case, produced in Court on the last day of a trial against a prisoner on a capital charge.

This last-minute evidence was not only to result in the conviction of Courvoisier, but was also to prove calamitous to Mr Phillips, and the history of what took place behind the scenes at the Old Bailey on that day makes almost as fascinating and dramatic a story as do the events which took place within

[1] Errors not infrequently creep into accounts of famous cases and are subsequently perpetuated. In his *Introduction to the Trial of Courvoisier,* already quoted, even Sir Harry Poland is sometimes guilty of giving the date of this disclosure as Thursday, 18th June. The same mistake is made by J. B. Atlay in his *Famous Trials of the Century* (1899), and this has recently been repeated by Lord Russell of Liverpool in *Though the Heavens Fall.* That it was in fact Friday, 19th, all contemporary accounts of the case, and the dramatic nature of its climax, make abundantly clear.

the Court itself, and it created almost as great a sensation. The controversy which ensued—a controversy hotly contested in the contemporary Press and as hotly argued in legal circles, remains even to this day a subject of debate. To the historian of crime it becomes a duty to rescue the facts from the fog of partisanship and the mire of prejudice. Let us, therefore, now observe what was taking place behind the scenes before the Court began to sit that day, for, with this knowledge in our minds, we can better understand and appreciate the drama of the *dénouement*.

One of our most reliable sources of information is Mr Serjeant Ballantine, who as we know was present in Court on all three days of the trial. He records that when he entered the robing room of the Old Bailey on that Saturday morning, shortly before the arrival of the Chief Justice and his Associate Judge, Mr Baron Parke, he was in ignorance of the overnight developments. 'I saw Phillips there,' he writes, 'who seemed in a great state of excitement.'

The Times provides an account of what had happened an hour or two earlier when two police officers had escorted Madame Piolaine to a room in Newgate overlooking the press-yard where Courvoisier was taking exercise among the other prisoners.

'Madame Piolaine came to Newgate and, having seen the prisoner in the press-yard, she at once identified him as the man by whom the parcel containing the missing plate had been left at her house. The fact of the plate having been discovered and the identity of the prisoner proved, a communication to that effect was made to the prisoner, and on hearing a piece of information so astonishing and unexpected he turned deathly pale and became extremely agitated, *and before the time arrived for his being placed at the bar he sent for Mr Phillips, his Counsel.*'[1]

A later edition of the same newspaper adds the following information:

[1] Author's italics.

'Courvoisier . . . requested an interview with his Counsel, and upon this occasion he admitted the correctness of the statement as to the discovery.'

That is to say *he admitted to his Counsel that the parcel contained the missing silver and that it was he who had deposited it with Madame Piolaine*,[1] and he made this admission '*before* the time arrived for his being placed at the bar'—before, in fact, the Judges had arrived; and it was this admission that had produced that 'great state of excitement' in Mr Phillips which Serjeant Ballantine had observed. The latter, indeed, thus corroborates and amplifies the foregoing account:

'*He* [Courvoisier] *did not, as was generally supposed and asserted at the time, avow that he had committed the murder*,[2] although doubtless what he did own was very stringent evidence of the fact, and the communication was certainly made, *not for the purpose of admitting his guilt, but merely to prepare his Counsel to deal with the evidence.*'

That is perfectly clear; by acknowledging his connection with the parcel of silver he implicitly admitted that no second person was concerned in the crime, and the only inference to be drawn from that was that he alone was guilty. But he did not admit that guilt in so many words, and therefore his Counsel was not absolved from continuing his defence.

It was the duty of the Prosecution to inform Mr Phillips of the new facts which had come into their possession, but they were not aware of them until late the previous evening, and they could not disclose them until they had been confirmed, and until Madame Piolaine had identified the prisoner. Consequently when Mr Phillips received Courvoisier's request for an interview on his arrival at the Old Bailey that morning neither he nor Mr Clarkson, his junior, had any idea of the nature of the revelation which awaited them, and, suddenly confronted with this unexpected development, the mercurial Mr Phillips lost his head. Mr Serjeant Ballantine writes:

[1] Author's italics.
[2] Author's italics.

89

'Mr Charles Phillips was a curious compound of intellectual strength and weakness. He possessed undoubted genius . . . but was deficient in moral courage and self-reliance. . . . The course pursued by Mr Phillips shewed the inherent weakness of his character. It was peculiarly a situation for self-reliance and sound judgment. He was bound to continue the defence, although his mode of conducting it could not but be materially affected by the new evidence. Mr Phillips, however, adopted a line that was wholly inexcusable.

'He sought an interview with Baron Parke—who . . . although not the presiding Judge, was assisting at the trial —communicated to him the confession of his client, and asked his advice. This conduct placed the Judge in a most painful position and was grievously unjust to the accused. It is possible that, if Baron Parke had not been taken by surprise, he would have declined to express an opinion. . . . Having learned that the prisoner did not intend to relieve his Counsel of the defence, the learned Baron said that of course he must go on with it. . . . This was the only advice he could give, and ought to have been patent to the inquirer.'

Mr Phillips' own account of this dramatic episode differs in certain most important particulars from those provided by *The Times* and by Mr Serjeant Ballantine, but its principal significance lies in the fact that, in spite of the controversy his conduct aroused, it was not until nine years later that he made it public, and this he did in a letter which appeared in *The Times* of 20th November 1849.

'Just before the Judges entered [*he wrote*], Courvoisier, *standing publicly in front of the dock*,[1] solicited an interview with his Counsel. My excellent friend and colleague, Mr Clarkson, and myself immediately approached him. . . . Up to that morning I believed most firmly in his innocence, and so did others as well as myself. "I have sent for you, gentlemen," said he, "*to tell you I committed the murder.*"[2]

[1] Author's italics.
[2] Author's italics.

When I could speak, which was not immediately, I said: "Of course, then, you are going to plead Guilty?" "No, sir," was the reply, "I expect you to defend me to the utmost."

'My position was, I believe, without parallel in the annals of the profession. . . . Mr Clarkson suggested obtaining the opinion of the learned Judge *who was not trying the case*,[1] upon what he considered to be the professional etiquette under circumstances so embarrassing. In this I willingly acquiesced. We obtained an interview, and Mr Baron Parke requested to know distinctly whether the prisoner insisted on my defending him, and, on hearing that he did, said I was bound to do so, and to use all fair arguments arising on the evidence. I therefore retained the brief.'

An adequate commentary upon this apologia is provided by no less an authority than Sir Harry Poland, who says:[2]

'Mr Baron Parke was, I know, much annoyed that he had been told of Courvoisier's confession, *for he was as much trying the case as the Chief Justice;* the practice at the Central Criminal Court in 1840, and for years afterwards, was that all the Judges on the rota sat together to try cases, and in this case Mr Baron Parke took an active part in the trial. . . .

'There can be no doubt that both Mr Phillips and Mr Clarkson committed a grave error of judgment in consulting Mr Baron Parke on the subject. In the first place any statement to the solicitor or Counsel is sacred, and ought not to be told to anyone, and yet he informed Mr Baron Parke, who was one of the Judges trying Courvoisier, of this confession. . . .'

In the light, therefore, of the contemporary accounts provided by *The Times* and by Mr Serjeant Ballantine, and in that of Sir Harry Poland's considered opinion, one is forced to the conclusion that Mr Phillips' own belated version of the incident, though specious, is inaccurate.

[1] Author's italics.
[2] *Op. cit.*

10

The Trial: Saturday, 20th June

'If the great criminals told the truth, they would very rarely tell
of their struggles against crime. Their struggles are towards it.
They buffet with opposing waves to gain the bloody shore—not to
recede from it.'[1]

I

The Times tells us that 'a rumour having got abroad that
some important discoveries had been made by the police,
at an early hour the crowd began to form before the
Court'.

The London underworld keeps a wary eye on police
activities, and police activities had been intense that Friday
night. Rumour flattens out and spreads low, like smoke in
a sudden squall; it eddied through taverns in mean streets; it
was spread by belated roisterers making their uncertain way
home; it was circulated by those whose work forced them out
of bed before the sun had risen. By the time the small tradesmen
of Snow Hill were taking down the shutters of their shops
rumour had caused a strangely assorted crowd to collect
beneath the walls of Newgate; a crowd palpitating with a sub-
dued excitement which communicated itself even to those who
did not fully understand its cause, so that even the ladies of
Mayfair in their gossamer India muslins, driving to take their
privileged places on the Bench at the Old Bailey, caught its
contagion and their pulses quickened. Their number was
greater than on the previous days, as was that of the gentlemen
who accompanied them, while from the number of barristers
present it might be inferred that no other case was being heard

[1] Charles Dickens.

in all the Courts of London that day, and every individual who entered the Old Bailey was immediately conscious of a peculiar thrilling sense of expectancy, which reached a new peak of intensity when the trim, erect, black-clad figure of the prisoner entered the dock, and it was noticed that, in spite of his composure, his face was deathly pale.

It was just after ten o'clock when, in the words of *The Times*:

'Immediately on their lordships taking their seats Mr Adolphus rose and said that in the course of yesterday afternoon a very important piece of evidence had come to the knowledge of the Prosecution, and, as that part of the case had not been opened, he was quite ready now, if their lordships thought it necessary, to make a short statement to the jury.'

Every eye had been fixed on Mr Adolphus; now all switched to the prisoner before turning with one accord to Mr Phillips as he swiftly rose to say in sharp protest:

'In justice to the prisoner a communication of the facts should have been made to me immediately they came to the knowledge of the Prosecution.'

Mr Adolphus: 'I believe the communication took place as soon as possible.'

Mr Phillips: 'I completely deprecate any fresh statement on the subject to the jury.'

The Chief Justice: 'It is quite unnecessary to make any additional statement to the jury, because the evidence must be such as should enable them to understand and apply it.'

Mr Phillips: 'I pledge my word that neither I nor Mr Clarkson received any information about the matter till within the last quarter of an hour. The prisoner's attorney is ready to take his oath that he received no communication whatever.'

The Chief Justice: 'Let us have no more argument about it. Call the witness.'

The Clerk of the Court: 'Call Charlotte Piolaine.'

'When the woman appeared in Court [*wrote Mr Adolphus in his diary*], and the prisoner, who had maintained throughout the trial the greatest composure, saw her,

93

he became most agitated, gushed out into a profuse per-
spiration and nearly fainted.'

It was not surprising; in Madame Piolaine he beheld the
one person in all the world whose evidence would be fatal to
him. As 'neatly attired in black' she entered the witness-box
and took the oath, he knew that, unless a miracle occurred, the
gallows awaited him. He, who had felt no compassion towards
the old man whom he had murdered while he slept, who had
given no thought to the shock and grief his act would cause his
victim's family, to whom deceit and treachery had never
occasioned a pang, now felt the arrow pierce his cold armour
at last. His appearance was so ghastly that he was told he might
be 'accommodated with a chair', but he 'declined the offer'
and, after an immense effort, 'appeared . . . to completely
recover his composure'.

In tense silence Mr Adolphus began his examination of the
witness, who thus replied to his questions:

Charlotte Piolaine: 'My husband's name is Louis Piolaine; he
keeps an hotel, in Leicester Place, Leicester Square. Mr Joseph
Vincent, his partner, is my cousin. I am of English birth. I
know the prisoner at the bar; I knew him about four years ago;
he came to our hotel to ask for a situation. I don't remember
that he gave me his name; we used to call him "*Jean*" in the
hotel—in English that is "John". French is generally spoken
in our hotel. He lived with us as a servant for about a month or
five weeks—not longer. I never saw him since that time until
about six weeks ago.

'He came to me at the Hotel Dieppe one Sunday morning
and knocked at the door of my room. I said, "Come in" and he
walked in. I did not recognize him at the moment, and he said:
"Don't you recognize me?" I said, "No", and he said: "I am
Jean who lived with you some time ago." I then recognized
him. I asked him if he was in a situation, and he said he was.
I said: "I'm glad of it." He soon went.

'I saw him again on the Sunday a week or a fortnight later.[1]
He came in the evening and asked me how I was. He had a
parcel—a brown-paper parcel—in his hand, and he asked me

[1] Sunday,—3rd May.

94

to take care of it, saying he would call for it on the Tuesday evening following. It was tied up and sealed. I said, "Certainly I will," and he left it and went away. I put it in a cupboard and locked it up. He did not call for it on the Tuesday following, and I never saw him again until today.

'In consequence of what was published in a French newspaper my cousin had some communication with me. My husband was absent in France. We consulted a friend[1] and I subsequently sent for Mr Cumming and another person[2] who came for the purpose of seeing what the parcel contained, and it was opened in their presence.'

A Court official exhibited the parcel, and Charlotte Piolaine continued in evidence:

'The parcel produced is the one the prisoner left with me. It contained some silver spoons and forks, two pairs of stockings, a gold instrument for assisting hearing, and a jacket. There was also some tow in the parcel which prevented the plate from being felt and kept it from rattling. We tied the parcel up again after taking an inventory. I signed the inventory.'

Courvoisier had composed his features into a mask-like rigidity, but they glistened moistly, and his long fingers gripped the edge of the dock so forcefully that they shewed livid against the dark wood.

Later on in his address to the jury Mr Phillips was to lay much stress on the fact that the Defence had been deprived of any opportunity to pursue inquiries as to the *bona fides* of Madame Piolaine and the proprietors of the Hotel Dieppe, and to remind the jury that, despite this, they, like everyone else, must be aware of the unsavoury reputation generally born by licensed premises in the vicinity of Leicester Square. Now he concentrated his cross-examination on trying to extract from Madame Piolaine some admission which would suggest that the Hotel Dieppe was a place of ill-repute, a gambling den, the refuge of thieves and fugitives from justice, and watched by the police, and that the testimony of persons connected with it should be regarded with suspicion, especially when so considerable a sum as £400 was involved. Sarah Mancer had been

[1] Louis Gardi.
[2] Mr Cumming's clerk.

confused, if not intimidated, by Mr Phillips' tactics, but Madame Piolaine was made of sterner stuff; she rebutted all his suggestions with complete imperturbability.

She and her cousin were English, she told him; her husband was French. All three of them resided at the Hotel Dieppe, though her husband's business sometimes took him to France. He had many acquaintances in both countries. No suspicious characters or undesirable aliens sought refuge at the Hotel Dieppe, nor had the police ever entered it. The foreigners who patronized it were engaged on lawful business. As for gambling, it was true there was a billiard table on the premises, but it was used solely for purposes of recreation.

What of backgammon? demanded Counsel. Backgammon, witness answered, was never played there; the hotel did not even possess a backgammon board.[1]

Mr Phillips next suggested that this eleventh hour production of the silver was a plot on the part of the witness, her husband and cousin, to incriminate the prisoner and so claim the reward. When, he asked, had she first heard of the murder?

'I heard of the murder the day after it occurred.'

'Were you not shocked? Did you not hear it discussed and discuss it with your husband?'

'I was very much shocked, but I cannot say that I spoke to my husband about it. I have no time to talk of such things.'

In answer to further questions witness said: 'I do not speak with people in the public rooms of the hotel; I did not speak of the murder to anybody; I never saw placards about rewards; I do not go out much, I am far too busy with my special occupations.'

Mr Phillips: 'Did your "special occupations" allow you to converse with your husband on any "special" topic during the three weeks after the murder?'

'My husband was in London for about three weeks after

---

[1] Backgammon had at that time an evil reputation. It had figured prominently at the trial of Thurtell for the murder of William Weare. Thurtell had invited Weare for a country visit, and thither he went complete with backgammon board. Weare's murder was said to have been due to the fact that he had been dunning Thurtell for debts incurred at backgammon. As already stated Mr Phillips had been one of the junior Counsel engaged in that case. Thurtell was convicted and hanged (1823).

the murder, but whether I spoke to him or not of the murder during that time I cannot say.'

'Will it please my lord to take notice of that answer?'

The next witness was *Louis Gardi*. He testified as follows: 'I am a modeller. I live in King Street, Soho. I am acquainted with Madame Piolaine of the Hotel Dieppe. I was present one Sunday when a parcel was brought there, but I did not pay much attention to it. . . . I cannot say positively that the prisoner was the man who brought it, because he stopped so short a time.

'I was at the hotel yesterday; Monsieur Piolaine's partner fetched me; he said something to me and we went together to Mr Cumming in the City, and Mr Cumming came back with us to the hotel. A parcel was then produced in the presence of Mr Vincent, Madame Piolaine and myself; the parcel, to the best of my recollection, was left at the hotel about the time of the murder, but I cannot say on what date.'

Richard Cumming, whom Mr Adolphus described in his diary as 'a respectable attorney', stated: 'I am a solicitor and reside at 17 Old Jewry. Mr Vincent and the last witness came to my office yesterday, and I accompanied them to the hotel in Leicester Place. When I got there a parcel was produced, and after my advice was asked about it, I opened it and made out a list of the articles it contained. Before I tied it up again I noted the crest which was on the spoons and forks: it was a goat, and having satisfied myself that a goat was the crest of the Bedford family I immediately proceeded to the police station in Marlborough Street, where I made a statement, and was directed to come here and see the Attorney for the Prosecution. Besides the spoons and forks there was one leather box containing a gold ear apparatus, two pairs of white stockings, one striped jacket and a quantity of tow.'

Joseph Vincent corroborated the evidence of the previous witnesses. He remembered that a young man called '*Jean*' had been employed about four years previously at the Hotel Dieppe for a few weeks; he believed the prisoner to be that person, but would not swear to it. He himself was of English birth, as was his cousin, Charlotte Piolaine; he was the partner of Monsieur Piolaine who had been absent in France for the past three weeks. 'After I had read something in a French newspaper I conversed with Madame Piolaine, and was subsequently present when the parcel was opened, after which I signed the paper produced.'

Henry Carr stated that he had seen the prisoner wearing a striped jacket, like the one produced, when they had both been in the employment of Mr Fector.

Lydia Banks, washerwoman, identified the stockings as belonging to the prisoner.

Thomas Davis identified the hearing-aid as one bought by Lord William Russell from witness' former employer, the late Mr Wilder, in June 1836.

James Ellis, now valet to Lord Mansfield, identified the hearing-aid as one which he had sometimes seen his lordship using when he had been in his employment. He also identified the forks and spoons as being Lord William's property. His evidence was corroborated by *Sarah Mancer*.

Mr Molteno, of Pall Mall, stated that he was an art-dealer and print seller. Lord William Russell, who was a connoisseur of art, often visited his shop and sometimes made purchases. About nine days before his murder his lordship had purchased a print of *The Vision of Ezekiel*. Witness had been shewn the brown paper in which the stolen articles had been wrapped; it was 'the very piece' in which he had packed up and sent the print to Lord William Russell.

In reply to *Mr Phillips* witness said: 'I recognize it as the wrapping of that print which was sent to Lord William Russell from my shop, as my label is stuck on it. I always stick such a label on all parcels sent to customers.'

The evidence of Mr Molteno provided the last link in the chain of circumstantial evidence against the prisoner. Eye-witnesses may be mistaken in their observations; their memories may play them false; they may perjure themselves; but here was an example of a chain of circumstantial evidence, unbroken at any point, every link of which was tested and proved, and consistent with the guilt of the accused. No jury could require more.

Apart from the sounds inseparable from such proceedings, the silence which had gripped the Court remained unbroken when *Mr Phillips* rose to make his speech.

'Mr Phillips' appeal to the jury [*Sir Harry Poland was to write*] is remarkable as coming from a man to whom Courvoisier had confessed his guilt. In fact such a speech would not be delivered by any barrister at the present day, but Mr Phillips was expected to make a fine speech, and the difficulty of his position, his excitement, and the crowded Court, certainly caused him, in my judgment, to go too far. . . . Mr Phillips is reported to have said, "The Omniscient God alone knows who did this crime," and again, "Even supposing him (Courvoisier) guilty of the murder, which was indeed known to Almighty God alone, and of which for the sake of his eternal soul he (Mr Phillips) hoped he was innocent." We may hope that he was not quite correctly reported.'[1]

Sir Harry Poland was born into the world after the event of which he was writing, but Mr Serjeant Ballantine had already had some thirty years' experience of the Criminal Courts before he heard that speech delivered, and he wrote of it as follows:

'I heard Phillips' speech. It was extremely eloquent. He made the most of some indiscretions in his opponent's opening, but he was overweighted by the facts, and certainly, since I have been at the Bar, juries have not shewn themselves apt to be carried away by flowers of rhetoric. Many of those used by him in his speech were not only in bad taste —whatever might have been the circumstances—but upon this occasion were utterly unjustifiable.'

After quoting those selfsame expressions which Sir Harry Poland was later to do, Serjeant Ballantine continues:

[1] *Op. cit.*

'Such expressions from the mouth of an advocate, possessing the knowledge that Phillips did at the time he used them, are not only offensive to good taste, but scarcely escape conveying a positive falsehood. . . . The only excuse I can find for Phillips is from the knowledge that he always composed his important speeches before he delivered them, and up to the morning of the last day he believed that Courvoisier was innocent. But whilst this may redeem him from the imputation of conveying a falsehood, it does not excuse the language in which he indulged. . . . He certainly laid himself open to very grave censure.'[1]

Where Mr Phillips' peculiar talents had established him in the forefront of his profession, so his marriage with a beautiful and aristocratic heiress had established him in Society, and there can be no doubt that he arrived at the Old Bailey that morning expecting to dazzle with his forensic eloquence both the Court itself and the greatest galaxy of fashion which had ever attended a criminal trial. His vanity, his unstable temperament, would not permit him to readjust himself to circumstances which had so suddenly and drastically altered since the night before, or to discard those 'flowers of rhetoric' he had so confidently and triumphantly prepared. Nor did he remember Mr Baron Parke's advice *'to use all fair arguments arising on the evidence'*.

Beginning 'low' by saying that 'after twenty years' experience of the criminal courts he had seldom risen to address a jury with more painful and anxious sensations'; that 'he left them to imagine how much that anxiety must be increased by the production—without any notice whatever—of evidence by which the life of the unhappy man at the bar might be placed in the greatest peril—and he said *"might"* because he did not consider the additional proof by any means conclusive'—he soon began to exceed this initial restraint. Referring to the 'bitter tone' of Mr Adolphus' opening speech, and to 'the prejudice which he endeavoured to raise against the prisoner by telling them, the jury, that it was the common practice of foreigners to murder where they robbed', and after pointing

[1] *Op. cit.*—see, however, Appendix I.

to the rarity of crime in Switzerland and 'the virtuous character of the prisoner's fellow-countrymen', his voice grew tremulous with emotion as he went on to say that he, his associates, and the jury themselves, were 'all embarked on the same cause: the life of a fellow-creature was entrusted to their keeping, and so surely as they dealt with that life, and justly so, so surely would they have to answer for it to the God who made them. When he looked around him on that crowded Court, and saw the intensity of the public gaze, and almost heard the throb of popular indignation, and when he turned him to the dock, where the wretched object of this outburst stood—alone amid the multitude, far from his native land, far from the friends who loved him . . . a poor, solitary, helpless foreigner—he did own that he could feel his spirits fainting fast within him, were it not for the anchor by which he held fast; an anchor that was centred in the hearts of the jury. . . .

'I rely upon your integrity,' he told them—and though he was addressing them collectively, he managed to convey the impression that his words were addressed to each member individually—'upon your sense of justice. I participate in the generous reliance which the prisoner shewed when he refused all foreign interference and entrusted his life to a jury of Englishmen. The prisoner was right and I myself have no fear of appealing to this tribunal. . . . I submit that in such a case as this, wrapped up in the clouds, in mystery and darkness, there is not only nothing upon which you can safely convict the prisoner, but here and there probabilities start up which might make you suspect that he had been the victim of an unjust and depraved conspiracy. . . .

'The Prosecution was bound to shew the prisoner's guilt—not by inference, not by subtle and refined ingenuity, but by downright, clear and palpable demonstration. How did they do this? What said Mr Adolphus and his witness, Sarah Mancer? . . . As for the prisoner, he had no motive of hatred, of jealousy, of revenge. Plunder had been suggested, and this expression brought up against him: "I wish I had old Billy's money: I would not be long in this country." Could there be a more innocent and natural expression from the lips of a foreigner far from his native land? . . .

'Who put the bloodstained gloves and shirt-front into the prisoner's box? I assert freely and fearlessly that they were placed there by some of the police. Baldwin lied on his oath; Inspector Pearce denied attempting to intimidate the prisoner, while in the same breath he admitted that he expected to share the plunder, and divide the reward of £400 over the coffin of Courvoisier. . . . And was it not singular that not a spot of blood, nor a scratch, had been discovered on the clothes or person of the prisoner?'

Turning to the evidence of Madame Piolaine, he said:

'If this be true, it is conclusive, not of *murder*, but of *robbery*. . . . If the prisoner is acquitted of the charge on the indictment, he will still be answerable for the robbery'—in which case, suggested Counsel, transportation would be an adequate punishment. 'Better far that the prisoner, in the dreadful solitude of exile should . . . before the presence of God, atone by a lingering repentance for the deed than that he should be sent, in the dawning of his manhood, to an ignoble death in a case where the truth was not clear. . . .'

Persuasively the 'golden voice' pressed its arguments, then, deepening its tone, it solemnly admonished the jury:

'To violate the living temple which the Lord has made, to quench the fire his breath has given, is an awful and tremendous responsibility. The word once gone forth is irrevocable. Speak not that word lightly; speak it not on suspicion, however strong; on moral conviction, however cogent; on inference—or on anything, but a clear irresistible, bright, noonday certainty. If you pronounce the word "Guilty" lightly, its meaning will never die within you; it will accompany you in your walks; it will follow you in your solitude like a shadow; it will haunt you in your sleep and hover over your beds; it will take the form of an accusing spirit, and confront and condemn you before the Judgment Seat of God.'

3

'Phillips [*noted Mr Adolphus in his diary*] made a speech of three hours in defence of the prisoner. I was engaged in another Court, and only heard the conclusion. Tindale summed up in a masterly manner. I heard him two hours and then was obliged to go away.'[1]

In the course of that summing up the Chief Justice warned the jury 'not to be misled by the speeches of Counsel on either side. . . . He left it to them to decide whether the murder and the robbery were perpetrated by different persons, or by one person, and whether it was a genuine robbery at all. . . . The evidence of Constable Baldwin was unworthy of credence, but that of Sarah Mancer ought to be observed. . . .

'Without the offer of a reward many crimes would remain undiscovered; it was for the jury to decide how far the credibility of witnesses was affected by the expectation of a reward.

'If it was a genuine robbery, the thief had not pursued the ordinary course. Instead of getting into the house by the glass-panelled door at the back of the dining-room floor, which afforded easy access, he appeared to have broken open the door into the lower area—and broken open that door with some violence. Moreover, if thieves had entered for the purpose of plunder, would they have left behind them so many articles of value which they might have disposed about their persons? . . .

'Little account could be taken of what servants said in their private talk about their masters, and the jury should give little weight to the agitation shewn by the prisoner, or to his remarks about "Old Billy", which were mere kitchen gossip. On the other hand, no importance should be attached to the discrepancies in Sarah Mancer's evidence, and she was entitled to be believed. As for the articles secreted in the prisoner's box, the jury would consider whether in their previous search of it —when all the shirts were taken out and placed on the bed— the gloves, handkerchiefs and shirt-front could have escaped notice. . . .

'The finding of the table silver at Madame Piolaine's destroyed the hypothesis that thieves had made off with *that* part of the plunder. Many of the articles found concealed in the pantry had been kept by the deceased—put away in drawers in his bedroom—how far was a stranger likely to know where to

[1] He was taken ill.

find them, or to choose such a place in which to conceal them? . . .

'Evidence of character was of great value in cases of doubt, but could not have much weight where proof of guilt was strong. It was for the jury to say whether in this case the facts proved the guilt of the prisoner beyond reasonable doubt. If they had any hesitation, then the prisoner ought to have the benefit of it.'

No judicial summing-up was ever more restrained and impartial. The jury took only an hour and twenty-five minutes to reach their decision and then returned to pronounce the verdict *Guilty*.

The Times was thus to describe the next scene:

'The prisoner heard the verdict with no visible traces of emotion. The Chief Justice himself seemed far more deeply moved when he addressed the prisoner before passing sentence. In tones of solemn admonition his lordship said:

' "The age of your victim, his situation as master, had no effect upon you. To atone to society, which has received a shock by your crime, to prevent the recurrence of such crimes, you must suffer an ignomious death. What may have been your precise and actual motive it is impossible to state. I fear it was the lust of filthy lucre. It has been demonstrated in this instance by the Providence of God that the crime committed in darkness shall be brought to light."

Under the stress of considerable emotion the Chief Justice then passed sentence of death, and, according to the custom then prevailing, fixed the date of execution for Monday, 6th July.

'The prisoner [*reported* The Times] listened to both pronouncements with no outward manifestation of feeling, and left the dock without faltering.'

II

The Condemned

'Murderers do not worry. . . . Some men who have undoubtedly been very anxious between the time of their crime and their arrest, told me they at once became quite calm within days, hours, or perhaps minutes, of their arrest.'[1]

I

READING evidence, even when it is reported *verbatim*, is a poor substitute for hearing it given in the atmosphere of the Court. The subtle *nuance* of the spoken word, the thrust and parry of question and answer, are lost to the millions who read the newspaper reports of criminal proceedings—for of necessity these have to be compressed into the space allotted to them, and however painstakingly this may be done, wherever there is compression there is distortion. Yet there always exists a number of persons who will argue with dogmatic persistence, and upon no firmer basis than newspaper reports and current gossip, that an accused person is innocent of the crime with which he is charged, and, should he be convicted, are prepared to maintain their opinion not only to the gallows foot, but after.

For this reason, if for no other, it is to be regretted that the former practice of publishing the confessions made by condemned felons awaiting execution has been abolished, for these would go a long way towards fortifying the public conscience against the insidious prejudice disseminated by those who decide for themselves that justice has miscarried. Indeed, it has come

---

[1] Dr J. A. Hobson in his address to the third international congress on crimin-nology: London, September 1956.

to be accepted that such confessions are now no longer made, and the question as to why this should be so is often asked. But such an impression is by no means correct. A case in point is that of Thomas Henry Alloway, convicted and hanged in 1922 for the murder, and sexual assault, of a young woman at Bournemouth. A voluble faction continued to protest his innocence, and, to try and prove it, even went to the extraordinary lengths, after his execution, of invoking the aid of spiritualism. Had the Authorites only published his last-minute confession of guilt, an end would have been put to this foolish clamour.

Courvoisier's persuasive personality, the good character which he enjoyed, the dramatic production of the final, clinching evidence against him, the extraordinary fact that no trace of blood had been discovered anywhere except within a short radius of the spot where the deceased's head lay, all provided the stuff of which such prejudices are composed; and it may, therefore, be safely assumed that, if his confession had not been published, many would have proclaimed his innocence and created a legend that his conviction and execution constituted a classic instance of a miscarriage of justice.

2

In all, Courvoisier made three distinct and separate confessions, and made them on different dates. In the *Annual Register* these have been compressed into a single, composite confession, thus creating a distortion which has deprived them of their significance. In order, therefore, to attain an understanding of the psychology of this remarkable young criminal one must make some examination of these documents in the order in which they were written—a task which, it would appear, has never before been undertaken.

The first of them, dated from Newgate on 22nd June—only two days after Courvoisier's conviction—was witnessed by Mr W. W. Cope, governor of the prison, the Reverend Mr Carver, the chaplain, and Mr T. Flower, one of the under-sheriffs, and was published in *The Times* of 26th June. It created something of a sensation; not, however, of the kind that its author expected, but because it was most unusual for a condemned man to make a confession so soon after sentence of death had been passed upon him. Yet as Thackeray was later to indicate it failed to impress the general public, in whose mind the facts of the case were still fresh.

Courvoisier knew that certain features of his crime still baffled the Authorities, and that he had a number of sympathizers who included persons of prominence. He accordingly hoped that by attributing his downfall to an unfortunate combination of circumstances he might induce these last to use their influence to have his sentence commuted to transportation.

The story he told on 22nd June was therefore to the effect that, while in attendance upon Lord William at the Castle Hotel, Richmond, during Easter, he had listened to the conversation of other servants describing the great country mansions of the aristocracy with which they were familiar, and telling of their travels with their employers from one fair city of Europe to another, and he had thus suffered the first pangs of envy, out of which had sprung temptation. Upon leaving Richmond, the confession continued, Lord William had gone to stay with friends at Campden Hill, and there Courvoisier had found a book describing the adventures of a profligate young man of respectable parentage—such as himself—who, having gambled away his possessions, moved with devil-may-care abandon from place to place, roistering, thieving and living on his wits. Already dissatisfied with the tedium of his existence in the service of an elderly and exacting employer, and with his moral stamina weakened by such literature as this, he had taken the first step on the downward path by purloining the gold locket. The ease with which he had accomplished this without awaking suspicion in his master's mind encouraged him to develop the idea of faking a burglary of the house in order to steal other valuables, and then embark upon a career similar to that of the hero of whom he had read.

With the intention of putting this plan into effect on 4th May, he had deposited the parcel of silver with Madame Piolaine on the previous day—Sunday, 3rd. On Monday night, however, having forced the back door his better feelings had prevailed, and he had put the door to rights again and gone up to bed. But next day Lord William's anger over the carriage incident had aroused his own and confirmed him in his resolve. As soon as he had left his master in bed that night, he had come downstairs, forced the back door once more, and was in process of creating the disorder in the dining-room when Lord William unexpectedly appeared on the scene.

'He came downstairs to the water-closet. He had his wax-light, but as he had his slippers on I did not hear him. . . . He opened the dining-room door and saw me. I could not escape his sight. He was quite struck and said: "What are you doing? You have no good intention in doing this. You will quit my service to-morrow, and I shall acquaint your friends with it." I made him no answer. He went to the water-closet. I put some of the things in order. I left the dining-room. I was on the corner of the stairs that go down to the kitchen. . . . I waited to see what he would do when he came out. . . .'

So far his story is plausible enough, but what he alleges next took place is a defiance of all probability.

'He went into the dining-room where he stayed a minute or two. I watched him go upstairs. . . . I thought it was all up with me. My character was gone, and I thought the only way I could cover my faults was by murdering him. . . .'

These last two sentences are the gist of the matter; they are intended to shew how a desperate young man, in a foreign country, was driven to commit murder in order to save his character. But let us examine this part of the story in the light of reason.

If Lord William had really caught this young foreigner—who had only been in his employment for a matter of five weeks—in such compromising circumstances as those described, what would he have been most likely to do? It was not yet midnight; on all sides he was surrounded by neighbours; there were two trustworthy women servants under his own roof, and a constable on patrol in the proximity.

True, he was a somewhat frail old man and might not have felt equal to risking attack should he attempt to summon help at the front door, as a younger man would have done, but he was a man of intelligence—and only a fool, after dismissing an obviously ill-disposed servant whom he had just discovered engaged in a criminal act, and coupling with that dismissal the threat to ruin his chances of further livelihood, would have left that man to his own devices, returned placidly upstairs and fallen into sound slumber without even taking the elementary precaution of turning the key, ready to his hand, on the inside of his bedroom door. Householders in those days possessed rattles to be sounded in cases of emergency. Surely what Lord William would have done would have been to fling open his bedroom window and sound his rattle, or else rouse the two women servants sleeping overhead?

It is equally difficult to believe that Courvoisier, with murder already in his heart, would have tamely permitted his master the opportunity of doing any of these things. It would have been the work of a moment to have seized one of the heavy silver candlesticks from the table and struck him down as he turned to leave the room—and furthermore, the body of the old gentleman, in his dressing-gown and slippers, with his wax-light lying beside him, and surrounded by overturned chairs and scattered silver, would have made a far more convincing picture of the householder murdered by burglars whom he had caught in the act, than the one which Courvoisier actually contrived in his attempt to create a similar impression.

While this confession was in process of being written,[1] Mr Cope voiced the general curiosity by asking Courvoisier how he had 'cut his master's throat without getting so much as a spot of blood upon his clothing or person'? Courvoisier accordingly included in his statement the reply: 'I turned up my coat- and shirt-sleeves of my right hand.'

But such a precaution would have been totally inadequate, nor could he have committed the crime with only one hand.

---

[1] Courvoisier wrote it in French, and it was translated at the Home Office before being issued to the Press.

To have inflicted the wound he made it would have been necessary to force his victim's head backwards with the other hand, and however quickly he afterwards interposed the pillow neither he nor his clothing could have escaped without some bloodstains. But not until he was being led to the scaffold did he reveal his secret, as we shall see.

Two days after the publication of this first document, Courvoisier, realizing that it had not achieved the desired result, concocted another, which seems to have been intended to appeal to the evangelical spirit of the age. Opening in a similar strain with the familiar picture of a young man labouring under severe temptation, he goes on to say that, unaccustomed to drinking anything more intoxicating than ale, and sparingly even of that, he had recently taken to sampling the wine from the cellarette in his pantry, and on that Tuesday his master's anger about the carriage had driven him to seek solace in it with more than usual freedom, and, as the evening wore on, to resort to it with ever-increasing frequency. The *Examiner* thus sums up the general trend of the second confession:

> 'The man who murdered his master . . . is made to say in one of these effusions that *he* is not the guilty person, but that Satan is to blame . . . that Christ is his friend, and promised him forgiveness and admission to the Kingdom of Heaven.'

But this confession in its turn wrought no miracle of deliverance, and as day succeeded day, each bringing that last dread one of all relentlessly nearer, he turned his thoughts to the only other means of escaping the fearful penalty he must pay. It was only when that in its turn failed that, on the very morning of his execution, he wrote the third confession.

3

In 1818 Parliament had adopted the articles of Elizabeth Fry regarding the treatment of prisoners, and by 1840 the conditions which had formerly prevailed at Newgate had been greatly improved. Courvoisier's cell, therefore, was furnished with a table, a couple of chairs, and a bunk with mattress and blankets. He was permitted to receive letters, and supplied with writing materials wherewith to answer them, and also provided with what was deemed suitable literature. Nor did he lack for company. Besides the daily visits of the prison chaplain and Mr Baup, and those of the prison governor, one or other of the under-sheriffs would frequently come to assure himself of the prisoner's welfare. He talked eagerly with his visitors, as he did with his gaolers, but manifested the greatest pleasure in the company of Mr Evans, one of the under-sheriffs, who used to converse with him in an unofficial and friendly way. Throughout his imprisonment his behaviour was exemplary.

Sunday, 5th July, the eve of his execution, dawned—as fair and fine a day as that on which, exactly two months before, he had plotted to commit his crime under cover of the coming night. Having breakfasted on bread-and-butter and coffee sent in from a nearby coffee-house, he made his Will, disposing of such trifles as he possessed, and wrote some letters, leaving the one to his mother to the last.

The two clergymen in turn spent some time with him; Mr Evans looked in to see him; the governor's visit was of rather longer duration than usual, for, as he was afterwards to state in an interview with the Press, there was something so abnormal in the condemned man's composure that Mr Cope 'felt assured that he would use all his ingenuity to take his own life on the eve of his execution'.

From time to time the prisoner, and everything in his cell, had been subjected to a close search and nothing of a suspicious nature had been found, and although Mr Cope had 'ordered a vigilant superintendence to be kept over him', his two gaolers, Locke and Sargent, had noticed nothing to report. None the less the governor's intuition persisted, so at 10 p.m. on that last night Courvoisier would spend on earth, he entered the cell. The prisoner, quill in hand, rose from the table where he had been writing and stood before him with his usual quiet defer-ence. Mr Cope bade him undress, 'which he seemed somewhat reluctant to do'.

His clothes, blankets and mattress were taken away and replaced by others. A search revealed nothing in the blankets, and though a sliver of wood was found in the mattress it attracted no attention. But wedged into a corner of the prisoner's coat pocket was a tightly rolled strip of the same material as the suit itself. Confronted with this Courvoisier admitted without hesitation that he had detached it from the inside seam of his trousers when he was in the privy and 'he submitted that to a person in his circumstances, with an ignominious death before his eyes, the alternative of a silent departure was the most eligible choice, and that, notwithstanding all the religious exhortations, public and private which he had received, he had made up his mind on the matter'.

Asked how he intended to carry out his intention Courvoisier said that, after going to bed that night, he proposed to tie the strip of cloth around his arm and open a vein.

'But how could you have bled yourself?' asked Mr Cope.

'The mattress which you have sent away had concealed in it a small piece of wood which I had sharpened in such a manner that I could easily have opened my arm with it.'

Apparently unperturbed by the foiling of his intention, Courvoisier took up his pen again on the governor's departure and continued writing until the bell of St Sepulchre's Church nearby struck eleven o'clock; then, rising and stretching himself, he said to Locke, the senior gaoler:

'I am going to sleep. Awake me at four o'clock, for I have still much to put down.'

His means of self-destruction gone, he had decided, now every flicker of hope had perished, to write a truthful account of his crime.

Locke, who was to give the Press an account of his last hours, said:

> 'He lay down and fell asleep in a few minutes, but awoke at midnight and asked what time it was. On hearing it, he laid down again, having repeated his request to be called at 4 a.m. . . . He slept quietly, unlike some other nights when sometimes in his sleep he would groan and grind his teeth.'

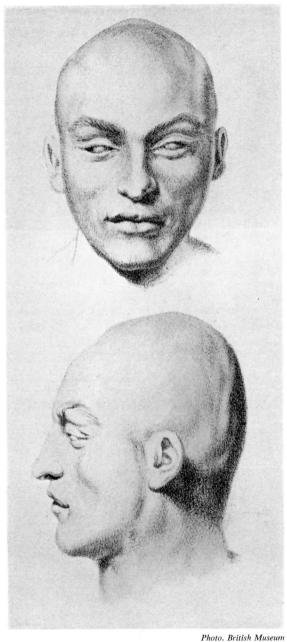

FRANÇOIS BENJAMIN COURVOISIER

An engraving taken from a cast made after his
execution.

12

The Execution: Monday, 6th July

'I have murdered; I have been in the company of notorious debauchees; I have robbed.'[1]

I

OUTSIDE the portals of Newgate the gaunt, black scaffold had been erected. Everywhere in London thousands who had discussed the case throughout the preceding weeks determined not to miss the last spectacle of all. Among them was Thackeray, who was to write:[2]

'X——,[3] who had voted with Mr Ewart for the abolition of capital punishment, was anxious to see the effect on the public mind of an execution and asked me to accompany him to see Courvoisier hanged. . . . As I was to rise at three in the morning I went to bed at ten . . . but as might be expected the event of the morrow was perpetually before my eyes through the night and kept them wide open. . . .

'I could not help thinking, as each clock sounded, "What is *he* doing now? Has *he* heard it in his little room in Newgate yonder. . . ."

'It is twenty minutes past four as we pass St Sepulchre's. . . . Before us lies Newgate prison; but something a great deal more awful to look at, which seizes the eyes at once and makes the heart beat, is the gallows. There it stands, black and ready, jutting out from a little door in the prison. As you see it you feel a kind of dumb electric shock, which causes one to start a little and give a little gasp of breath. . . .

---

[1] Courvoisier's confession.
[2] *Op. cit.*
[3] Richard Monckton-Milnes, 2nd Lord Houghton.

'We went down into the crowd which was very enormous, but not dense as yet. . . . People sauntered up and formed groups and talked, the newcomers asking those who seemed *habitués* of the place about former executions. . . . Throughout the whole four hours the mob was extraordinarily gentle and good-humoured. . . .

'What good sense and intelligence have most of the people by whom you are surrounded; how much good humour does one hear bandied about from one to another! . . . The crowd has grown very dense by this time, it is six o'clock, and there is a great heaving and pushing, and swaying to and fro; but round the women the men have formed a circle, and keep them as much as possible out of the rush and trample.

'In one of the houses near us a gallery has been formed on the roof. Seats were here put out, and a number of persons of varying degrees were occupying them. Some tipsy, dissolute-looking young men of the Dick Swiveller cast were in this gallery . . . a party which had evidently not been to bed. . . . The debauch was not over yet, and the women of the party were giggling, drinking and romping . . . sprawling here and there, and falling upon the knees of one or other of the males. Their scarfs were off their shoulders, and you saw the sun shining down upon the bare white flesh, and the shoulder-points glittering like burning glasses. The people about us were very indignant at some of the proceedings of this debauched crew, and at last raised up such a yell as frightened them into shame, and they were more orderly. . . .

'The character of the crowd was as yet, however, quite festive; jokes bandying about here and there, and jolly laughter breaking out. . . . Really the time passed away with extraordinary quickness. . . . The workmen were knocking and hammering at the scaffold, a mysterious clattering of blows was heard within it, and a ladder, painted black, was carried round and into the interior of the edifice by a small side-door. We all looked at this little ladder, and at each other. . . .

'Soon came a squad of policemen, stalwart, rosy-looking

men, saying much for city-feeding; well-dressed, well-built
and of admirable good-humour. They paced about the open
space between the prison and the barriers which kept back
the crowd from the scaffold. The front line, as far as I could
see, was chiefly occupied by blackguards and boys . . . who
saluted the policemen on their appearance with a volley of
jokes and ribaldry. As far as I could judge from their faces
there were more blackguards of sixteen and seventeen than
of any maturer age, stunted, sallow, ill-grown lads. . . . There
were a considerable number of girls, too, of the same age;
some that Cruikshank and Boz might have taken as a study
for Nancy. . . .

'But yonder, glittering through the crowd in Newgate
Street, see the sheriffs' carriages are slowly making their
way. . . . Close to the barriers, where we are, the mob has
become so dense that it is with difficulty that a man can
keep his feet. Each man, however, is very careful in pro-
tecting the women, and all are full of jokes and good-
humour. The windows of the shops opposite are now
pretty nearly filled by the persons who hired them. Many
young dandies are there, with mustachios and cigars; some
quiet, fat, family parties of simple, honest tradesmen and
their wives . . . who are looking on with the greatest
imaginable calmness and sipping their tea. . . .

'Scarcely a word has been said about Courvoisier all
this time. It was past seven now; the quarters rang and
passed away; the crowd began to grow very eager and more
quiet, and we turned back every now and then and looked
at St Sepulchre's clock. Half an hour; 25 minutes. What is
he doing now? . . .

'As the clock began to strike an immense sway and
movement swept over the whole of that vast, dense crowd.
They were all uncovered directly, and a great murmur
arose, more awful, *bizarre*, and indescribable than any
sound I had ever heard before. Women and children began
to shriek horribly. I don't know whether it was the bell[1]
I heard, but a dreadful quick, feverish kind of jangling

---

[1] Years before a sum of money had been bequeathed to St. Sepulchre's to pay
for the tolling of the bell at executions.

noise mingled with the noise of the people and lasted about two minutes. The scaffold stood before us, tenantless and black; the block chain was hanging down ready from the beam. Nobody came. "He has been reprieved," someone said; another said: "He has killed himself in prison."

'Just then, from under the black prison door, a pale, quiet head peered out. . . . A man in black appeared on the scaffold, and was silently followed by about four more dark figures. The first was a tall, grave man; we all knew who the second was. . . .

'He was dressed in a new black suit, as it seemed; his shirt was open. His arms were tied in front of him. He opened his hands in a helpless kind of way, and clasped them once or twice together. He turned his head here and there, and looked about him for an instant with a wild, imploring look. His mouth was contracted into a sort of pitiful smile. He went and placed himself at once under the beam. . . .'

2

But let us now look into the condemned cell.

The forefinger of sunrise, which was to usher in a radiant day, had hardly touched the clear sky, nor had it penetrated at all into the cell, when Locke placed a hand upon the sleeping prisoner's shoulder and awoke him, saying kindly:

'Courvoisier, it is four o'clock now, and I have woke you as you told me; but there is no call for you to get up yet unless you wish.'

The prisoner sat up and asked 'if he could be got a pot of coffee and some thinly cut bread and butter, which was brought in from the coffee-house'. While it was being brought he 'made his last toilet' and then settled himself down, as Thackeray wrote, 'to tell the world how he did the crime for which he suffered. This time he will tell the truth and the whole truth'.

But he did not, even in those last minutes, tell *quite* the whole truth, for he repeated his former assertion that he turned back the right sleeves of his shirt and jacket to commit the murder. The whole truth he was to reserve for a last-moment communication to Mr Evans, the under-sheriff.

In neither of the two long documents which he had already written, nor in this final one, did he utter one word of remorse for the life he had so ruthlessly exterminated. And it is significant that neither Thackeray in 1840, nor our own sentimentalists today, more than a century later, ever have a thought to spare, a word to utter, or a tear to shed for anyone but the criminal about to undergo a just punishment and, to the very end, concerned with no one but himself alone.

When he had finished this last confession, Courvoisier wrote his last letter which he addressed to Mr Evans; then, from among the books which had been given him, he selected five and in each of them he inscribed the words: '*Ce 6 juillet 1840. François Benjamin Courvoisier vous donne ceci, mon ami, pour souvenir.*'

At six o'clock, while that great concourse outside in Newgate Street was good-humouredly beguiling the hours of waiting, the two clergymen entered the cell. Courvoisier greeted them calmly, but after an hour of prayer he cried: 'O God! how could I have committed so dreadful a crime? It was madness! When I think of it I cannot believe it!'

Invited to take the Sacrament he eagerly acquiesced, and Mr Wheelton, the High Sheriff, Mr Evans, Mr Cope, and the Swiss Minister of State, all partook of it with him.

The clock at St Sepulchre's chimed the last quarter before eight as they rose from their knees, and, drawing from his pocket that last letter he had written, Courvoisier scribbled on the back of it his full name and the words, 'the day of my execution', and gave it, with one of the books he had inscribed, into the hands of Mr Evans. The other books he gave to Mr Cope, the two clergymen and Locke.

At 7.55 the death-bell at St Sepulchre's began to toll, sounding so weirdly to the over-taut nerves of Thackeray. Locke stepped forward to bind the prisoner's wrists, and then in silence, with Mr Cope leading, the clergymen following, and the prisoner with Locke and Sargent, the other warder, on either side of him bringing up the rear, a procession was formed which wended its solemn way to that door beyond which the little black ladder led up to the scaffold. There the hangman was waiting, and the prisoner, before following him up the ladder, turned and shook hands with each member of his escort, except Mr Baup who accompanied him on to the scaffold; in another moment the sunshine of that July morning was striking down upon his shaven head.

'It was stated [*so says the* Annual Register], that some six hundred persons of distinction, including several members of the House of Commons, were admitted inside the precincts of the prison to witness the execution. The crowd outside was estimated to number at a moderate calculation 20,000 pressed together in the compactest mass. . . . The number of menservants present was remarkable as evincing the fearful interest taken in the culprit's fate by the class to which he belonged. . . . It was impossible to behold the mob, with their heads all bared and their eyes all eagerly directed towards the gallows, without the deepest feeling of awe, and the spectacle thus exhibited was enough to strike terror to the heart of the miserable felon whose ignominious fate rendered him the sole gaze of such an immense mass of human beings. . . .

'On his appearance a few yells of execration escaped from a portion of the crowd, but the general body of the people, great as must have been their abhorrence of his atrocious crime, remained silent. . . . His step was steady and collected, and his movements free from the slightest agitation or indecision. His countenance, indeed, was pale, and bore traces of dejection, but it was at the same time calm and unmoved.

'When the executioner was placing him on the drop he slightly moved his hands—which were tied in front of him and strongly clasped one within the other—up and down two or three times, and this was the only visible sympton of any emotion or mental anguish which the wretched man endured. His face was covered with the cap, fitting so closely as not to conceal the outline of his countenance, and the noose adjusted. . . . During this operation he lifted up his head and raised his hands to his breast, as if in the action of fervent prayer. In a moment the fatal bolt was withdrawn, the drop fell, and in this attitude the murderer perished.

'He died without any violent struggle. Two minutes after he had fallen his legs were twice slightly convulsed, but no further motion was observable, excepting that his raised arms, gradually losing their vitality, sank down from their own lifeless weight.

'After hanging one hour the body was cut down and removed within the prison.'

And so at the early age of twenty-three perished this man who had never known hunger or want, who had been well-educated, was well-liked, and well-endowed with those talents which could have made him a profitable career. His sorry story affords a classic instance of one who had everything in his favour, yet preferred to 'buffet with opposing waves to gain the bloody shore, not to recede from it'.

13

Epilogue

'The mind of man is far from the nature of a clear and equal glass. . . . I say, it is rather like an enchanted glass, full of superstitions and imposture.'[1]

I

COURVOISIER's epitaph was thus pronounced by the *Observer*:

'Courvoisier is dead; he died as he had lived, a villain: a lie in his mouth. Peace be to his ashes. We war not with the dead.'

The 'lie in his mouth' was the story he repeated even in his final confession; that all he had done when he committed the murder was 'to turn up his coat- and shirt-sleeves'. It was wholly unconvincing, yet he had repeated it several times to the prison officials and the two clergymen.

Only to Mr Evans did he reveal the truth. Whether it was contained in that letter he gave him as he was leaving the condemned cell for the scaffold it is impossible to say, but it seems likely; and it seems equally likely that Mr Evans passed on the information to Mr Adolphus, for the latter entered this in his diary without any reservation:

'. . . He was asked by the under-sheriff how it was possible he could cut the throat of his unfortunate master without leaving a trace of blood on his clothes, and that

[1] Francis Bacon.

120

nothing should be discovered newly washed. His answer was that he had no clothes on: he committed the crime in a complete state of nudity, and he only had to wash himself at the sink on coming down.'[1]

The truth of this is supported by the story of the 'young nobleman' paying his clandestine visit to the house opposite 14 Norfolk Street on the night of the crime. That story, like so many others, has suffered distortion in the process of time, and Mr Alan Brock in *A Casebook of Crime* writes:

'Although the evidence was not forthcoming at the trial, there is reason to believe that Courvoisier avoided the risk of bloodstains being found on his clothing . . . by stripping for his work and afterwards having a bath. The latter process was observed from the bedroom of a lady friend by a certain famous General, who, for obvious reasons, preferred to remain silent.'

There is not much difference between an anonymous nobleman and an anonymous General, but there was no bathroom at 14 Norfolk Street, and Courvoisier would hardly have cleansed himself in his victim's bedroom, the drawing-room or the dining-room, which were the only rooms—except the maidservants' bedroom—facing Norfolk Street and therefore visible from the other side of it.

What actually happened would seem to be that as the clandestine visitor—were he nobleman or General—was taking a discreet departure from his lady-friend's house at about 1 a.m. on Wednesday, 6th May, he happened to see through the uncurtained window of the landing the figure of a naked man carrying a lighted candle go by the corresponding window of Lord William's house.

It was as simple as that! And, as J. B. Atlay observes: 'Had this piece of information come out at the trial, it would have supplied another link in the chain and cast a further difficulty in the way of the unlucky Phillips.'[2]

[1] *Op. cit.*
[2] *See* Appendix I.

There are two other matters arising out of this case which are of considerable interest to the student of crime: firstly, what prompted that callous young murderer to make the seemingly reverent gesture of covering his victim's face; secondly, was the technique he employed, in committing the crime naked, original?

With regard to the first, the case of Danny Karrigan affords a close analogy. He was shot and killed by an unseen assailant while strolling with his sweetheart along a wooded lane on the outskirts of Perth. The girl fled to give the alarm, and when helpers reached the spot it was found that the murderer had rifled the dead youth's pockets and also spread his victim's handkerchief carefully over his face.

Later a man with gypsy blood was arrested and charged, and in his account of the case Mr William Roughead observes:

> 'No explanation of the singular fact was offered by the evidence given at the trial. It was astonishing that the murderer having . . . rifled the body, should have shewn such respect for the dead as to cover the face of his victim. But I am informed that the solution is simple: it is the inveterate custom of members of the tinker clan to do so by the dead.'

The custom of covering the face of the dead is not confined to the tinker clan; it is widespread throughout the world, but where a murderer is concerned the action may arise from a superstition, common in the Orient, that the brain remains alive, and the eyes retain their powers of vision, for some hours after the heart has ceased to beat.

According to Lady Burton, she and her husband, Sir Richard Burton, the famous explorer and Oriental scholar, both held this belief, and she related in her autobiography how Sir Richard having died at dawn on 20th October 1890, in the presence of his doctor and herself, his eyes retained the brilliance and penetration for which they had always been notable until the sunset of that day, when all light left them.

It has been claimed—and also denied—that the murderers of P.C. Gutteridge shot out his eyes after they had killed him in the belief that the retina might retain an image of themselves. That Courvoisier was responding to an identical impulse when he covered up his master's face before possessing himself of his property seems possible.

As for our second question—was Courvoisier's technique original?—sometime about the middle of the eighteenth century, another servant, named James Hall, murdered his master, a Mr Penney, Principal of Clement's Inn and Deputy Paymaster of the Forces. While this unfortunate man was undressing to go to bed James Hall crept up behind him, stunned him with a cudgel, and then, having first stripped himself naked, cut his victim's throat. He too washed himself at the sink.

It seems by no means improbable that Courvoisier who, by his own confession, was an avid reader of books on crime and criminals, derived the method he employed from that of James Hall who, in his subsequent confession, gave the fullest details of his crime which, like Courvoisier himself, he was to expiate on the gallows.[1]

---

[1] In the course of that confession James Hall provided the information that *cold* water is the most effective means of removing bloodstains: information of which the late Edgar Wallace made use in compiling one of his famous thrillers.

APPENDIX I

Mr Charles Phillips

Samuel Warren, Q.C., who wrote several monographs on criminal trials under the *nom-de-plume* 'Barrister-at-Law', was a staunch supporter of Mr Phillips and had this to say concerning his alleged conduct at the trail of Courvoisier in a letter which he wrote to him, and which was published in *The Times* of *20th November 1849*.

'Some time ago I was dining with Lord Denman, when I mentioned to him the report in question. His lordship immediately stated that he inquired into the matter and found the charge to be utterly unfounded, that he had spoken on the subject to Mr Baron Parke . . . and that Baron Parke told him he had for reasons of his own most carefully watched every word that you uttered, and assured Lord Denman that your address was perfectly unexceptionable, and that you made no such statements as those attributed to you.

'Lord Denman told me that I was at liberty to mention this fact to anyone, and expressed in noble and generous terms his concern at the existence of such serious and unfounded imputations on your character and honour.'

In *Famous Trials of the Century* (1899) J. B. Atlay tells us that Mr Phillips took a newspaper report of his speech to the Judges who had presided over the trial:

'. . . and in the presence of many witnesses asked them whether he had made use of any such expressions. "You certainly did not," replied Tindale, "and I will be your voucher whenever you choose to call me. To which Baron Parke added: "And I had a reason, which the Chief Justice did not know, for watching you narrowly, and he will remember my saying to him when you sat down: 'Did you notice how carefully Phillips abstained from giving a personal opinion of the case?' " '

Samuel Warren's and J. B. Atlay's contributions to this controversy were made nine years and fifty-nine years, respectively, after the event, and the latter does not even quote an authority for his statement. If Mr Phillips were innocent of the charges made against him, it is odd that he and his friends should have made so little attempt to rebut them at the time. There would not, then, appear to be any good reason for doubting the accuracy of contemporary reports and opinions concerning his speech, as expressed by such an unimpeachable *ear-witness* as Serjeant Ballantine—a view evidently taken by the author of the reference to Mr Phillips in the *Dictionary of National Biography*,

APPENDIX II

From *John o' London's Weekly*, 10th May 1924.

The Murder of Lord William Russell

'Sir,
Mr Moreton Frewen in his delightful book, *Melton Mowbray and Other Memories*, gives an account of the murder of Lord William Russell by his butler, Courvoisier. The victim was the great-uncle of the late G. W. E. Russell, who told Mr Frewen a detail which did not transpire at the trial. The murderer was naked when he killed Lord William with a knife, and so there were no stains on his clothes. Courvoisier's Counsel impressed the jury by pointing out that, although the bed was drenched in blood, there was not a stain on the prisoner's garments.

'At this stage there waited on the Lord Chancellor a profligate young lord from Sussex. He said that he was with a lady in a house opposite to Lord William's on the night of the murder, and clearly saw a stark-naked figure come for an instant between the curtain and the blind, which was not completely drawn down: this room he had since identified as the bedroom of the murdered man. The lord in question wanted to know what was his duty—to offer evidence and compromise the lady or remain silent? The Lord Chancellor advised that if serious suspicion was attached to any innocent man the peer must come forward, but he thought the circumstantial evidence was sufficient to hang the accused, as indeed it did.

'Mr Frewen's version is incorrect in one or two facts. The following is the true story:

'Lord X. was visiting a married lady on the other side of the street. Going down the stairs in the dark, and looking through the window at the opposite side of the road, he saw a man going down the staircase naked. Suspicion for the murder attached to one of the housemaids. Lord X. thereupon consulted his lawyer, and asked him what he should do, as, if he disclosed himself, he would ruin the lady's reputation. The lawyer said: "Wait a little, and see what happens. If the housemaid is in serious danger, you must come forward at all costs." A few days afterwards Courvoisier was tracked by reason of his having pawned [*sic*] some of the things stolen. So Lord X. was able to remain silent.

'Yours etc.

'INTERESTED.'

The Murder of Julia Wallace

THE ACCUSED

William Herbert Wallace

'In a criminal case the rules are fairly precise and one
rarely has occasion to bother one's head about morality.
If you are prosecuting you must conceal nothing from
your opponent. If you have collected fresh evidence,
which was not given before the magistrates who committed the accused person for trial, you must serve your
opponent with a copy of it. If you deem it unnecessary
to call one of the witnesses who did give evidence before
the magistrates, you must nevertheless offer to call him so
that your opponent may cross-examine him if he wishes.
In opening the case to the jury you must conceal nothing
which tells in favour of the prisoner. On the other hand,
if you are defending you can do almost anything you
like and you have no duty whatever to let the jury know
the whole truth of the matter. On the contrary, it is
positively your duty not to do so.'

C. P. HARVEY, Q.C.
(*The Advocate's Devil*)

Contents

ILLUSTRATIONS

MAPS

I

Preview

'For he who lives more lives than one
More deaths than one must die.'[1]

I

IN *Ego 6* James Agate wrote of the murder of Julia Wallace that it 'was planned with extreme care and extraordinary imagination. Either the murderer was Wallace or it wasn't. If it wasn't, then here at last is the perfect murder. If it was, then here is the murder so nearly perfect that the Court of Criminal Appeal . . . decided to quash Wallace's conviction.'

No case within living memory has been debated more keenly and persistently than this one, yet so far no theory has been advanced to account for the apparent *senselessness of the act itself*. Not even the Prosecution suggested a motive, and subsequent speculations on the point have been characterized mainly by their wildness.

But behind every murder there must lie a motive, unless the killer be insane—an eventuality which in this instance the Defence declared themselves ready to disprove. The question, therefore, which arises, which penetrates to the very heart of the matter, and which still remains unanswered, is '*Why* was Julia Wallace killed?'

That question we will proceed to make our own, and we will keep it in the forefront of our mind as we reconsider the case.

The crime was committed on the evening of Tuesday, 20th January 1931, when William Herbert Wallace and Julia, his wife—a childless couple—had been married almost exactly seventeen years. For all but the first year of that period they

[1] *The Ballad of Reading Gaol*—Oscar Wilde.

had lived together, in apparent harmony, in the small feature-less villa, in a rather drab quarter of Liverpool, which was the scene of the crime; and during the whole of that period Wallace had been employed by the Prudential Assurance Company as a full-time agent in charge of a nearby working-class district.

According to the evidence of the boy who delivered the milk Julia Wallace was alive at 6.30 on that fatal evening. Some time between then and 8.45 p.m. she was struck down and killed in the front parlour of that little house.

P.C. Williams, on duty close by, was informed of the tragedy by Mr J. S. Johnston, Wallace's next-door neighbour, and reached the house at nine o'clock. Wallace admitted him and made the following brief and lucid statement:

'At 6.45 p.m. I left the house in order to go to Menlove Gardens, and my wife accompanied me to the backyard door. She walked a little way down the alley with me, then she returned and bolted the backyard door. She would then be alone in the house. I went to Menlove Gardens to find the address which had been given me was wrong. Becoming suspicious I returned home and went to the front door. I inserted my key to find I could not open it. I went round to the backyard door: it was closed, but not bolted. I went up the backyard and tried the back door, but it would not open. I again went to the front door, and this time found the door to be bolted. I hurried round to the back and up the backyard, and tried the back door, and this time found it would open. I entered the house and this is what I found.'

With a gesture he indicated the body of his wife lying on the hearthrug at their feet, her battered head islanded in blood, and strands of hair torn from her scalp.

Closing the door on that stark picture of violent death Wallace conducted the officer into the kitchen-living-room, where he took down a small cash-box from the top of a tall bookcase and, displaying it, declared that the sum of £4, a crossed cheque and a postal order were missing from it; thus suggesting that robbery had been the motive for the crime.

The Topical Press Agency Ltd.

WILLIAM HERBERT WALLACE

At the age of about thirty-four. Note the intensity of the gaze,
and the taut line of the jaw.

This suggestion constituted the hypothesis eventually put forward by the Defence. It was an hypothesis conducive to scepticism. There could be no doubt that the assassin had contracted considerable bloodstains upon his person and his apparel, and the closest examination failed to shew that he had washed those stains away; yet he had seemingly moved upstairs and down in the narrow confines of that house, creating here and there apparently purposeless disorder; had for some inexplicable reason extinguished the gas-lights in the ground-floor rooms, and, having thus enveloped himself in their curtained darkness, had contrived to make his exit without leaving a trace of blood on any door-handle, wall or other object, to mark his progress. Not only that: he had killed like a madman, yet without making a sound to attract the attention of the neighbours on the other side of the thin party wall, and, taking his weapon with him, had vanished like a wraith, utterly and for ever!

2

The question which confronted the Criminal Investigation Department of the City of Liverpool was: '*Who* killed Julia Wallace?' They worked assiduously to discover the answer. The result was Wallace's arrest. They worked no less assiduously to find the answer to that second question which we have made our own: '*Why* was Julia Wallace killed?' Their apparent failure to do so was made manifest by Mr Justice Wright[1] himself in the course of his address to the jury at the trial.

'The evidence is that the prisoner and his wife, to all appearances, were living together in happiness and amity. . . . There is nothing that he could gain, so far as one can see, by her death. It can also be pointed out that there is no one else, so far as can be seen, who had anything to gain

[1] *Robert Alderson Wright, P.C., b.* 1869. Called to Bar, Inner Temple, 1900; K.C. 1917; Bencher of the Inner Temple 1923; Judge of the High Court of Justice, King's Bench Division, 1925–1932; Created a Life Peer 1932; Master of the Rolls 1935–1937; Chairman, United Nations War Crimes Commission 1945. Publications: *Legal Essays and Addresses.*

by her death, if you exclude the hypothesis of the unknown robber who, it is suggested—and it is a suggestion you will have to consider carefully—may have committed this crime.'

The trial of William Herbert Wallace for the murder of his wife occupied four days of the Liverpool Assizes. It was conducted with scrupulous regard for all those rules which have been specially designed for the protection of an accused person in our criminal courts. Particular care was taken to select the jury of ten men and two women from persons residing outside the city boundaries. Yet, despite the absence of motive and the circumstantial nature of the evidence, that jury returned a verdict of *Guilty* after an absence of only one hour. Sentence of death was then passed upon the prisoner without comment from his lordship.

Wallace entered an appeal, the hearing of which lasted two days. In the course of pronouncing the judgment of that Court the Lord Chief Justice, Lord Hewart, made the following observations:

'. . . Three facts are obvious. The first is that at the conclusion of the case for the Crown no submission was made on behalf of the appellant that there was no case to go to the jury. The second fact which seems to be obvious is that the evidence was summed up by the learned Judge with complete fairness and accuracy, and it would not have been at all surprising if the result had been an acquittal of the prisoner. The third obvious fact is that the case is eminently one of difficulty and doubt.

'Now the whole of the material evidence has been closely and critically examined before us, and . . . suffice it to say that we are not concerned here with suspicion, however grave, or with theories, however ingenious. Section 4 of the Court of Criminal Appeal Act of 1907 provides that the Court of Criminal Appeal shall allow the appeal if they think that the verdict of the jury should be set aside on the ground that it cannot be supported having regard to the evidence.

'The decision at which we have arrived is that the case against the appellant . . . was not proved with that certainty which is necessary in order to justify a verdict of Guilty. . . . The result is that this appeal will be allowed and the conviction quashed.'

But while that decision terminated once and for all the legal issue, and Wallace went forth a free man, his subsequent position was entirely different from that of an individual who has been acquitted of the charge against him *on the evidence submitted at his trial.* A stigma attached to him; a stigma similar to that attached to someone upon whom a Scottish jury has passed the verdict of Not Proven.

3

Some writers on this case have created the impression that, from the very beginning, it aroused enormous public excitement, and that this, combined with a strong local feeling against Wallace, prejudiced the jury. There is no ground for either of these contentions.

With regard to the first of them, naturally the Liverpool Press printed day-to-day reports of the investigations and made a feature of the trial—but without undue sensationalism. The London newspapers treated the case with greater brevity—*The Times* reporting it not at all and confining its observations to a short leading article concerning the findings of the Court of Criminal Appeal.

With regard to the second, suffice it to say that in one Liverpool church a collection was taken to assist Wallace with the costs of his defence, while on the eve of the appeal the permission of the Bishop of Liverpool was sought and obtained for the offering of prayers in the Cathedral that the Lords of Appeal might be guided to a *right* judgment, *whatever that judgment might be.*

It was only after his liberation that feeling against Wallace began to manifest itself in Liverpool, and this was *partly* due to the publication of what he called his *Life Story* in the pages of *John Bull*.

Written in a mawkish, emotional strain, especially when his wife is the subject, this is an unconvincing document, obviously designed to excite public sympathy for himself. Between its publication and his death—which occurred only a handful of days after the second anniversary of his wife's murder—he contributed some shorter articles in a similar vein to other organs of the popular Press. With his death all who cared to do so were at liberty to publish freely their own opinions of his case.

In the quarter of a century which has elapsed since then many have done so—both factually and fictionally—and how singular a thing it is that, although the case has become firmly established as a classic in the annals of crime, all, from first to last, dispensing with original research, have based their accounts, without quibble or question, upon Wallace's own writings! In composing the stories of our lives even the most virtuous of us are apt to skate gracefully over incidents which do not reflect as greatly to our credit as we should like; even the most truthful of us are apt to exaggerate incidents which do; and all of us tend to omit altogether those which, for one reason or another, we deem it politic to leave unrecorded. Wallace, as we shall see, did all this, and his *Life Story*, therefore, hardly constitutes the source from which the truth, the whole truth and nothing but the truth can be expected to emerge.

4

Mr Edgar Lustgarten, whose legal erudition is combined with a lucid literary style which makes his books on criminal matters as delightful to read as they are informative, in the course of an account of the Wallace case observes: 'As a mental exercise, as a challenge to one's powers of deduction and analysis, the Wallace murder is in a class by itself.'[1] It is, he says, 'the perfect scientific puzzle', and so it is. But one must dissent from his assertion that 'it is perfect because it hasn't a solution', for the very good reason that no puzzle ever

[1] *Verdict in Dispute* (Andre Deutsch).

devised by one human brain is incapable of solution by some other human brain.

The only way to accomplish this is by an intensive study of the individual who stood accused of propounding the puzzle, and the first step must be to discover all one can about his antecedents and background; the influences to which he has been subjected in youth; the basic equipment with which he has started life. One must then follow as closely as possible his subsequent career, marking his predilections and antipathies, noting his successes and failures; studying his medical history, if possible, and learning all one can about those whose lives have impinged most closely upon his own.

When, as in this case, the individual concerned is to all appearances merely a middle-aged insurance agent who has been suddenly hoisted out of obscurity to become the central figure in a drama so spectacular, yet so subtle, the limelight tends to become focused upon his recent life to the exclusion of his formative years, with the result that, as time goes by, facts which may be of inestimable value to the investigator become buried ever deeper in oblivion, while errors multiply and persist.

Nevertheless, even if the spade of the investigator turns up little of sensational interest in the way of fresh material, it is astonishing how many new fragments come to light which, when pieced together, shew the shape and pattern of the whole design. Thus it is that we may at least achieve a more funda-mental knowledge of our individual's process of thought and behaviour, and what has conditioned both; and this, taken in conjunction with the facts revealed through the legal proceed-ings, is of immeasurable assistance in helping us to find the answer to the problem he has posed.

'Crime [*says Mr Lustgarten*] yields many of its secrets to pure logic. The orthodox processes of deductive reasoning are among every competent inquirer's tools. By their appli-cation one can draw assured inferences, not only from the material facts, but from human temperament. . . . One may assume, for instance, that a strong-willed and courageous burglar has dominated a feeble-willed and cowardly accomplice. One may assume that a squeamish and fastidious murderer has not adopted from choice the bloodiest method of despatch. . . . The chance of error flowing from such assumptions, though not totally excluded, is infinitesimal.'[1]

In the Wallace case there are four points of outstanding importance, quite apart from the question of motive. They are:

1. The crime was carefully planned, and the first step towards putting it into execution was taken twenty-four hours in advance of the act itself.

2. It was planned with a scientific detachment and a mathematical precision.

3. The first blow was struck with a cool and calculated aim upon the left temple, and it killed the victim almost instantaneously.

4. It was followed by ten more blows delivered with all the symptoms of frenzy.

[1] *The Woman in the Case* (Andre Deutsch, 1955).

2

William Herbert Wallace

'The question is not: "Who did this crime?" The question is: "Did the prisoner do it?" ' [1]

I

IN ORDER to repair a faulty structure it is essential to demolish some of the existing fabric. Some of the structure which has been built up about the Wallace case is faulty owing partly to the uncritical acceptance of Wallace's *Life Story* on the one hand, and to lack of any original research on the other. These faults must be repaired as we proceed.

His *Life Story* opens with the words: 'I was born in the year 1878. We lived in the Lakeland District, and my early days were spent in that glorious country of mountain, lake and fell.' Out of this has arisen the legend that he was born at Keswick.[2] The truth is as follows: William Herbert Wallace was born on the 29th August 1878 at 44 Newton Street, Millom, which is not in the Lake District at all, but is a small town on the Cumberland bank of the Duddon estuary, which divides that county from the Furness peninsula of Lancashire.

Wallace tells us nothing about his family, but Mr Nigel Morland[3] states that Wallace's parents were 'respectable, middle-class people who saw that their two sons—William had a brother—received an education in keeping with their social level'; and he goes on to repeat an assertion made by Mr John

[1] Mr Justice Wright in his address to the jury.
[2] 'William Herbert Wallace was born in 1878 at Keswick,' states Mr Nigel Morland in *Background to Murder* (Werner Laurie, 1955). Mr. Morland seeks to prove Wallace's guilt.
[3] *Op. cit.*

Rowland,[1] presumably on no other authority than Wallace himself, that at the age of fourteen he was 'apprenticed' to a draper.

These are the facts which, it would seem, are making their appearance for the first time: Wallace was the eldest of the three surviving children of Benjamin and Margery Wallace (*née* Hall), the other two being Joseph Edwin and Jessie. Newton Street consisted of artisan's cottages, and Benjamin Wallace was employed in a printing works. Later in life he became a part-time agent for an insurance company—perhaps the Prudential, for at the time of his death in 1915 he held five small Industrial Life Policies with that company. There is nothing to suggest that the Wallace family were other than respectable people.

In those days the school-leaving age for a boy of the class to which the Wallaces belonged was fourteen, and thenceforth he must earn his own living. At that age, therefore, Wallace left the local school and a job was found for him in the neighbourhood, probably as errand boy to a local tradesman. Being particularly good at mathematics, and quick and eager to learn, he soon improved his position by obtaining employment with a linen-draper, possibly in Keswick; in a couple of years he had made himself thoroughly acquainted with the business, and he left the situation for a better one; a performance which he repeated until he had obtained sufficient experience to qualify him for the post of salesman with a large wholesale firm in Manchester.

In his *Life Story* he compresses the whole of this period into the following somewhat euphemistic paragraph:

'At the age of fourteen I was apprenticed for five years to the drapery trade. After several assistanceships in various towns the *wanderlust* which had obsessed me in earlier years grew to fever heat, and at the age of twenty-three I sailed for India, to take up a position as salesman in Calcutta.'

Everything we know of Wallace emphasizes the fact that

---

[1] *The Wallace Case* (Carrol & Nicholson, 1949). Mr Rowland seeks to prove Wallace's innocence.

wanderlust was an emotion singularly unlikely to have wrought him to 'fever heat'; if it did, his experiences abroad quickly effected a total cure, for once he returned to England he never attempted to leave its shores again, or even to venture beyond its northern counties. He is more likely to have been influenced —like anybody else—by the fact that the situation offered him better pay and prospects.

But before proceeding we must glean some idea as to the personality of this young man. From boyhood he had possessed a reverential regard for learning, and since his circumstances had restricted his education to a minimum, he sought to remedy the deficiency with a concentrated persistence which he retained throughout his life. He never took the least interest, or part, in athletics and popular pastimes, and while his school-mates had been spinning their tops or playing marbles on the pavements of Millom he had sought solitude in which to pursue his quest for knowledge, and in reading everything upon which he could lay his hands, from the newspapers to the classics, from tales of adventure to science and philosophy.

Introspective and reflective, he had innate powers of discrimination and perception, and of accurate observation, while he possessed a remarkable memory for detail. His favourite relaxation was to take long, solitary walks over the countryside, or about those cities to which his subsequent career took him, learning their highways and byways, alleys and short-cuts; paying keen, but critical, attention to all which lay along his path, whether it took the form of a road accident on the Yorkshire moors, a bargain over a handful of rice in a Shanghai bazaar, the behaviour of multitudes thronging the streets of Calcutta in the throes of religious fervour, or the sight of a piece of woodland on the outskirts of Liverpool held in the glittering and brittle stillness of a bitter frost. The beautiful and the ugly, the usual and the unusual, turmoil and tranquillity, were all noted by the watchful and rather staring eyes behind the spectacles, and analysed by the active brain behind the high, wide forehead.

At nineteen he stood a couple of inches over six feet, was sallow of complexion, thin and rather narrow-shouldered; but he was tough and wiry in spite of the fact that even before he had reached his 'teens he had suffered periodically from a weakness which was traced to his kidneys. This had been treated with apparent success while he was employed at Manchester, and when he sailed for India he entertained high hopes that he had been cured.

Neat and precise in his personal appearance, he was neat and precise in his work, and in his mode of speech. His manner, though formal and chilly, was civil, and he conveyed the impression of being what his class and generation termed 'gentleman-like'. While he seems to have made no enemies, neither does he seem to have made any friends.

How long he remained as a salesman with the firm of Whiteway, Laidlaw and Company at their Calcutta branch it is impossible to say. He himself tells us that he eventually fell ill. There is no evidence to suggest that his life was in the least danger at this time, or that it had been on those former occasions when the complaint in his kidney had troubled him, so one can only suppose that he was indulging his gift for picturesque exaggeration when he later wrote:

'Sentenced to death for the third time by a council of doctors, I had to leave India and seek the milder [sic] climate of China.[1]

And here we come to a point which is of primary importance in the study of his case: *neither in his* Life Story, *nor in any of his other published writings, did Wallace at any time give the slightest hint as to the name or nature of his illness.*

'In Shanghai [*he continues*] I worked as advertising manager for a general store. My illness, however, reached its climax, and I made up my mind to leave China and return at once to England. If I had to die, I preferred the the land of my fathers as my final resting-place. I arrived home seriously ill, and entered Guy's Hospital.'

Now, indeed, he *was* seriously ill; an operation had become imperative, and the only choice he had in the matter was

[1] This and other quotations, unless stated to the contrary, are from Wallace's *Life Story*.

whether it should be performed in China or in England. He chose the latter alternative, caught the first ship home, and at Guy's Hospital his left kidney was removed. The year was 1907.

With that began what was to prove the most decisive four years of Wallace's life.

2

As soon as he could, after his operation, he travelled north to his people. Before his convalescence was over it had become plain that with the removal of the diseased organ there was a marked improvement in his physical state, and a corresponding change in his mental outlook. His bony figure took on some flesh; his complexion lost its extreme sallowness; and he now sought, rather than shunned, contact with his fellows. The reading matter which now absorbed him was principally concerned with political and social questions, which he seized every opportunity to debate. He had developed into an ardent politician; a persistent and purposeful Liberal.

Before that year of congenial convalescence was over he had ceased to be an observer, watching the play of politics from the wings; he had taken a place upon the stage—even though one suspects that he is again exaggerating when he claims that he was soon 'addressing meetings in all parts of the North Lonsdale constituency'. But there is much reason to believe that, as he says, his 'financial position becoming precarious' he had to find fresh employment. It seems, indeed, possible that he may even have had to borrow money to tide him over till he did so. He presently found a situation, again in Manchester, but he had now lost all desire for a commercial career and had begun to entertain political ambitions. And why not? The Liberal Party was in power and looked like remaining there for years to come; men whose origins were as humble as his own, and who were endowed with no greater intrinsic ability, were rising to eminence. Lloyd George and others like him sat on the Government front benches. Why should not William Herbert Wallace achieve what they had achieved?

Twenty years later, with the chill of his narrow escape from the gallows still upon him, he recorded the event which was to alter the course of his life with a brevity and simplicity which indicates how deeply it affected him: 'To my delight I was eventually appointed Liberal Agent for the Ripon Division, West Riding of Yorkshire.'

In the same sentence he continues: 'Here began the happiest years of my life, for in Harrogate I met at this time my future wife.' But two years elapsed before his marriage to Julia took place, and in the events of those two years the seeds of the tragedy were sown.

3

We have already noticed that Wallace avoided giving the name of his birthplace and avoided disclosing the nature of his illness. He is equally reticent with regard to his connection with Harrogate, diverting the attention of his readers from those most vital four years of his life with sentimental gush. So reticent is he that a total misapprehension has arisen which is embodied in these words of Mr Rowland:[1]

'It is worth noting that Wallace, like so many North-countrymen, seems to have had a real aversion for the South of England, and never apparently sought a job there. . . . Even his holidays were the typical North-countryman's, spent at Harrogate: it was there, in 1911, that he met the lady who was two years later to become his wife.'

Wallace's connection with Harrogate and his consequent meeting with Julia had absolutely nothing to do with holidays; Harrogate was the party headquarters in the Ripon Division— the office being at 5a Raglan Street—and it was at Harrogate therefore that Wallace, on his appointment as secretary and agent, took up his abode.

At first he lived in lodgings, but towards the end of 1910 a house—9 Belmont Road—was taken in his father's name, and, his mother having died, here he, his father and his sister Jessie

[1] Op. cit.

all lived together. None of this was ever revealed by Wallace. When he left Harrogate all that had happened there became a closed book, which has remained closed ever since; but everything which had been written on its pages was indelibly impressed upon the minds—and, we may believe, upon the hearts —of Julia and himself, influencing the whole of their subsequent life together.

Wallace was now in his thirty-third year. Since he was sixteen he had never known—except during his recent period of convalescence—that sense of security and well-being that is derived from a settled background and family solidarity. In their undemonstrative way the Wallaces were united. Joseph Edwin hastened back from the Far East as soon as possible after his brother's arrest. When Wallace's conviction was quashed he left the Court of Appeal supported on one side by Joseph and on the other by Joseph's son. In appearance all three bore a strong resemblance to each other, but William was by a head the tallest.

One may feel sure that the whole family was proud and gratified at Wallace's selection to fill this new post, and were no doubt as sanguine as himself that it would lead to still greater opportunites. One may feel sure that Jessie, with the practical good sense of the North-countrywoman, provided nourishing and wholesome food for him, and looked after his general comfort; while, knowing Wallace's expansive literary style, we may picture him writing glowing accounts of his prospects to his brother out in Malaya.

It would have infuriated him could he have known that, after his death, even the warmest advocates of his innocence would write so condescendingly of his intellectual powers. It has been left to Mr F. J. P. Veale, in his monograph on the case,[1] to strike a proper balance.

'The plain truth is that Wallace was a victim of the educational system in force during the first years of his life. With his capacity for study and keen interest in intellectual subjects he could not have failed to have done well had proper training been within his reach. . . . Had he been

[1] *The Wallace Case* (printed privately, 1950).

born half a century later Wallace's life would certainly have
been on very different lines. . . . In these days a young man
of his type would have risen stage by stage with the aid of
State scholarships and grants.'

Wallace's recent experience in addressing audiences was of
great benefit to him. Like so many self-educated people of
humble origin, whose intelligence is above the average, he
suffered from that hyper-sensitiveness which invests its subjects
with, on the one hand, an exaggerated consciousness of their
powers, and, on the other, with an acute awareness of their
limitations. Like all such people he was filled with a passionate
longing to shine, to dazzle, and to be the centre of attention;
but, like them, too, he was held in check by the dread of
rebuffs. It is the personal, the individual, element which is
affrighting; something composite, like an audience hanging
on one's words, provides an unique sensation, stimulating and
inspiring, and bestowing that confidence which stiffens the
morale.

Established in his post at Harrogate, and in contact with
a different world from that purely commercial one he had
formerly occupied, Wallace was quick to perceive his lack of
poise and polish. He determined to remedy this, and presently
gained the *entrée* into one of those literary and artistic circles
which flourish in spas and watering-places such as Harrogate;
and there, in the person of one of its most enthusiastic members,
he met the woman who became his wife and was destined to
become the victim of that apparently motiveless murder which,
Mr Lustgarten tells us, James Agate never tired of debating.

3

The Victim of the Crime

'Women . . . partly through a tradition of inscrutability—
partly through an over-developed defensive mechanism—as a
sex are often deliberately secretive about their motivating thoughts,
however unexceptionable. . . . Parallelled, though, with an
analysis of the woman goes, of necessity, an analysis of events, for
the latter and the former interact.'[1]

I

THE first blow of the weapon which struck down Julia
Wallace was delivered so swiftly, and with such accuracy
of aim, upon her temple that she was dead before she
knew that it was about to be administered. In that sense her
violent end might be deemed merciful, but it makes the deed
all the more treacherous and abominable.

'Any description of Julia Wallace [*writes Mr Veale*[2]]
must necessarily be brief, since practically nothing is known
about her characteristics and tastes, apart from what her
husband has recorded.'

Quite so, and there the matter has been allowed to rest; but
all through the years a number of facts concerning her have
lain gathering dust in the limbo of oblivion, while guess-work
has embellished what her husband's pen recorded.

'She was a lady of good birth and social position [*wrote
Wallace magniloquently*], whose tastes were very similar to

[1] *The Woman in the Case*—Edgar Lustgarten.
[2] *Op. cit.*

my own. Dark-haired, dark-eyed, full of energy and vivaciousness, she filled in every corner of the picture I had dreamed of "that one woman in all the world" most men enshrine in their hearts. She was an excellent pianist, no mean artist in water-colour, a fluent French scholar, and of a cultured literary taste.'

Unimpressed by this eulogy Mr Veale suggests:

'Apparently she came of a somewhat higher social class than her husband. The general impression given by Julia Wallace is of a lower middle-class woman of the Edwardian governess type.'[1]

Although Wallace, as usual, gilded the lily, there would appear to be some truth in his description of Julia. She *was*, in those days, 'energetic and vivacious'; besides playing the piano she possessed a trained voice and often sang at concerts; she had some talent with her paint-brush. And, moreover, she sought to improve her accomplishments. She may, or may not, have been fluent in French, and there is no evidence that her taste in literature was anything out of the ordinary. She would certainly have been qualified to hold the post of governess; whether she ever did so there is now no means of deciding, for at the time she enters the orbit of this narrative she was already established in comfortable independence at 11 St Mary's Avenue, Harrogate.

This, as the accompanying illustration shows, was a pleasant, well-constructed stone villa of three floors above a semi-basement. A low stone wall and a little strip of garden separate it from the road and a flight of stone steps leads up to a front door agreeably recessed in an arched porch. The generous proportions of the windows suggest airy, well-lighted rooms eminently suitable for those musical evenings to which she invited her friends.

She also accompanied them to plays and concerts, and on sketching expeditions to beauty spots in the surrounding countryside. Nor did her activities end there; possessing deep religious instincts she was a regular attendant at her parish church

[1] *Op. cit.*

JULIA WALLACE

'A gentle personality . . . wistfully anxious to please, nervously
restrained.'

of St Mary and took an active part in parochial affairs; while being endowed with a strong civic conscience she regularly registered her name on the Burgess Roll.

So little effort has hitherto been made to discover anything about Julia that only one person, Mr Nigel Morland, has hazarded a suggestion as to her maiden name, and he has got it wrong. He gives it as Thorpe;[1] it was, in fact, Dennis. Her father, William George Dennis, was a veterinary surgeon; Julia would appear to have been his only child, and he would seem to have given her every chance to develop her latent talents and to have left her adequately provided for.

There was a quality about Julia which drew people to her. Even in death, those whom her terrible end brought to her side, accustomed though many of them were to such sights, found themselves peculiarly affected. In life this quality seems to have resided in a warm and gentle manner, which, in her portrait, looks out, rather wistfully, from her dark eyes and lurks in the trace of a smile about her sensitive lips. With its well-cut features it is the face of a woman of refinement, anxious to please, nervously restrained. According to the fashions of 1910 she is well and tastefully dressed: her hat, with its ostrich plume, is of good quality; her fur stole of ample proportions, while the tucks and embroidery which embellish her blouse are hand-done.

'The possibility has been raised [*writes Mr Veale*[2]] that she may have been killed by a former lover, or by a blackmailer who knew some dark secret of her former life. As to this possibility, which is unsupported by evidence of any kind, one can only say with Mr Rowland that it is hard to think of her as having "aroused dangerous passions in the breast of any man".'

Such a possibility was in fact investigated by the police with an entirely negative result, and so melodramatic a notion only persists in the minds of those who hanker after the sensational.

[1] *Op. cit.*
[2] *Op. cit.*

Undoubtedly Julia Dennis was the type of woman to whom the mere notion of arousing 'dangerous passions in the breast of any man' would have been abhorrent. On the other hand she looks the type of woman whom a man of perception might feel proud and happy to make his wife. And it can never be said of Wallace that he was lacking in perception. Her air of gentility, her accomplishments, her security and independence, all represented those very things that he lacked, and which he needed more than ever at that particular moment to establish him in his new position and assist him in the career which he hoped might be opening out before him.

'The courtship lasted two years and was idyllic [*he wrote in his* Life Story]. From the first moment we met we found in each other that friendship, companionship and love we needed.'

If this ecstatic picture of love at first sight be true, why, one may ask, did the lovers wait two years before they married? There was no legal impediment in their way.

Did Julia hesitate? And, if so, were her reasons concerned with the personality of Wallace himself; or was it merely that, at her age—she was a year his senior—she was reluctant to exchange her independence, and the niche she had created for herself, in order to marry anyone at all?

If the first were her reason, did her reluctance spring from what Mr Lustgarten terms a woman's 'over-developed defensive mechanism'—in other words that intuition, or instinct, which in a sensitive woman, like Julia, living alone, is often very acute? Did she, in spite of appreciating Wallace's attributes, experience that instinctive recoil from him, which many people undoubtedly did?

'Wallace [*writes Mr Veale*[1]] was a highbrow: not, indeed, an academic highbrow, but nevertheless a genuine and persistent highbrow. . . . The only apparent result of his intellectual interests was that they seem to have made him faintly disliked by most of his acquaintances.'

[1] *Op. cit.*

Research has elicited a number of facts which throw light upon these questions, and upon others relating to the vital four years which Wallace spent in Harrogate. It shews, for one thing, that with a pen in his hand Wallace was a past-master of the art of creating illusions favourable to himself out of material that was unfavourable, as he does in the following passage of his *Life Story*.

'These were the days when all the future seemed rose-coloured, sun-lit, and steeped in everlasting happiness. Nothing could ever change! But through this Eldorado of a lover's dreams the wheel of fate was turning, turning . . .'

The wheel of fate? It will be suggested that *fate* had little to do with the tide in his affairs which was to sweep him—with Julia at his side—away from his moorings and out of Harrogate; and it will further be suggested that therein lies the first clue as to what is the answer to the question—'*why* was Julia Wallace killed?' Seeking this clue is a delicate task, and at first its significance can only be somewhat hazily discerned, though later with the addition of others it will grow in clarity.

2

When one has gathered together a number of isolated facts the difficulty is to relate them to each other in such a way as to show cause and effect. Perhaps the best method is to begin at the end of the period to which they apply and work backwards. Let us, then, begin with the following quotation from Wallace's *Life Story*:

'A blissful year of marriage preceded the outbreak of the Great War. We set up house in a quiet quarter of Harrogate, little dreaming of the maelstrom which was destined to uproot us within a very few months. The war, crashing into our quiet lives, brought politics to the ground, and I was once again thrown on my beam ends.'

The first illusion which this passage creates is that the setting up of a house in Harrogate had been his responsibility; it is nowhere suggested that in reality all he did was to pack up his effects at 9 Belmont Road, transport them to the house already owned and occupied by his bride, and there hang up his hat. The second illusion is that the Great War constituted that 'maelstrom' which was the cause of the 'uprooting', and that he was thereby 'thrown on his beam ends'—in other words lost his post as Liberal party agent—because it 'brought politics to the ground'. That illusion persists to this day, and we find it thus gravely stated by Mr Rowland.[1]

'With Wallace working for the Liberal party—work he enjoyed and that he thought well worth while from the point of view of the country as a whole—his life appeared to be set on peaceful lines. There was no chance, he thought, that things could go seriously wrong. But then, like a bolt from the blue, which it appeared to so many people, came the First Great War. At once Wallace's livelihood was gone, for it was clear that under the threat of German aggression all political activity would come to a standstill: no one would any longer think of employing a full-time political agent. . . . It was time for him to go job-hunting again. He was thirty-six years of age. He had given all his thoughts to politics in recent years.'

When writing this paragraph Mr Rowland appears to have been under the impression that Wallace lost his job as soon as war broke out. *He did not do so until a year later*—towards the end of 1915, and when he was thirty-seven. Moreover, Mr Rowland overlooks two facts: it takes more than wars to 'bring politics to the ground', and Wallace, as a man medically unfit for active service, would have been the ideal person to keep the party organization in being until peace returned. But the most important fact of all was, of course, unknown to Mr Rowland, which is that *immediately Wallace had been 'thrown on his beam ends' he was succeeded in the post he had held by one Mr A. Cotterill.*

[1] *Op. cit.*

So the illusion created by Wallace, and subscribed to by others, that he lost his much-prized post, which he had held since 1910, as a direct result of the war would appear to be false, and the only alternative is that the reason was a personal, not a national, one. In order to form an opinion as to what it might have been *il faut reculer pour mieux sauter.*

It will be recalled that, referring to his political activities after his convalescence, Wallace wrote, 'my financial position becoming somewhat precarious I took a situation in Manchester', and it was then suggested that he might have had to borrow money to tide him over a period in which he was undoubtedly devoting every shilling to further his political ambitions. In the commercial world which he had inhabited all his life he must have learned that much business is done on the strength of an affluent appearance and an affable manner, and having secured the appointment at Harrogate, it may well have seemed to him that, by setting up house at 9 Belmont Road and adopting an attitude of open-handedness, he would do much to further his chances of advancement towards a political career. But when a man has no financial resources to draw upon, such indulgences are liable to land him in debt— and thence into the clutches of money-lenders, who, in default of adequate security, charge exorbitant rates of interest. It is suggested that this is what happened to Wallace, and that marriage with Julia offered him the chance of escape from a very precarious position. This opinion is based upon a number of facts, each one small in itself, but incontestable, and forming in the aggregate a forceful argument.

1. It was Julia Dennis' practice to enter her name each year on the Burgess Roll in respect of 11 St Mary's Avenue. It appears for 1911—the year in which she first made the acquaintance of Wallace. It appears again in 1912—when Wallace, according to himself, was well launched on his courtship. It does *not* appear for 1913, while for 1914 the name *Wallace* is substituted, *without any distinguishing Christian name, or even an initial.* How are we to interpret these facts in the light of what we have learned of these two persons' stories? May it not be that the reason why Julia Dennis did not register her name for 1913 was because she was expecting very shortly to

change it to Wallace? If so, then it is only logical to assume that some hitch—or even crisis—intervened. And why was the registration for 1914 made in that strangely tentative form? May not the explanation of that be that Julia Dennis was then in process of transferring her property by Deed to the man she had now decided to marry, and to whom she was married on 24th March of that year? If Wallace was literally 'thrown on his beam ends' when he lost his post only eighteen months later, whither had Julia's capital vanished—and vanished, it is plain, for ever?

2. The wedding itself, which was to herald what Wallace describes as 'a blissful year of marriage', was solemnized in the parish church of St Mary by the vicar, the Reverend E. A. Chard, on the 24th March 1914. The register was signed by Jessie Wallace and an unspecified person, J. S. Allanson.

3. Neither the usual formal announcement, nor any report of the marriage having taken place, appeared in the local Press.

4. The newly wedded couple took up residence in the bride's home, 11 St Mary's Avenue.

5. The tenancy of 9 Belmont Road was given up, and Benjamin and Jessie Wallace also took up their abode at 11 St. Mary's Avenue.

6. At that address, a year all but twelve days later, Benjamin Wallace made a Will in the presence of the vicar. He had suffered a stroke and could only attach his mark, not his signature, to the document. By this Will his estate was to be equally divided between his son, William Herbert, and his daughter, Jessie, the former being appointed executor.

7. Ten days after that—on 22nd March 1915—Benjamin Wallace died of cerebral haemorrhage, aged 79, *in the workhouse infirmary at Knaresborough*.

How do these facts strike the inquirer?

Does it not seem curious that the bridegroom who had resided in Harrogate with his family for the past four years and held a post which must have brought him quite often into the public eye and made him acquainted with a considerable number of people; and that the bride who, for even longer, had taken an active part in parochial affairs and moved among a

Photo. Bertram Unné

11 ST MARY'S AVENUE, HARROGATE

'A well-constructed stone villa set in pleasant surroundings.'

fairly wide circle of friends, should have married so very un-
obtrusively that the event should have escaped *all* notice in
the local Press? Does it not seem strange that, as soon as the
marriage had been performed, Benjamin Wallace should have
given up his own home, where he had his daughter to look
after him, and that both he and she should have gone to live
under Julia's roof? But strangest of all—and savouring of that
callousness which was so to strike observers on the night of his
wife's murder—is surely Wallace's action in arranging for his
dying father to be removed to meet his end in the infirmary of
a distant workhouse!

How, too, did it come about that Benjamin Wallace, who
had been registered as a houscholder at 9 Belmont Road until
a year before his death, should die possessed of no more than
£56, all derived from six Industrial Life Insurance Policies?
Does it not suggest that his savings, along with the capital
which Julia had inherited from her father, had both been
whirled away by that 'maelstrom' which was created—not by
the Great War—but by the burden of Wallace's debts? And
may it not have been this self-same 'maelstrom' which swept
him out of his post?

4

29 Wolverton Street, Liverpool

'We know very little about the private lives of people, or of their thoughts.'[1]

I

TWICE before Wallace's career had been brought to an abrupt halt, but these were little more than temporary setbacks. The third time was calamitous. His employment at Harrogate had not only provided him with ample opportunity to develop his intellectual interests and accustomed him to a higher standard of living than he had previously enjoyed, but had also conferred upon him the prestige of a semi-public appointment. If the loss of his post really arose from the cause to which he attributed it in his *Life Story*, not only would that prestige still have been attached to him when he sought re-engagement, but it is surely a remarkable thing that the Liberal party, which he had served for four years and was still the party in power, should have made no attempt to find him an alternative post in, for instance, one of the many ministries then being set up in connection with the war effort, and copiously staffed?

Nothing of the sort happened. With his pride in his pocket Wallace left Harrogate and the wreckage of his hopes, in order to start 'job-hunting again'. That he obtained a situation with the Prudential Assurance Company in Liverpool may have been due, to some extent, to the posthumous influence of his father, who in later life had been a part-time insurance agent, and, since five of the six policies of which he died possessed were held with the Prudential, it was probably that company

[1] Professor J. E. W. MacFall in evidence at the trial.

by which he was employed. Wallace's way, too, would also be rendered easier by reason of the fact that the younger men who would normally have been his competitors were serving with the armed forces.

He was placed in charge of the working-class district of Clubmoor. It was an agency usually given to a junior employee, but he was in no position to pick and choose, and it would at least enable him to preserve his self-respect, while he could cherish hopes of promotion.

He and Julia took up their abode at 29 Wolverton Street, a *cul-de-sac* of small terrace-houses in the rather drab neighbouring district of Anfield. For the first decade of their existence in Liverpool Wallace made the narrow confines of his house a refuge from which he could exclude the world; a refuge in which he could brood over the ruins of his castles in the air, and find solace during his leisure hours in study, particularly of chemistry and physics, to promote which he immediately converted the smallest of the three bedrooms into a combined laboratory and workshop. In those days no one but Julia and himself ever crossed the threshold of No. 29.

Mr Veale says of Wallace that it is 'wrong to assume his isolation was from choice and that he only brought himself to maintain contact with his fellow men in order to earn his living', adding that 'he was a regular attendant at the chess club of which he was a member, and when given an opportunity he gave talks on chemistry at a local technical institute'[1]. But it was not until *1923* that Wallace joined the chess club, and the date at which he gave his lectures was later still. Moreover, both these activities were merely an extension of his intellectual life and outside the private one in which he immured his spirit. Chess, indeed, was not only a pastime to which he had been addicted since boyhood, but was also one over which silence predominated; while his talks on chemistry constituted a tribute to his intellectual superiority which was gratifying to his self-esteem and, at the same time, brought in a small but useful addition to his income in the way of fees.

Mr Rowland remarks of Wallace that he was 'an aloof, slightly priggish man', but there was more than that to account

[1] *Op. cit.*

for the feeling of constraint, if not actual antipathy, which his acquaintances had towards him. There was something metallic about him. He approached everything with a cold precision which drained it of all colour. He had an inquiring mind, but his curiosity had nothing warm about it; it was the curiosity of the analyst, or vivisectionist, and in all his mental make-up there was not a grain of humour. The general impression he gave was of a disdainful superiority which made no attempt to disguise the fact that he despised his fellow-men's preoccupations with such things as the events of the racing calendar, cricket and football fixtures, and despised, too, their robust and commonplace geniality.

But what must have permeated his whole being like the venom injected by the adder's fang was the sense of stagnation in his own life. Every week, year in and year out, he was compelled to trudge the pavements of Clubmoor, knocking upon some five hundred and sixty of its doors and entering its squalid dwellings to pay out small sums in Sick Benefit, to explain the filling in of forms, and to collect the few pennies due as premiums on petty Industrial Life Policies, while with each succeeding year the hope of promotion—or, at least, of transfer to another district less drab and more lucrative—dwindled and finally died.

The downdrag of that dreary treadmill of routine could induce a feeling of mortification even in an apathetic mind; to a man of Wallace's lively intelligence it must have been purgatory. And as the drop of venom in the adder's fang can permeate a man's whole system, so, too, must the sense of frustration and defeat have poisoned Wallace's whole mind as hope perished in his heart. Yet he must choke down his mortification as he trod the treadmill of his life—which tread he must if he were to survive—and now the drudgery grew more bitter still with the knowledge that his health again was failing, that he was middle-aged, and that the younger generation was pressing hard upon his heels. Did he but stumble, and one out of the thousands of unemployed would elbow him aside.

Less than this has caused a man to take his own life. But has it ever set a man, who is not insane, to evolve an elaborate plot to murder his wife by violence within the walls of their own home, knowing full well that her death would bring him nothing to mitigate his circumstances? *'We know very little about the private lives of people, or of their thoughts.'*

Every writer on this case is agreed—and there were witnesses to testify—that Wallace never shirked his work and his accounts were never a penny wrong; yet the fact remains that at the end of sixteen years of faithful service he was still doing the same job, and that one usually done by a junior man.

What was the reason for this? The successful insurance agent should possess that quality called 'the common touch'. Wallace conspicuously lacked it. He should be endowed with geniality; the police investigations revealed that Wallace's clients in Clubmoor regarded him as 'surly', and when he attempted to resume work among them after the quashing of his conviction they shut their doors in his face. Can this have been entirely due to prejudice? Would he have been the object of such concerted hostility if he had made himself liked in his district? Nor was this hostility confined to Clubmoor; it manifested itself even within the offices of the Prudential when he was compassionately transferred there to a clerical post. Indeed, the more one studies Wallace's life and personality, the more it would appear that there was something about him similar to that which inspired the famous jingle:

> 'I do not like thee, Dr Fell;
> The reason why I cannot tell:
> But this I know, and know full well:
> I do not like thee, Dr Fell.'

2

Through the pages of *John Bull* Wallace presented the public with a picture of the life which he and his wife led at 29 Wolverton Street as illusionary as that in which he had depicted the Harrogate scene. This is what he says:

'Here we lived in perfect happiness and harmony for sixteen years. Our days and months and years were filled with complete enjoyment, placid perhaps, but with all the happiness of quietude, and mutual interests and affection. Neither of us cared much for entertaining other people, or for being entertained; we were sufficient in ourselves. My wife had an artist's natural love of colour: landscape, seascape and flowers appealed to her. . . .'

The eye of the artist can, of course, find beauty and colour in the most unexpected places and objects, but Julia must have had to look very hard to find either the one or the other in her surroundings at Wolverton Street. That little two-storeyed villa in a row, flanked and confronted by its counter-parts, was where she spent practically the whole of her days during those sixteen years. Throughout the whole street the dingy brick façades were unrelieved by so much as a blade of grass, though by craning out of the window she could see a pair of sad-looking trees rising above the brick wall which blocked the end of Wolverton Street and made it into a *cul-de-sac*.

From her bedroom window the only view she could command was of a chequer-board of backyards extending on either hand, and on both sides of a central alley, each one the repository of battered dust-bins and the site of ramshackle coal-sheds. Here not even a stunted tree put out a hopeful leaf in spring, and the only colour to regale Julia's eye was provided by the washing flapping from the clothes-lines every Monday.

How stultifying that background! How different to the one which had been hers at 11 St Mary's Avenue, with its wide windows, pleasant little garden and trim surroundings!

And what of those 'mutual interests' she and her husband shared with all the 'happiness of quietude'?

On six mornings a week he left the house soon after break-fast, returned for his dinner at midday, and, on every weekday but Saturday, went about his work again until 6 p.m. Usually on Mondays, and sometimes on Thursday as well, he would depart again about an hour later and spend the evening playing chess at the club which met in a café in the city, while on other evenings he might be absent delivering his lectures at the technical institute.

29 WOLVERTON STREET, LIVERPOOL—NO. 31 IS
ON THE RIGHT

'A two-storied villa of dingy brick, flanked and confronted
by its counterparts.'

Such were his principal activities and diversions. Julia's activities were confined to household chores, and of diversions she had hardly any. With rare exceptions all the days of her year were the mirror image of each other. Apparently the Wallaces took no annual holiday. Wallace's diary mentions only a day trip to Settle, in the North Yorkshire moors, which would seem to have afforded the only opportunity for Julia to indulge her love of landscape. As for seascape, it would seem that she had to content herself with the murky waters of the Mersey.

Wallace's diary also mentions that on three or four occasions they took a tram across the city to Calderstones, to see the roses in bloom in the public gardens; otherwise Julia's chances to enjoy the sight of flowers must have been limited to the occasions when she went shopping in Breck Road and beheld them displayed in florists' or standing in buckets outside the greengrocers'; or, if she ever ventured the four hundred yards from her door to the junction of Breck and Rochester Roads, her eyes may have been gladdened by the sight of the formal flower-beds with which the municipal authorities had enlivened a triangular plot of grass, at the apex of which she would also have seen—brighter even than the Corporation's geraniums—a scarlet telephone kiosk; that very kiosk from which at 7.15 on the evening of Monday, 19th January 1931, there went forth the mysterious message which fixed the day and hour of her death.

In all those sixteen years of her existence in Wolverton Street feminine fashions underwent many changes, but, winter and summer, Julia continued to wear those dresses with long, flared skirts and hems almost touching the ground, which had been the vogue at the time of her marriage. Such an one was she wearing when she was murdered, and after it had been removed at the mortuary her underclothing was found to be in a pitiable state. This had been awkwardly contrived by herself out of the cheapest material, and was clumsily darned and patched, for she did not number sewing among her accomplishments. It was then, too, that the pathetic little hoard of some thirty shillings was discovered stitched into her ragged corsets. But more pathetic still was the emaciated condition of her body, bearing as it did all the signs of chronic undernourishment. At fifty-two, though suffering from no disease, she had become a 'feeble, weak woman'.[1]

But though in Liverpool she moved in no artistic circle, went on no sketching expeditions, and attended no concerts with her friends—there were no friends—at least she reguarly attended Holy Trinity Church in Breck Road, and there were women among the congregation who, the police investigations revealed, would have liked to be on friendly terms with her. She was, indeed, always ready for a chat with them after Service was over, but these exchanges went no further; Julia returned to Wolverton Street like a hermit to a cell.

Next door to the Wallaces, at No. 31, lived the Johnstons, both of whom were to be important witnesses at the trial. Mrs Johnston and her husband—an engineer by profession—were a likable couple with two children of school age. At the time of the crime they were on the point of moving to a better neighbourhood, but during the ten years they had lived at No. 31 Mrs Johnston had made a number of friendly advances towards Julia.

'Have you ever been in the Wallaces' house?' *Mr Hemmerde*, Counsel for the Crown, asked her in the course of her evidence.

'Yes, about three times.'

'In how many years?'

'In ten years.'

'In ten years you have only been in there three times?' repeated Counsel in tones of astonishment.

'Yes—in the front room only.'

'Were they both there on those three occasions?'

'No; only Mrs Wallace.'

'Have you ever seen them together?'

'No.'

Three times Mrs Johnston had called to see Julia, had been invited into the formal little parlour, and had sat there conversing. Like Julia's other acquaintances Mrs Johnston received the impression that she was sadly lonely—yet none of them was encouraged to renew her visits. None the less it is not unlikely that Wallace's words, 'we were sufficient in ourselves',

[1] Professor J. E. W. MacFall in evidence.

expresses a view of his own which he forced upon his unwilling wife.

Just as there was something faintly repellent about Wallace, so there was something about Julia which instinctively attracted and aroused sympathy. On the night of 20th January 1931 the Johnstons were to be the first persons—apart from Wallace himself—to behold Julia lying murdered in that same little parlour. The manner of her death had made her a sight terrible to behold—a sight from which Mrs. Johnston might excusably have recoiled; yet she fell at once upon her knees beside the body, and, taking a lifeless hand between her own, had cried deeply moved: 'Oh, you poor darling!'

In cross-examination *Mr Roland Oliver*, Counsel for the Defence, asked her:

'Were you a friend of Mrs Wallace?'

'Yes, as neighbours.'

'You liked her, did you not?'

'Yes.'

'When you saw her dead you exclaimed: "Oh, you poor darling!"?'

'Yes—but it is a word I have never used except under strong emotion.'

3

During the nineteen-twenties Wallace developed what appears to have been his nearest approach to friendship with one of his fellow-men. This was Mr Joseph Crewe, one of the senior clerks in the Prudential office, with whom his work brought him into frequent contact; and in 1927, when he began to experience trouble in his remaining kidney, and it seemed likely that he would have to become an in-patient at a Liverpool hospital, Mr Crewe had been sympathetic and helpful.

The following year the latter was promoted to the rank of supervisor and became Wallace's immediate superior. He then went to live in Green Lane, Mossley Hill—a district some four miles by tram from Wolverton Street and in close proximity to those Menlove Gardens which were to figure so conspicuously in the case for the Prosecution as the scene of Wallace's alibi.

In that same year, 1928, Wallace was at length compelled to enter hospital for some weeks, and a junior agent temporarily took over his district.

Just as Wallace's discharge from Guy's Hospital in 1907 had marked the beginning of a second cycle in his life, and his departure from Harrogate in 1915 that of a third, so now did his emergence from hospital in 1928 mark the beginning of the fourth and last.

As he had plunged into politics in 1907, as though urged by the need to expand, so now, as though compelled by some irresistible impulse to put his powers to the severest possible test, and at the same time arouse the wonder and admiration of his acquaintances, he suddenly determined, at the age of fifty, to master the technique of playing that most difficult of all instruments, the violin.

He had shewn no particular musical genius before; he shewed none now, but with the assistance of Mr Crewe, himself a competent amateur, who helped him in the choice of an instrument and gave him a few lessons at his house in Green Lane during the ensuing winter, Wallace, by dint of indefatigable persistence, achieved a remarkable proficiency. Julia's long-neglected talent for the piano was called into being to play his accompaniments, and there were few evenings in the week when the wail of the violin and the soft strumming of the piano did not beat upon the ears of the Johnstons on the other side of the thin party wall.

5

The Telephone Call: 19th January 1931

'The lady supervisor has produced an official note which they keep when there is a difficulty of getting a reply. So we get 7.15 as fixing that time, and no doubt some little time before whoever rang up must have been in that kiosk.'[1]

I

BY 6th November 1930 a small, hand-written notice had been pinned up by the captain of the chess club, a Mr Beattie, on the board beside the telephone in the City Café giving the names of the members selected to play in the second-class tournament which was to begin on 10th November and continue on alternate Mondays until 21st February 1931. Wallace was down to play his first contest on 19th January.

The club was a small one, and the commitments of its members did not always allow them to keep the fixtures. For this reason it was the rule that if they were not in their places by 7.40 p.m. substitutes were found for them. Mr Beattie had already had to find a substitute to take the place of Wallace's opponent, and as Wallace himself had not attended the club meetings for the past fortnight Mr Beattie was uncertain as to whether he would turn up that night.

Wallace was to state that, on the night of 19th January, he left his house for the City Café at 7.15, but there was no one to corroborate this evidence or any of his movements until he appeared among his fellow-members. At about that time, however, a man entered that telephone kiosk at the junction of Breck and Rochester Roads. It had no interior lighting and was dependent for illumination on a street-lamp some twenty-five

[1] Mr Justice Wright in his address to the jury.

feet away. To passers-by on the pavement the man behind that plate-glass would present no more than an indistinguishable shadow, but he himself could clearly see the tide of life outside and watch the tramcars clanking to a halt at the stop just opposite—so the kiosk was a handy vantage-point for one wanting to send a message and then quickly catch a tram into the city.

Whoever that man might have been, when he inserted his two pennies into the slot of the call-box he was deliberately putting into execution a carefully premeditated plot which was to culminate in Julia's death—a plot which had been worked out to the last detail. But machinery, like man, is fallible. The man in the kiosk knew that when he had pressed the two coins into the slot he would automatically become connected with the Exchange, and he asked the answering voice of the operator for Bank 3381—the number of the Cify Café. A couple of minutes later the Supervisor, Miss Lilian Kelly, answered a complaint. Its somewhat unusual phraseology, she told the Court, impressed it on her memory.

'Operator,' said a man's voice, 'I have pressed Button A, but have not had my correspondent yet.'

The official record of the incident reads as follows:

> 'When the caller was first plugged through he received no answer, necessitating a second call. He complained to the operator of not being put through properly in the first place, and after some conversation the supervisor refunded the twopence he had paid for the second call. These two different operators testified that the man who booked the call had "an ordinary voice and was rather polite".'

As soon as Miss Kelly had obtained the number required by the caller she made an official note that at 7.15 p.m. a defect had been reported from public call-box Anfield 1672, and accordingly next morning Leslie Heaton, a telephone mechanic, was sent to inspect the instrument, subsequently reporting that he had found 'a fault in the mechanism which he had corrected'.

Miss Dorothy L. Sayers, in her account of the Wallace case,

(Based by permission of the Ordnance Survey and 'Geographia' Ltd., on the Plan of Greater Liverpool.)

PLAN OF ANFIELD, LIVERPOOL.

1. Telephone kiosk.   2. Holy Trinity Church.   3. Public Library.   4. St Margaret's Church.

has written: 'She' (Miss Kelly) 'was spoken to by a caller who said, "Operator, I have pressed Button A, but have not had my correspondent yet". *She then connected him and thought no more about it.*'[1] This, as we have seen, is incorrect. It has also been asserted in other accounts of the case that Miss Kelly would have had no means of knowing from what call-box the call had emanated unless she had asked the caller for his number. This, too, is incorrect; when a public call-box is used, its number is automatically recorded at the Exchange.

The importance of this incident is twofold; but for that hitch in the mechanism the time, and place, from which emanated the message that heralded Julia's death would never have been known, while it established that, whoever its sender was, it would have taken him no more than four minutes to reach that kiosk from 29 Wolverton Street.

Gladys Harley, waitress at the City Café, answered the call when it came through. A voice, which she later described as 'just an ordinary voice—a man's voice', asked to speak to Mr Wallace. Glancing around the room she said that Mr Wallace was not there, whereupon the voice expressed a wish to leave a message for him.

'Then I had better fetch Mr Beattie,' she replied, and did so. The latter, too, informed the voice that Mr Wallace had not arrived, but added:

'If you care to leave a message, I'll give it to him as soon as he gets here.'

'I want to see him urgently. I've got something in the nature of his business that I want to talk to him about.'

'What name shall I say?'

'Qualtrough—R. M. Qualtrough.'

The name was sufficiently unusual for Mr Beattie to be uncertain of its spelling, so fishing an envelope out of his pocket he asked the caller to spell it out to him. This the voice did, slowly and distinctly, adding with equal emphasis: 'And the address is 25 Menlove Gardens *East*, Mossley Hill.'

Having noted all this down on his envelope Mr Beattie said:

'Wallace should be here within the next half-hour—though

[1] *The Anatomy of Murder*: author's italics.

I can't be certain he will come. Couldn't you ring up again later?'

'No, I'm too busy for that. I've got my girl's twenty-first birthday on. But I want to speak to Mr Wallace on a matter of business.'

'I see. What would you like me to tell him?'

'Could you ask him to come round and see me at about half past seven tomorrow night?'

Promising to do so Mr Beattie hung up the receiver, pocketed the envelope and resumed his interrupted occupations.

In the magistrates' court he was to give a description of that voice totally at variance with that given by the two telephone operators and Gladys Harley. It was, he stated, 'confident and strong'. At the trial he said it was 'strong and rather gruff', an answer which he elaborated in reply to the Judge as meaning 'a confident voice—sure of himself'.

Asked by Counsel for the Defence, *Mr Roland Oliver*, if, at the time, the voice had struck him as being 'not a natural one', witness replied:

'No, I had no reason for doubting it.'

Thus encouraged Mr Oliver took something of a risk.

'Did it occur to you that this voice was anything like Mr Wallace's?' he asked.

Had the witness hesitated or shewn doubt the effect might have been highly detrimental to his client's cause, but the answer came promptly:

'Certainly not.'

Immediately Mr Oliver took a still greater risk.

'Does it occur to you *now* that it was anything like his voice?'

'It would be a great stretch of imagination for me to say anything like that.'

Counsel had scored a distinct triumph which more than offset his failure to shake the testimony of the other witnesses.

Mr Beattie was unable to give the Court any clearer idea of the time at which he had spoken to that voice than that it was 'seven or shortly after seven'.

Asked if he had seen Wallace arrive witness replied that he had not seen Wallace 'until about half an hour after I had received the message, say a quarter to eight'.

Mr Hemmerde (for the Crown): 'When you saw him what was he doing?'

'He had commenced to play a game with an opponent named McCartney.'

According to the evidence of another member of the club, Mr James Caird, Wallace was still deliberating his opening move when Mr Beattie gave him the message. Mr Caird had spoken to Wallace before the latter had taken his place at the chess board, but neither he nor anyone else in the club, or in the café, had observed Wallace's arrival.

'I have a message for you,' said Mr Beattie to Wallace and had to repeat his words before he attracted his attention.

'What?' he asked without looking up. 'Who from?'

'A man named Qualtrough.'

'Qualtrough? Qualtrough? Who's Qualtrough?'

'Well if you don't know, I certainly don't.'

At that Wallace glanced up and asked:

'What did he want?'

Mr Beattie consulted the envelope.

'He said he wanted to see you tomorrow evening at half past seven about something in the nature of your business. His address is R. M. Qualtrough, 25 Menlove Gardens East, Mossley Hill.'

'I don't know the chap. Where is Menlove Gardens East, anyhow? Is it Menlove Avenue?'

'No—Menlove Gardens East.'

'Where is Menlove Gardens East? I don't know it.'

'Wait a minute,' said Mr Beattie. 'I'll see if Deyes knows where it is.'

As he went off to consult a fellow-member, taking his envelope with him, Wallace produced a pocket diary and Mr Caird saw him write across the spaces for both Monday and Tuesday, 19th and 20th January: '*R. M. Qualtrough, 25 Menlove Gardens EAST. 7.30.*'

Returning from his errand Mr Beattie said:

'Deyes knows Menlove Gardens North, South and West, but has never heard of Menlove Gardens *East*. He knows the district well and says it is not the sort of place to be knocking about in after dark.'

'Oh well,' said Wallace, 'I belong to Liverpool. I've got a tongue in my head and can find out where it is.' And with that he turned his attention to the game.

Mr Hemmerde (to Mr Beattie): 'The name Qualtrough was spelt out to you over the telephone; did you spell it out to the accused?'

'No.'

'So,' commented Counsel significantly, 'although it was such an uncommon name, and Wallace protested "I don't know the chap", he knew how to spell his name?'[1]

Wallace won his match and, according to Mr Caird, 'appeared very pleased at having done so'. He and Wallace travelled homeward on the same tram, together with another member named Bethurn. The last left them when they all alighted at the tram-stop, and, according to the evidence of Mr Caird, the following conversation then ensued between him and Wallace.

'Wallace asked me if I had ever heard the name Qualtrough. I said I had only heard of one person of that name. . . . He said: "I wonder what is the best way of going to Menlove Gardens East, where this fellow Qualtrough lives?" I said: "I should think the best way would be to get a bus from Queens Drive. That will take you in the right general direction, and you can inquire as to the actual address when you get to Menlove Avenue." . . . "If I go," he answered, "I shall come into town and then get a tram out to Menlove Avenue." . . . I said: "I take it you have made up your mind to go then?" He said: "Frankly I have not quite made up my mind about it. If I go I shall go the way I suggested. After all, I have to think twice before I throw away what may be some paying business." '

In reply to *Mr Roland Oliver*, cross-examining, witness said that he had observed nothing unusual in the accused's demeanour that evening. He had been to the Wallaces' house, the last occasion being about a year previously. He had seen Wallace and his wife out walking together.

'I should say they were a happy couple, a very happy couple.'

---

[1] Qualtrough is a common enough name in the Isle of Man, but in Liverpool at that date the police could find only fourteen persons who possessed it.

Mr Oliver: 'What sort of man is he as known to you?'

Witness seemed to have some difficulty in clothing his ideas on the subject in suitable words.

'Well . . . well, a man who is intellectual and varied in his interests—and that sort of thing.'

'Is he a violent person?'

'Oh no, not at all—a placid man.'

2

No shadow of doubt has ever existed that the sender of that telephone message was the murderer of Julia Wallace. In view of this let us give careful consideration to the following points:

A. Assuming the sender to have been Wallace:

1. The purpose of the message was to prepare an alibi for the following night.

2. The great advantage of the message was that it committed him to nothing.

3. He could be certain of having the message delivered to him by Mr Beattie, in the presence of witnesses.

4. Police tests shewed that Wallace could have reached the telephone kiosk from his house in four or five minutes; and that, after leaving the kiosk, he would have had ample time to reach the City Café by 7.40.

B. Assuming the sender to have been 'R. M. Qualtrough':

1. The purpose of the message was to decoy Wallace away from his house in order that the sender might enter it with evil intent.

2. The sender could have seen by the notice posted in the City Café that Wallace was due to play his match in the chess tournament on that night. He could not, however, be *certain* that Wallace would keep the engagement unless he watched him leave his house and saw him board a tram bound in that direction.

3. In that case, if Wallace, as he stated, did not leave his

house until 7.15, the sender could not have made the telephone call at 7.15, as officially recorded by the operator.

4. Since the whole plan depended upon decoying Wallace away from home the *next* night, surely the only way of making *certain* he got the message would have been for the sender to go to the City Café himself, watch for Wallace to arrive, and then go and put through a call to him from the nearest public call-box? If he were a man known to Wallace he could as easily have disguised his voice when speaking to him as Wallace did—if he were the sender—when speaking to Mr Beattie.

In short, if 'R. M. Qualtrough' was the author of that telephone message he took a great deal too much for granted; not least of which was the assumption that Wallace, before setting out to keep an appointment with a stranger at a dubious address, would not take the elementary precaution of consulting a directory beforehand.

6

Tuesday, 20th January 1931

'History maketh the man wise, mathematics maketh men subtle.'[1]

I

'Agate's interest in Wallace [*explains his friend, Mr Edgar Lustgarten, with whom he had tirelessly discussed the case*] was not at all surprising. It was a case to delight that hard and lucid brain which had allied itself so oddly to a subtle sense of art. The latter had become the instrument of his profession; the former he made the foundation of his hobby, and he loved to dedicate his scanty leisure hours to exercising a prodigious gift of logic. He doted on detective problems of the higher type; he could meditate for hours over a cunning move at chess; he was, in fact, a devotee of scientific puzzles.'[2]

IN describing these particular characteristics of Mr Agate, his friend was, incidentally, describing some of Wallace's own. He, too, had a hard and lucid brain; he, too, was a devotee of scientific puzzles, of detective problems, and of chess; he, too, possessed a considerable gift of logic, and the illogicalities resident in that unexpected telephone call would surely have struck him forcibly. As we see from Mr Caird's evidence, the matter was in the forefront of Wallace's mind when they parted that night. It is therefore to be expected that, on awaking next morning, it would still be there, for during that day he would have to decide whether or not to keep the

[1] Francis Bacon.
[2] *Verdict in Dispute.*

appointment so irregularly made with the unknown Qualtrough.

The first thing which would surely have occurred even to a tyro in the insurance business—not to mention a man with sixteen years' experience behind him—as remarkably odd was that this mysterious stranger should require an agent *with whom he was unacquainted and who was in charge of a district on the other side of the city from that in which he himself resided to call on him out of business hours,* when all he had to do was to contact the agent in charge of his own district or communicate direct with the Company's offices. And although he had insisted that the matter was 'urgent', he was willing to delay it for twenty-four hours in order to follow this unusual procedure.

It did not make sense. Either the sender of the message was strangely eccentric, or he was up to something which boded no good.

Wallace, too, was a cautious man. All the members of the chess club were Liverpool men, yet not one of them had ever heard of Menlove Gardens *East.* Mr Deyes, who knew that district best, was emphatic that there were Menlove Gardens North, South and West, but no Menlove Gardens East, adding the warning that the district 'was not one to be knocking about in after dark'.

Surely this information would have prompted most of us to make further inquiries, of which the most obvious would have been to telephone to our friend, Mr Crewe, who was not only our immediate superior but actually lived within a stone's-throw of those various Menlove Gardens and would be certain to know the whereabouts, if it existed, of Menlove Gardens East? Or, failing that, would we not have availed ourselves of the public library in Breck Road, only a few minutes' walk from our own door, and consulted a directory, and a plan of the city, in order to verify the existence of R. M. Qualtrough and the address he had given?

Had William Herbert Wallace taken either of these obvious precautions he would quickly have learned that *there was no such person as R. M. Qualtrough, and no such place as Menlove Gardens East.*

The normal being finds it incredible that anyone of sane mind can be so cool-headed and callous as to partake of breakfast, dinner and tea with his intended victim without betraying some signs of emotion. Only Julia herself could have said how the man who was to be accused of her murder conducted himself towards her on that day: whether he had been abstracted, more impatient and irritable—or more considerate —than usual, or whether he had emanated anything which had aroused her apprehensions.

Two people saw her on that last afternoon of her life: her sister-in-law, Amy, wife of Joseph Edwin Wallace, who was living in Liverpool while her husband was in Malaya, and paid her a visit, departing at 4.30: and Alan Close, the milk-boy, to whom Julia spoke a kindly word when she took in the milk from him two hours later. To both Julia appeared much as usual.

What of the accused himself? If he had planned and was preparing to commit this crime he must have been exercising enormous self-control in the presence of all those who knew him, but when he was off his guard might there not have been a swift access of emotion? Neither Amy nor Alan Close saw Wallace himself, and searching for some grain of evidence as to his demeanour one comes upon an incident contributed by a police constable named Rothwell who stated that he had seen Wallace that afternoon, about 3.30, in the Clubmoor district.

'I have known the accused as a collector for the Prudential for about two years,' he told the Court. 'His face was haggard and drawn, and he seemed very much distressed; he was dabbing his eyes with his coat-sleeve and appeared to me as if he had been crying. I have never seen him like that before. I was quite close to him.'

This evidence was strongly challenged by the Defence.

Mr Oliver: 'If I were to call about twenty-five people who saw him that afternoon round about that time, and they said he was just as usual, would you say you had made a mistake?'

'No, I should stick to my opinion.'

Wallace himself, in the course of his evidence, emphatically denied this allegation, and agreed with his Counsel's suggestion that his eyes might have been watering. Mr Oliver also called three of Wallace's Clubmoor clients whom he had visited that afternoon.

The first of these, *Louisa Harrison*, stated that Wallace paid her a routine visit 'soon after 3.30'.

Mr Oliver: 'Did he appear to have been crying?'

'He was joking with me.'[1]

Amy Lawrence testified that when Wallace called at her house her husband was having a cup of tea, and he offered him one which he accepted.

Mr Oliver: 'What was he like?'

'He was the same as usual.'

The evidence of the third witness, *Margaret Martin*, is of interest in that she appears to have been the last person, except Julia, to see Wallace until he boarded a tramcar in the City at 7.10 on his way to Menlove Gardens. She stated that she had known him for two years, and that he had called that afternoon concerning the surrender of a policy. She found him 'just the same as he has ever been; calm and the same in appearance'. Asked the time at which he had called she replied: 'I cannot give the correct time.'

Mr Oliver: 'Approximately?'

'About half past five; it might be anything up to ten minutes.'

'Up to ten to six?'

'No, not up to ten to six; between half past five and ten to.'

It seems unfortunate that Mr Hemmerde did not think it worth while to try and clear up this point in cross-examination, for on the time Wallace left Margaret Martin's house would depend the time at which he returned to Wolverton Street, and

[1] In this connection Mr Veale observes (*op. cit.*): 'It is much to be regretted that no specimen of Wallace's usual jokes has been recorded. . . . Are we right in suspecting that he joked as part of a carefully selected business technique? It is perhaps significant that, whereas his diary abounds in sentimental, melodramatic and didactic observations, it contains no traces of anything remotely approaching a jest.'

the length of time he had at his disposal after doing so is a matter of considerable importance. He himself stated in evidence that after leaving Margaret Martin he had taken a tram-car home.

Mr Oliver: 'You reached home about six?'

'Shortly after six—possibly five past.'

'What time did you leave your home again that evening?'

'At a quarter to seven.'

'Between something after six, when you got back from your work, and a quarter to seven you say your wife was there. Had you had a meal?'

'I had my tea.'

'With her?'

'Yes.'

Asked if he had washed and changed, Wallace said he had washed his face and hands in the bathroom, changed his collar and brushed his hair in the bedroom.

'When you went out was your wife alive?'

'Certainly.' To further questions from his Counsel he replied: 'She came down the backyard with me, as far as the backyard door, and I left her standing there *with an instruction to her to bolt the door after me.* That was our usual practice.'

The Wallaces' house was the fourth one from the *cul-de-sac* end of Wolverton Street. This *cul-de-sac* was pierced by a footway leading to Breck Road and giving access to an alley which passed behind the houses on the Wallaces' side of Wolverton Street and led into Richmond Park Road. It was the door into this alley to which Wallace's evidence referred. Some confusion has arisen between the backyard door from the yard into the alley, and the back door from the yard into the house, both of which, together with the front door, were to play prominent parts in the events of that night. The *backyard door* was furnished with an ordinary thumb-latch and the bolt to which Wallace's evidence referred; the *back door* and front door of the house were both equipped with rim locks with bolts below them.

Since Wallace, and soon afterwards Mr and Mrs Johnston, were to enter the house by that back door and discover the body of Julia, it may be useful to take a brief survey of it.

The back door opened into a small scullery lighted by a gas-jet on the wall above the sink. Beside the sink was a gas-cooker, the use of which had superseded the range in the adjoining kitchen which was now used solely as a general living-room. This was lighted by a gas-lamp pendent from the centre of the ceiling, and furnished principally with a table, at which the Wallaces took their meals, and a couple of wicker armchairs, one on each side of the hearth. The recess on one side of the chimney-breast had been fitted with shelves, on one of which stood a radio set and on another a small cupboard which Wallace had constructed out of a wooden box, hinging its lid to form a door. The other recess was filled by a mahogany bookcase seven feet two inches high. The window, overlooking the backyard, was heavily curtained to exclude draughts.

Out of this living-room another door opened into a narrow passage which led past the parlour to the front door. No means of illuminating this passage had been provided, presumably because it was considered that in a house of that size, if the living-room door were open, the light there provided sufficient illumination; as in fact it did, and even cast a shaft of light into the parlour as well.

This room—the one in which Julia was murdered—measured fourteen feet by eighteen feet, inclusive of the bow-window facing Wolverton Street. Its door opened to the right and within it, immediately on the left, stood a sideboard on which were a few pieces of china and some framed photographs. Opposite the door and slightly to the right was the fireplace fitted with an upright gas-fire, and a gas-bracket on either side. Beneath these, drawn back to the wall, were a couple of armchairs, and between the one on the right of the fireplace and the bow-window was a piano. In the bow itself was an oval table with more photographs and ornaments, and facing it across the room was its pair, flanked by a couple of occasional chairs. Framed examples of Julia's water-colour studies of 'landscape, seascape and flowers' adorned the walls at regular intervals.

Close by the living-room door a narrow flight of stairs led up to a diminutive landing off which opened two bedrooms, and a bathroom with wash-basin and water-closet, all overlooking the backyard. There was a larger bedroom above the parlour. This room, though the best furnished, was, according to Wallace, unused.[1] The middle bedroom was Julia's and the smallest was the one Wallace had converted into a laboratory.

Upstairs and down each of these rooms was to present the police with its own peculiar puzzle, and most of these puzzles were mutually conflicting. Much could be deduced from that circumstance alone, but though such deductions might be sufficient to convince the minds of the investigators, they did not necessarily constitute admissible evidence against a man on trial for his life.

The puzzle which struck their minds most forcibly was the curious state of the parlour. Julia's body lay diagonally across the hearthrug, her feet close to the fender, her head towards the door; she had been the victim of a particularly brutal assault, yet nothing in that room was disordered—not even the hearthrug on which she lay.

The blinds of the bow-window had been pulled down and the curtains drawn across them. The keyboard of the piano was exposed, and upon its music-rest had been arranged, side by side, the violin score and piano accompaniment of one of Mozart's sonatas. Across the arms of the chair to the right of the fireplace had been laid the violin-case, and the chair itself had been drawn forward towards the fire, as though someone had done so in order to perch on the edge of the seat and hold out chilled fingers to the warmth. It all looked as though those arrangements had been recently made—and made, could it be doubted, by the hands of the woman who lay there dead?

---

[1] In *Six Trials* Miss Winifred Duke suggests that Wallace was actually sleeping apart from his wife and occupying this room—a fact he would naturally be anxious to conceal.

7

Tuesday, 20th January 1931 (continued)

'This murder, I should imagine, must be almost unexampled in
the annals of crime. Here you have a murder committed sometime
on an evening in January, committed in a populous neighbourhood, in a house, and you have that murder so devised and so
arranged that nothing remains which would point to anyone as
the murderer . . . no finger-prints . . . and no weapon that can be
traced anywhere, and, so far as can be ascertained, no conceivable
motive in any human being.'[1]

I

THERE was no one to corroborate Wallace's statement
that, after leaving Margaret Martin's house in Clubmoor
he had travelled home by tram; there was no witness
to confirm his allegation that he had arrived there at 6.5 p.m.;
no one in all those tightly wedged houses appears to have seen
him cross his backyard with Julia at 6.45 or have heard him
'instruct' her to bolt its door; no one seems to have noticed him
walking along the alley, board any public conveyance at any
point in the vicinity of Wolverton Street and travel upon it
to the tram junction at Smithdown Road and Lodge Lane. In
all those comings and goings he might have been wrapped in a
mantle of invisibility. It was only when he boarded a tram-car
at that junction at 7.10 that he once more became not only
visible, but, for a man of his reputed taciturnity, remarkably
audible—a state which endured throughout his exploration of
the Menlove Gardens district until 8.15, after which he was not
seen or heard again until half an hour later when, rounding the
Breck Road end of the alley, he announced his presence to Mr

[1] Mr Justice Wright in his address to the jury.

and Mrs. Johnston who were just leaving their house to spend the evening with friends.[1]

Mr Johnston was able to testify that it was 8.45 when he and his wife saw Wallace approaching, as he had looked at their kitchen clock a few moments before. Allowing half an hour for his journey to Menlove Gardens and another half hour for his journey home, Wallace had spent a full hour there roaming about within a radius of a quarter of a mile from the spot at which he alighted from the tramcar. Nor was that the tram he had originally boarded at Lodge Lane. That one he had climbed upon in spite of its conductor's warning that it did not pass Menlove Gardens and his giving him the numbers of those that did.[2] In return for this information Wallace gratuitously told him that he 'was a stranger in the district, that he had some important business calls and wanted Menlove Gardens East'—reminding the conductor of this last fact no less than three times in the course of a mile. When, therefore, they reached Penny Lane—where Wallace would have to change trams—the latter called out: 'Menlove Gardens, change here.' He further stated in evidence:

'I looked around and saw the No. 7 car in the loop, heading for Calderstones, and I told him if he hurried he would get that car.'

Wallace did get it, and impressed upon the conductor of that tram, too, that he was a stranger in the district and wanted Menlove Gardens East. Yet he was travelling over exactly the same route he had taken with Julia when they had gone to see the roses in bloom at Calderstones—the same route, too, for some, if not all, of the way, he had taken when he had gone for his music lessons to Mr Crewe in Green Lane, one end of which was exactly opposite the entrance to Menlove Gardens North.

Yet though 'a stranger in the district' he did not, as Mr Hemmerde succinctly pointed out, approach the policeman on point duty standing within a few yards of the spot at which he alighted from the No. 7 tram—the very person, one would have

---

[1] *See*, however, page 193.

[2] *Thomas Phillips* (conductor), in evidence: 'He asked me if the car went to Menlove Gardens East, and I said: "No; you can get a No. 5, 5A, 5W, or a No. 7 car." '

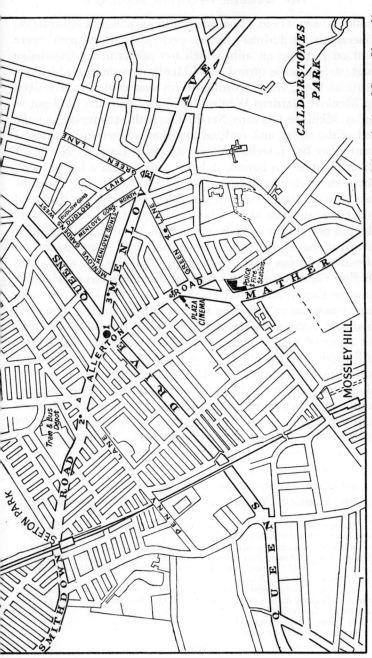

(*Based by permission of the Ordnance Survey and 'Geographia' Ltd., on the plan of Greater Liverpool.*)

PLAN OF MOSSLEY HILL, LIVERPOOL

1. Policeman on point duty. 2. Where Wallace changed trams. 3. Where Wallace alighted from second tram. 4. Mr. Crewe's house. 5. Where Wallace caught tram home.

thought, from whom a stranger would have sought information concerning an address—unless, perhaps that 'stranger' were bent on creating an alibi which too premature a knowledge might defeat. So he turned out of Menlove Avenue into Menlove Gardens West, and, according to his own evidence: 'I walked up Menlove Gardens West on the right-hand side till I got as far as Menlove Gardens North. I saw the nameplate on the end of the street, and realized that that was not quite where I wanted to be. I walked down Menlove Gardens North for about eight or ten houses. A lady[1] came out of a house there, about the eighth house down, and I waited till she got to the gate, then I stepped across into the middle of the road and asked her, did she know where Menlove Gardens East was? She did not appear to know very much about it, but suggested it might be along this road—meaning a continuation of Menlove Gardens West. . . . I retraced my steps and went along Dudlow Gardens . . . then I realized that there was no Menlove Gardens East in that direction. About that time I saw a gentleman I now know to be the witness Green[2] coming along the road and I stopped him and asked him, and he said he did not know of such a place as Menlove Gardens East. I said: "All right; I suppose I had better inquire at No. 25 *West*." A lady answered the door. We had a little conversation and she could not help me.[3] Then I went along Menlove Gardens South, and they were even numbers. I turned into Menlove Gardens North . . . and I noticed that they were even numbers also, and therefore my number could not be among them, and I was a bit puzzled to know what to do. I did not know where I was going to find myself.'

Mr Oliver: 'Where did you find yourself then?'

'In Menlove Avenue, at that tram-stop' (pointing to

[1] She was the only person out of all those Wallace spoke to that night whom the police were unable to trace.

[2] *Sidney Green*, a clerk, stated that the accused had accosted him in Menlove Gardens West, explained that he was seeking a Mr Qualtrough at 25 Menlove Gardens East. 'I told him there was no such place. The accused then said he would try 25 Menlove Gardens *West*.'

[3] *Mrs Katie Mather* stated that on opening the door she saw a 'tall, slight man. . . . He asked me if a man of the name of Qualtrough lived there, *and if that was Menlove Gardens East*.'

The Judge: 'I suppose you said "No"?'

'Yes, my lord, and he went away.'

the plan and indicating the tram-stop opposite Green Lane).

'Where did you go next?'

'Down Green Lane.'

'What did you know about Green Lane?'

'I knew that my superintendent lived there.'

'You had been there before?'

'I had.'

'. . . Finding yourself in Green Lane did you do anything with regard to Mr Crewe's house?'

'Yes, I rang the bell, or knocked—I don't remember which —and could get no answer and walked down to the bottom end of Green Lane.'[1]

In his evidence on the first day of the trial Mr Crewe had stated that Wallace had visited his house for violin lessons; but, more important still, he informed the Court that he had been absent from home on the evening of Tuesday, 20th January. In the course of his cross-examination of Wallace, therefore, *Mr Hemmerde* asked:

'. . . You knew that halfway up Green Lane lived Mr Crewe. . . . Did it not occur to you when you were in difficulties on the night of the 20th, and you could not find Menlove Gardens East, to look in and ask Mr Crewe where it was?'

'. . . I have given evidence that I did look in. . . . I knocked on the door, but could get no answer.'

'When did you do that?'

'I should say it was about 7.40.'

'Do you say that you stated elsewhere that you called on Mr Crewe that night . . . stated it to anyone before you gave evidence here today?'

'I think that it is in the evidence in one of my statements to the police.'

'I will find out if it is there.'

Counsel proceeded to read aloud the account Wallace had given the police of his movements in and about Menlove Gardens. This account was a model of lucidity and precision which had enabled them to find, without difficulty or delay, the

[1] The Allerton Road end.

people to whom he said he had spoken. But it contained no reference to Green Lane, to the fact that Mr Crewe lived there, or to his having knocked on any door other than that of 25 Menlove Gardens West.

Concluding this task Mr Hemmerde laid aside the statement and declared himself ready to read all the prisoner's other statements in order to demonstrate that none of them contained any mention of Green Lane or Mr Crewe. This, however, was not required of him since the Judge had the relevant documents before him and could confirm Counsel's assertion. Turning, therefore, to the prisoner Counsel said:

'I put it to you that you never said so until today. Of course you realize the importance of the point; that you were quite near your superintendent, who would know the district well, and you are walking about asking everyone else where it is. . . .'

Counsel had forcefully demonstrated his suggestion that the prisoner had fabricated the story of having knocked on Mr Crewe's door *only after* hearing the letter give evidence two days previously that he had been at the cinema on the night of the murder. He went on to develop an even more forceful line of interrogation.

'. . . "Mr Qualtrough",' he asked the prisoner, 'had no possible means of knowing whether you would ever get the message. or whether you would ever go to Menlove Gardens East; yet apparently he was ready and waiting for your departure the next night?'

'It would look like it.'

'Did it ever occur to you that he would have to watch both doors, front and back?'

'No, it did not.'

'You are a man of business instincts—you could hardly be a Prudential agent if you were not?'

'That is so.'

'. . . Not only could he not know you would go, but he could not have known that you would not look up a directory and find there was no such place?'

'No.'

188

'He would have to risk all that?'

'Yes.'

'And, of course, you could have found at once, if you had looked at the directory, where Menlove Gardens East was, or wasn't?'

'I could have done.'

'. . . Where is Mr Crewe generally during the day?'

'At his office.'

'And that office is on the telephone?'

'The office is on the telephone.'

'You had only to ring up Mr Crewe and find out where Menlove Gardens East was, if it was near him?'

'I could have done that, but I did not think of it.'

'. . . Does not the whole thing strike you as very remarkable, that a man who does not know you should ring you up for business in another district, and expect you to go there, and yet, without knowing whether you were going there or not, come and wait outside your house for the chance of murdering your wife?'

'Yes.'

'. . . The wrong address is essential to the creation of an alibi—do you follow that?'

'No, I do not follow you.'

'If you had been told Menlove Gardens *West*, the first inquiry would have landed you there?'

'Yes.'

'If you are told of an address which does not exist, you can ask seven or eight people, everyone of whom would be a witness as to where you were?'

'Yes.'

Those who have disparaged Wallace's intelligence have only to read these extracts from his evidence to realize that, even from the witness-box, on trial for his life, he never attempted to contest an obvious truth.

'. . . You used to go to Calderstones—very often, or fairly often?'

'. . . We generally went about twice a year, the time the roses were out.'

'How used you to go?'

Take a car to Lodge Lane and change over.'[1]
'The only route is down Menlove Avenue, is it not?'
'I couldn't really tell you that.'
'Couldn't you?'
'No.'
'I put it to you that you can only get to Calderstones by tramcar *via* Menlove Avenue?'
'I could not say that definitely. There may be two routes. . . .'

2

To revert to Wallace's narrative concerning his movements, he stated that when he could get no answer at Mr Crewe's house he had 'walked down to the bottom end[2] of Green Lane, and somewhere round about the bottom there was a policeman coming across the road. . . . I stepped into the road and asked him, could he tell me where Menlove Gardens East was . . .'

Mr Oliver: 'Did you talk quite a long time?'
'Yes. I responded to his geniality, and he responded to the invitation. . . .'
'Did he tell you there was no Menlove Gardens East?'
'Yes . . . and that he did not know the name Qualtrough. Then it occurred to me, as I was about to leave him, that possibly I might be able to get a directory at some local post office.'

There was, however, no directory at the post office in Allerton Road, which the officer had suggested he should visit, so he went instead to the newsagency next door.

P.C. James Sargent gave a detailed account of the conversation which had taken place between the accused and himself, the gist of which was that he had told Wallace: 'There is no Menlove Gardens East; there are Menlove Gardens North, South and West.'

[1] The route he travelled on the night of the murder, only on that occasion he chose a tram which did *not* go down Menlove Avenue, so he had to change again at Penny Lane.
[2] The Allerton Road end.

Mr Hemmerde (to this witness)*:* 'Had he said anything to you about who he was?'

'He said: "I am an insurance agent looking for a Mr Qualtrough who rang up the club and left a message with my colleague to go to Mr Qualtrough up at 25 Menlove Gardens East." '

To further questions from Counsel the officer replied:

'He then said, "It is not eight o'clock yet", and pulled out his watch. I also did the same. He said: "It is just a quarter to." I glanced at my watch and said it *was* just a quarter to. He then left me and walked across and down Allerton Road. I did not see the accused afterwards.'

The Prosecution suggested that Wallace had called the police constable's attention to the time for the purpose of strengthening his alibi; Wallace contended that he had compared watches with the officer because he thought that, if it were after eight o'clock, he would find the post office shut, but he does not appear to have mentioned this to P.C. Sargent himself.

The time-factor in this case, let it be repeated, is of first importance. That which surrounds the murder itself will be considered in its proper place; here it needs to be checked against Wallace's alleged movements in and around Menlove Gardens, for the very cogent reason that Julia's assassin had carried away with him the weapon of death. From the nature of the wounds it was apparent that they had been inflicted with a piece of metal, approximately an inch and a half wide, a quarter of an inch thick, and about fifteen inches long. Despite an intensive search by the police this article was never discovered, which is scarcely surprising since it was easily portable if carried up a sleeve or in the inner pocket of an overcoat, and it could be just as easily rammed into the ground at some spot convenient to the criminal. If Wallace were that criminal, he had, as the Judge pointed out, to get away from the house and to the tram very quickly indeed in order to establish his alibi, and it is doubtful if he would have had time to dispose of it in any open space between those two points. But there were many vacant sites on which building was either in progress or was about to begin in the Menlove district, and we must ask ourselves if Wallace would have had the time to conceal the instrument there.[1]

Sydney Green stated that Wallace spoke to him at about 7.20; P.C. Sargent said that he had spoken to him at between 7.40 and 7.45. Mrs Mather was unable to give any idea as to the time at which Wallace had rung her bell, and there is only his word for it that he did so *after* speaking to Sydney Green. At a minimum Wallace had a quarter of an hour in which to dispose of the weapon, and much can be done in that time. If it had eventually come to light in the course of building operations, there would have been nothing to identify it, even if it had attracted attention.

Wallace parted from P.C. Sargent almost immediately after they had compared watches, and, according to the evidence of the latter, he crossed Allerton Road and walked along it. Miss Lily Pinches, manageress of a newsagency at No. 130, stated that he entered her establishment 'just after eight o'clock'. By this reckoning it had taken Wallace a quarter of an hour to walk a hundred yards to the post office, inquire for a directory which they did not possess, and then enter the newsagency next door. Lily Pinches testified that Wallace asked to see a directory, and had inquired for 25 Menlove Gardens East—to be assured once more that it did exist. She even looked through her books to see if the shop delivered papers at such an address. This took about ten minutes, during which Wallace watched her without —according to her—mentioning that the man he was searching for was named Qualtrough; she was the only person to whom he did not do so.

---

[1] Miss Dorothy L. Sayers justly points out that there was extraordinarily little object in the murderer, whoever he may have been, carrying away the weapon. Obviously Julie had been killed by something in the nature of an iron bar, and so long as the murderer had wiped off his finger-prints, the presence of that something beside the body was unlikely to provide any evidence against him. Nevertheless, it must be remembered that the murderer, if he were someone from outside, could hardly have picked the iron bar out of the fireplace without Julia seeing him do so and being consequently warned of the impending assault. In that case the attitude of her body, and the condition of the room, would surely have shewn some signs of a struggle. There were no such signs. Had Wallace, as the police believed, faked the appearance of robbery to cover his own crime, he might have decided to get rid of the weapon with the object of creating the impression that the murderer had arrived armed and had carried it away with him. As we shall soon see, Wallace himself drew attention to the absence of a weapon, as well as to the presence of the mackintosh.

Mr Oliver suggested that the times she had given were utterly wrong, for Wallace had stated that at eight o'clock he had caught a homeward-bound tram at the stop 'near the cinema' in Allerton Road.[1] It was the word of one against the word of another.

It was the same in the case of the evidence of Miss Lily Hall, a stenographer, who alleged that she had seen Wallace at 8.35 talking to a man at the Richmond Park Road end of the alley. She and her mother attended Holy Trinity Church and used to chat to Julia after Service was over. She had never met Wallace, but she said she claimed to know him by sight; she said she could see him plainly, as he and the other man were standing within the radius of the light from a street-lamp. She was also certain of the time, because she had just left home to attend the second programme at the local cinema. As she crossed the road the men parted, and one—she had not noticed which—had turned into the alley.

Wallace denied the whole of her allegation, the point of which, if it could have been substantiated, was this: if Wallace was at the Richmond Park Road end of the alley at the time Lily Hall gave, he was not, as he claimed to have been, approaching his house from the opposite direction. Nor was he 'hurrying back', as he said he was, having been at last convinced that there was no such place as Menlove Gardens East and that 'there was something fishy about the telephone message'. But her evidence was, as his lordship told the jury, 'word against word . . . you will give it such weight as you think right', because, in spite of appeals on the part of the police, no one ever came forward to corroborate her testimony.

As to Wallace's contention that he was 'hurrying back', the first question which Counsel for the Crown put to Mr Johnston, who, with his wife, had seen him approaching them from the Breck Road end of the alley at 8.45 was this:

'Tell me exactly . . . was he hurrying—walking, running?'
'Walking in an ordinary way towards his back door.'

---

[1] Under cross-examination Wallace denied that he knew the name of the cinema, but Mr Hemmerde produced the diary and read a passage which shewed that he had visited it with Mr Crewe after one of his violin lessons. The passage read: 'We went to the Plaza Cinema, a wonderfully well got up place.'

8

The Murder

'There can be no doubt at all that this poor woman was done to death by, first, a very crushing blow, and then, if she was not already dead, by a succession of ten other blows.'[1]

I

WALLACE told the police that, when he went out at night, it was always his habit to do so by the back way; that his wife would always accompany him across the backyard for the purpose of bolting the backyard door into the alley behind him. Being thus protected she did not lock the back door of the house. Always when he returned he let himself in at the front door with his latch-key.

In his statement he said that, when he parted from his wife in the alley at 6.45 on the night of her murder, he had 'instructed' her to bolt the alley door as usual, and—also as usual—on his return he had gone to the front door. But after inserting his latch-key into the lock he found the door would not open. He had therefore rapped 'gently' with the knocker. This producing no response he had gone round by the alley to the back, found that the backyard door, though closed, was *not* bolted, walked up the yard and tried the back door. It was 'fastened against him' and he' beat upon it with his hands'. This, too, evoking no response, round he went to the front again. This time, after vainly inserting his key, he came to the conclusion that the door 'was bolted against him'.

Let us submit this statement to the commonsense comparison of how you or I would have behaved in such a predicament:

1. On returning to our home and finding, to our surprise

[1] Mr Justice Wright.

194

and irritation, that for some reason the front door would not yield to our key as it had done over a period of sixteen years, and knowing that, the time being only 8.40, our wife could hardly have yet gone to bed, would we not have used that knocker *smartly*, not *gently*, and—or—pressed our thumb with some vigour on the doorbell, before going round to the back?

2. And when, disconcerted and troubled by our failure to get an answer, we at last did go round to the back, would we not have been more disconcerted and troubled still to find that the backyard door, which we had 'instructed' our wife to *bolt* —as she had done for sixteen years—yielded to the pressure of our thumb upon the latch?

3. And what would have been our reactions on discovering, after hurrying up the backyard, that the back door of our house, which we had expected to be unbolted and unlocked— as it had always been in the previous sixteen years—was 'fastened against us'?

4. Would we not have remembered with a sick feeling of apprehension and alarm that mysterious telephone message, luring us away to a non-existent address; and would not the uncanny silence within our house increase that feeling to a grisly dread?

5. Would we not have felt an impelling urgency to get into that silent house—and get into it with the forces of law and order at our side? And would we not therefore have rushed away to summon the policeman whom we would have known —after sixteen years—to be on his beat nearby?

Would not these have been the instinctive reactions of any honest householder in the circumstances in which Wallace said he found himself that night? But all he did, according to his story, was to return and try the front door once again, and come now to the conclusion that it 'was bolted against him'.

The normal indignation of the householder locked out of his own home; the chill fear of the husband with nameless apprehensions in his heart[1]—would they not have impelled instant

---

[1] Wallace told the police that when he found there was no such place as Menlove Gardens East he had remembered cases in which men had been decoyed away from home for purposes of robbery; that a case of robbery had occurred 'not long ago' in the Anfield district itself and 'things had happened in its streets sometimes'.

action? But still Wallace did not go for the police. He returned to try the back door yet again, and this time, *under the eyes of Mr and Mrs Johnston, it was to open as soon as he turned the handle.*

Why did Wallace not call the police? It is here suggested that he did not do so, *because the officer would have entered the house with him; because he wished to do so alone—though with witnesses in the background;* and it is also suggested that he already had the Johnstons in mind. Then, with them in the offing, he would enter his house in the innocent guise of the puzzled and anxious householder, and give the impression of moving hither and thither, calling and searching for his wife. He would do so as rapidly as possible, that the evidence might shew he had had no time or opportunity to destroy, or dispose of, anything incriminating, but, at the same time, this swift survey would be able to assure him that he had left undone none of those things which he ought to have done. Then he would raise the alarm.

A mackintosh of his was to play an important part in that case. Unnoticed at first, it was 'bunched up' under the right shoulder of the corpse. It was heavily stained with blood, but the most puzzling feature of those stains was that many of them were on its interior. It was to be suggested by the Prosecution that Wallace wore it to protect himself from blood splashes when committing the crime, stripping it off afterwards and leaving it in the parlour. It is the present suggestion that, if this were so, Wallace threw it over Julia's body; that it contracted its interior stains from Julia's battered head, and that Wallace, entering the parlour on his return, decided, for some reason, to 'bunch it up' and thrust it under his victim's right shoulder before admitting the Johnstons.

2

Wallace, it has already been suggested, had the Johnstons in mind as witnesses. It is unlikely that he would have known that they were going out on that particular night—unless they had a regular engagement—but after living next-door to them for ten years he would know their habits, and would be able to guess from a little observation what their intended movements were likely to be. He would know that the children were put to bed at 8 p.m. or 8.30—as children were in those pre-television days—and if, just after that, there were no lights upstairs he could conclude that the Johnstons were spending the evening at home; if, on the other hand, he saw lights in their bedroom he could as easily deduce that they were on the point of going out. There *were* lights in their bedroom that night; therefore, if he also knew that, like himself, they always went out by the back, then he would know that he had only to lurk in the shadows of that unlighted alley in order to intercept them as they made their exit. That, their evidence suggested, was exactly what he did.

Now let us see what was going on in the Johnstons' house meanwhile, through their own evidence, and remembering that their house and the Wallaces' were twins to each other.

Mr Oliver (to Mrs Johnston in cross-examination)*:* 'You heard knocking on the back door; was that before you went out?'

'Yes, just a few minutes; we were getting ready to go out.'

'That would support his story so far when he said he knocked at the back door, and could not get in and went round to the front?'

'Yes; it was so usual we didn't take any notice.'

'What sort of knock was it?'

'Either with the flat of his hand or his clenched fist.'

Her husband, she stated, went downstairs and soon afterwards called out to her to 'hurry up'; she called back, 'I'm coming', extinguished the light, and joined him downstairs.

Even as Mrs Johnston had heard Wallace knocking on his back door almost directly below her bedroom window, so could Wallace have heard her calling to her husband that she 'was coming'. That would inform him that the Johnstons were on the very point of going out, and that he must slip away and then advance to meet them as they emerged into the alley, giving the impression that he was coming round from the front of his house, by way of the alley, to the back.

Counsel for the Crown (to Mr Johnston)*:* 'Which way did you go out that night?'

'The back way.'

'Can you say what you saw when you went out?'

'As I opened the door[1] to let Mrs Johnston go out Mr Wallace just passed.

'Had he come from the top of the alley?'

'From the Breck Road end.'

'Did your wife say anything to him?'

'My wife said: "Good evening, Mr Wallace." '

'Did you think there was anything unusual from his manner?'

'He seemed anxious when he asked Mrs Johnston a question. . . .'

'. . . . What did he say?'

'He said: "Have you heard anything unusual tonight?" '

'What did your wife say?'

'She said: "No—why? What has happened?" '

To further questions from Counsel Mr Johnston replied:

'He said he had been round to the front door and also to the back and could not get in; the doors were fastened against him. I suggested that he tried the back door again and, if he could not open it, I would get the key of my back door and try it.'

'Whereabouts were you when this conversation took place?'

'We were all standing in the alley, before the door into his backyard had been opened.'

'Did Mr Wallace say anything when he went up the yard?'

'When he got to the door he called out: "It opens now." '[2]

'Were you able to hear, from where you were, whether he tried with his key or anything?'

'He did not seem to try with a key; he seemed to turn the knob in the usual way and said: "It opens now." '

The Judge: 'Could you see?'

'Yes; I could see him at the door, my lord.'

'And it seemed to open quite easily?'

'Yes; there was no violence in the action of opening the door.'

Continuing his evidence witness said that Wallace had 'asked them to wait while he went inside'. Asked if he had

---

[1] The backyard door—into the alley.

[2] In reply to a similar question from Counsel, Mrs Johnston said: 'He looked over his shoulder and said: "She [meaning Mrs Wallace] will not be out; she has such a bad cold." '

noticed anything in particular about the house witness replied: 'Yes, the light in the middle bedroom[1] was low, and in the small backroom as well.'[2]

'Did you hear anything when Mr Wallace had gone in?'

'I heard him call out a name twice. I couldn't make out the name. I didn't know Mrs Wallace's Christian name.'

'Did you notice anything else?'

'Yes; just after he had called out the light was turned up in the middle bedroom.'

The Judge: 'You couldn't say, I suppose, where he was when he called out?'

'I should say he would be at the top of the stairs.'

Counsel: 'Did you notice anything else after the light had been turned up?'

'Yes; a match was struck in the smaller room at the top of the stairs.'[3]

Both the Johnstons were rather vague as to how long it might have been after Wallace had entered the house that they saw the flare of the match, and equally vague as to how long it was between then and his reappearance. Mr Johnston said that he 'roughly' estimated it at 'about a minute and a half' in both cases—about three minutes in all. Mrs Johnston put it at 'two or three minutes' in both cases, adding that 'it seemed of course a very long time'. One can only say, therefore, that Wallace was not absent for more than six minutes, and possibly less.

'We asked if the house was lighted,'[4] stated Mrs Johnston, 'and Mr Wallace said, no; he had to light the kitchen[5] and the parlour—and I particularly noticed the matches lying there.' She explained that she had seen 'one spent match in the kitchen . . . on the mat near the scullery door' and 'two spent matches just in the doorway of the parlour'.

How strange all that was! The intruder, having committed a brutal murder in order to rob the house—and a bitterly chagrined man he must have been to find himself

[1] Julia's.
[2] Bathroom.
[3] The room used as a laboratory.
[4] i.e. downstairs.
[5] Living-room.

only £4 the richer for his night's work—carefully extinguished the fire in the parlour[1] and all the lights on the ground-floor! And how, having plunged himself in that curtained darkness, had he made his way through those furniture-crowded rooms and out of the house without upsetting anything or brushing his bloody clothes against a door-frame or some other object?

How strange it was, too, that Wallace, with the gas-lamp he had lighted in the living-room illuminating the passage and throwing sufficient light into the parlour, when he opened the door, to disclose the mutilated condition of Julia's head—as the police tests proved it did—had not instantly cried out in horror and alarm to summon his waiting neighbours to his side! We find ourselves as interested as Counsel for the Crown in the bereaved husband's demeanour when, instead of that anguished shout to the Johnstons which we would have expected, he emerged from the house to acquaint them with the tragedy.

Counsel for the Crown (to Mr Johnston) : 'Did he run out, or just walk out?'

'He hurried out. He said: "Come and see; she has been killed." '

'What was his manner when he said that?'

'He seemed a bit excited.'

'When he said that, did you go into the house?'

'Yes, we all went in.'

The Judge: 'You all went in, through the kitchen, into the parlour?'

'Yes, my lord, right into the front room.'

Counsel for the Crown: 'Just say exactly what you saw.'

'As we went in I saw the body lying diagonally across the room, the feet towards the fireplace and the head towards the door.'

'I want you to tell me, if you can, how far the head would be from the door?'

'I should say eighteen inches from the edge of the door when it stood open.'

The torso, continued witness, was in a rather twisted attitude, the left arm outflung and the left side of the face uppermost, with bone and brain substance protruding from the wound in the temple. The right arm alongside the body, and

---

[1] There was ample evidence to prove that this had been lighted, as we shall see.

the right shoulder somewhat hunched. The crown of the head was battered in, and some strands of hair had been torn away from the scalp and lay in the pool of blood surrounding it. Julia's long, old-fashioned skirt was charred along one side above the hem, as though when she fell it had come in contact with the lighted fire.

Counsel for the Crown: 'What did your wife do?'

'My wife knelt down and took Mrs Wallace's hand and said: "Oh, you poor darling!" '

The Johnstons were standing on the left of the body. Wallace had lighted the gas-bracket before their entrance and had not turned it up fully, so they did not observe that a mackintosh had been 'pushed as with a hand' under the deceased's right shoulder. Like Julia's skirt it, too, was burned on one side.

Counsel for the Crown: 'You went out then, the three of you?'

'Yes, we went into the kitchen.'

While that scene was being enacted in the parlour Wallace had stood in the doorway. In a statement made to the police later that night he was to say that his wife 'had not an enemy in the world'; yet he shewed none of that stark bewilderment, which would have been natural, as to who could have killed her with such appalling brutality. Nor did he shew any rage against her unknown assailant, or urgent anxiety to set the police upon his trail. He seemed mainly concerned to demonstrate a motive for the crime.

Mr Johnston told the Court that, on entering the kitchen living-room, Wallace 'pointed to a door on the floor which belonged to a small cupboard[1] and had been wrenched off'.

Counsel for the Crown: 'He pointed that out and said it had been wrenched off?'

'Yes.' Witness then described how Wallace had reached up and taken down the small cash-box from the top of the bookcase in the chimney-recess, and removed its lid. 'I asked him if anything was missing. He replied "about £4", but he could not say exactly until he had seen his books. I said: "Will you look upstairs and see if everything is all right before I go for

---

[1] The cupboard referred to on page 181. It had no lock and contained nothing of value.

the police and the doctor?" He went upstairs; he didn't stay any length of time at all; he said: "There is £5 in a jar they haven't taken." I then went for the police.'

Asked to describe Wallace's demeanour during these proceedings witness said: 'He was very quiet, walking around; he didn't shout or anything.'

Under cross-examination, witness said that he had never been in the Wallaces' house until that night; he had never heard quarrelling going on between them; he had sometimes met them when they were out walking together.

Mr Oliver: 'So far as you could judge what were their relations?'

'A very loving couple; very affectionate, I thought.'

3

Counsel for the Crown put the following questions to Mrs Johnston:

'When your husband had gone for the doctor and the police, what did you and Mr Wallace do?'

'We were in the kitchen for a few moments, and then Mr Wallace returned to the parlour. I did also. Mr Wallace went first and I went right behind him—almost together, you see.'

'What did Mr Wallace do then?'

'Mr Wallace stooped over Mrs. Wallace and he said: "They have finished her; look at the brains".'

What terrible words those are! They would have sounded terrible enough—callous enough—had one heard them spoken of some unknown victim of an accident. Yet they were uttered by a husband gazing upon the battered skull and protruding brains of 'that one woman in all the world most men enshrine in their hearts'.

'He said,' continued Mrs. Johnston, ' "Whatever have they used?"—glancing round the room.'

'Did he say anything further?'

Wallace had been stooping over the body to the left of it; Mrs Johnston had been on the other side.

'Mr Wallace rose and came to the other side to leave the

room, and he said: "Why, whatever was she doing with her mackintosh, or my mackintosh?" '[1]

'He came round the body and said: "Whatever was she doing with her mackintosh, or my mackintosh"?'

'Yes.'

To further questions witness replied that until Wallace had drawn her attention to the mackintosh she had not noticed it, any more than her husband had done. It was almost the same colour as the hearthrug. 'It appeared to be something roughed-up, you know; it was almost hidden by the body, you see. Then he stooped down and said: "It is mine." '

Mr Roland Oliver (cross-examining): 'He did not pull it out from under the body?'

'No, he only fingered it.'

The Judge: 'It was when he fingered it that you noticed it?'

'Yes; when he remarked on it I looked at it.'

After this Wallace and the witness had returned to the living-room where, as the latter told Counsel for the Crown, the fire 'was very nearly out—just a few embers. . . . I said: "Well, we'll have a fire." I felt I must do something; inaction was terrible.'

In those three last words are concentrated the feelings of shock and horror which this kindly neighbour, setting out with her husband to spend a pleasant evening with some friends, had undergone during the last ten minutes. Wallace helped her to rekindle the fire, and this was scarcely done when there was a knock on the front door. Followed by Wallace, Mrs Johnston went to answer it.

Counsel for the Crown: 'Were you able to open it?'

'No; it is a different lock to mine and I think I was agitated, and I drew back and let Mr Wallace open it.'

Nor was witness able to say whether the door had been bolted, and was unbolted by Wallace.

Outside it stood P.C. Williams of the Liverpool City Police, who was to state in evidence: 'After a few seconds' fumbling by someone inside the door was opened by the accused.' Asked by *Mr Hemmerde* if he had heard a bolt withdrawn, he replied: 'I did not.'

---

[1] He later stated that his wife did not possess a mackintosh.

The Prosecution's suggestion was to be that Wallace's professed inability to get into his house was sheer pretence, and part of his plan. The Defence suggested that the murderer, having watched Wallace depart, had rung the bell and, on some plausible pretext, had been admitted by Julia into the parlour, where she had lighted one of the gas-brackets and then the fire. Having killed her he had bolted both the front and back doors lest Wallace should return before he had finished ransacking the house. Wallace did so, and the second time the murderer heard the front door being tried he had fled out by the back one—thus it had opened at once when Wallace had turned the knob in the presence of the Johnstons.

The main flaw in this argument lies in the fact that Wallace found the *backyard door* unbolted—that door which he had 'instructed' Julia to bolt, as was their 'invariable practice'—the *first time* he went round to the back—that is to say, *before* the murderer had escaped. And that the backyard door *was* then unbolted is proved by Mrs Johnston's evidence that she heard him 'beating with his hands' on the back door of the house.

However, the Defence is not required to put up any theory at all, so, should they advance one, it hardly matters if it be riddled with flaws. Their task is to disprove—to make nonsense if they can—of the Prosecution's case. Furthermore, the material which the Prosecution possesses must be put at the disposal of the Defence before the case comes to Court, as well as any fresh evidence which may develop after the trial has begun, but the evidence which the Defence possesses belongs solely to them and the Prosecution is not even informed of what witnesses they intend to call. And upon the Prosecution rests the onus of proving their case *beyond all reasonable doubt*.

9

The Investigations

'It is a fallacy to say: "If the prisoner did not do it, who did?"
It is a fallacy to look at it and say: "It is very difficult to think that
the prisoner did not do it." And it may be equally difficult to think
that the prisoner did do it. The Prosecution have to discharge the
onus cast upon them of establishing the guilt of the prisoner . . .
beyond a peradventure, beyond all reasonable doubt.'[1]

I

WALLACE greeted P.C. Williams with the words, 'Something terrible has happened', and led him to the
parlour. Williams, having glanced swiftly about him,
stooped and felt the deceased's right wrist. The flesh was
'slightly warm, but there was no pulsation'.[2]

'How did this happen?' he asked.

Wallace thereupon made that first statement of his which
has already been quoted,[3] and to which he adhered without
any substantial alteration throughout the case. He was standing
in the doorway while he did so, and immediately afterwards,
carefully avoiding treading in the blood about the victim's
head, 'he stepped round the body, near the sideboard, and lit
the other gas-mantle'.

Mr Hemmerde: 'Did you then proceed, accompanied by the
accused, to examine the house?'

'Yes, sir. . . . In the middle bedroom the gas-jet was lit. I
asked the accused if this light was burning when he entered
the house. He replied: "Yes; I changed in this room before
leaving." On the mantelpiece I noticed an ornament from

---

[1] Mr Justice Wright in his address to the jury.
[2] This and subsequent quotations are from the officer's evidence.
[3] *See* Chapter 1, page 134.

which four or five £1-notes were protruding; the accused took hold of this ornament, partly extracted the notes and said: "Here is some money which has not been taken." I requested him to replace the ornament and the notes in their original position, and this he did.[1] To the right of the fireplace I noticed a curtained recess. I approached this and the accused said: "My wife's clothes are there; they have not been touched."[2] I looked into the recess and apparently they were undisturbed. The accused said: "There seems to have been no one here." '

No *thief* had been there, anyhow, for besides this money some articles of jewellery lay untouched on the dressing-table. Thence Wallace and the officer moved on to the laboratory, where the former remarked: 'Everything seems all right here.' Next they entered the bathroom; the bath and the wash-basin were clean and dry; so was the towel.[3] P.C. Williams asked, 'Is this light usually kept on?' to which Wallace replied, 'We usually have a light here.'

Mr Hemmerde: 'Did you then go into the front bedroom?'

'Yes, sir.'

The state of that room was so astonishing and unexpected that, anticipating a little, we will quote the detailed description of it given in evidence by *Detective-Superintendent Moore*, who was soon to behold it.

'There was no light burning in the front bedroom and the blinds were not drawn. The bed was on the left of the door. The bedding was disordered on that side. It appeared to me as though a person had come in, taken the two pillows and flung them across the bed to the window side of the fireplace; one was practically on top of the other, and the bedclothing was pushed over towards the fireplace, exposing a portion of the mattress.[4]

[1] There were four £1-notes folded together. Wallace drew them out of the jar and later it was found that there was a smudge of blood across the inmost one, of the same blood-group as Julia's. This, and a small blood-clot on the side of the lavatory-pan in the bathroom were absolutely the only signs of blood anywhere in the house, apart from that in the proximity of the corpse. But there were no means of *proving* how and when they had got where they were found.

[2] Had Wallace assured himself of this when he went upstairs after leaving the Johnstons at the back door?

[3] If the blood-clot on the side of the lavatory-pan was then present it evidently escaped P. C. Williams' notice.

[4] If Miss Winifred Duke's suggestion that Wallace occupied this room be correct (*vide* footnote on page 182), then one may suppose that he stripped off the sheets and disordered the bed to conceal this fact.

There were three ladies' hats and a handbag lying about. There was a dressing-table in the room, containing drawers and a mirror, and also a wardrobe; the drawers of the dressing-table were shut, and the door of the wardrobe was shut. I asked the accused if the bedroom was like that in the daytime and he said: "I cannot say; I have not been in this room for a fort-night." '

Mr Hemmerde: 'Looking at the bed, and the condition of the room, what impression did it make on you?'

'It did not give me the impression of a thief looking for valuables.'

'Nothing had been disturbed in the drawers, or in the wardrobe?'

'Nothing had been disturbed there at all.'

If we credit R. M. Qualtrough with planning and executing this crime, and if we assume that his primary purpose was robbery, how astonishing and unaccountable his actions become. Why should he have omitted to enter what was, ostensibly, the only occupied bedroom, and therefore the most likely place for valuables wherewith to augment his meagre haul downstairs; and why should he have disordered a bed in an, ostensibly, unoccupied room? Had he slashed the mattress, or flung the contents of the drawers about, it might logically be supposed that he was searching for some specific object which he might have had reason to believe was hidden there. But he had done no such thing. And how miraculous it was that, with the blood of his victim unwashed from his person, he had seized those bedclothes and flung them about without their contracting the faintest stain, while in the bedroom which he had apparently *not* entered there was a bloodstained £1-note!

His behaviour in the living-room below, to which Wallace now conducted the constable, seems equally unaccountable.

'I noticed,' stated P.C Williams, 'the door of a small cupboard, broken in two pieces, lying on the floor. The accused pointed out to me a small cash-box which was on top of the book-case; he said there had been about £4 in it, and it was gone. The accused picked up a lady's handbag, which was lying on a chair near the table, and took out a £1-note and some silver. I noticed some silver coins scattered on the floor. I noticed the window was covered with heavy curtains. . . .

I said to the accused: "Did you notice any lights in the house when you entered?" He said: "With the exception of the lights upstairs the house was in darkness." '

The thief had disregarded Julia's handbag lying on a chair under his very eyes, but had perceived a small cash-box almost hidden from sight on the top of a book-case over seven feet high. Having possessed himself of its contents, he had carefully replaced its lid and neatly returned it whence it had come. But for no reason at all he had wrenched the door from an *unlocked* cupboard, wantonly broken it in two and flung the pieces on the floor.

As one considers the many strange actions of Julia's assassin they awake a memory in the mind; how similar they are in pattern to the actions performed by the assassin of Lord William Russell!

There were some other things in that room, of which mention must be made. Beside the smaller of the two armchairs which faced each other across the hearth, was a work-basket with a threaded needle stuck into some protruding mending, on top of which was a thimble. There was a copy of that evening's *Liverpool Echo* lying open on the table. Beside it was a sugar-bowl and a small plate which had evidently been left behind when the rest of the crockery used at that last meal husband and wife had eaten together had been cleared away. All the rest had been stacked, unwashed, on the draining-board of the scullery sink. The impression created was that the clearing away had been hastily done. Among the things in the scullery was a small jug containing a little stale milk—the fresh supply, which had been delivered at 6.30 that evening and taken in by Julia herself, had been poured into another jug and set aside, which suggests that the meal had been eaten *before* the fresh milk was delivered.

2

It had been nine o'clock when P.C. Williams arrived at the house; twenty minutes later his superior, Sergeant Breslin, also appeared. They entered the parlour together, and Wallace stood on the threshold, watching. It was then that Williams caught sight of 'something' under the deceased's right shoulder. Stooping to peer closer he exclaimed: 'That looks like a mackintosh.'

Mr Hemmerde: 'What did the accused say?'

'The accused was standing in the doorway. He looked into the hall and said: "Yes, it's an old one of mine; it usually hangs here." '

Wallace indicated some pegs just inside the front door.

Before P.C. Williams left the witness-box Mr Hemmerde asked him to describe Wallace's demeanour when they had first stood together beside his wife's dead body. The officer answered:

'He was cool and calm. I thought he was extraordinarily cool and calm.'

3

At 9.50 Professor J. E. Wheatley MacFall reached the scene. He was a distinguished academic personality, for besides occupying the Chair of Forensic Medicine at the University of Liverpool, he was Examiner in Medical Jurisprudence in the universities of Manchester, Birmingham, Edinburgh and Glasgow, while his *Textbook of Forensic Medicine and Toxicology* remains a standard work on those subjects. In addition to all this he held the post of honorary adviser to the Liverpool Criminal Investigation Department, and, in that capacity, had had considerable experience of crimes of violence. It so happened that at the time of Julia's murder he was also acting as police surgeon to the Liverpool City Police, and so the medical side of the case was in his hands from first to last.

Mr Hemmerde was to put the following questions to this witness.

'Can you tell my lord and the jury what was the demeanour of the accused?'

'I was very struck with it; it was abnormal.'

'In what way?'

'He was too quiet, too collected, for a person whose wife

had been killed in the way he described. He was not nearly so affected as I was myself.'

'Do you happen to remember anything in particular that led you to that conclusion?'

'Whilst I was in the room examining the body and the blood he came in smoking a cigarette, and he leaned over in front of the sideboard and flicked the ash into a little bowl on the sideboard. It struck me as being unnatural; he did not *come* forward; he *leaned* forward, so as not to step in the blood-clot.'

Could any *normal* individual have conducted himself in a manner such as this; smoking cigarettes and leaning forward to watch, with apparent detachment, the medical examination being conducted on the body of that woman with whom—as he was later to proclaim for the edification of the public—he had spent 'all those happy, industrious years' up to that very night?

Soon after eleven o'clock Professor MacFall sent for a colleague, Dr Hugh Price, who arrived accompanied by Professor Roberts, the City Analyst. Dr Price took Professor MacFall's place beside the body for the purpose of observing the progress of *rigor mortis*, so that the other two medical experts might give their attention to an inspection of the premises.

At that hour, crowded together in that little villa, were, besides the medical authorities, no less than six police officers, including the photographer and finger-print expert. When those officers first entered that small villa in one of the poorer residential districts of Liverpool, to find that the wife of an obscure insurance agent had been murdered early in the evening during her husband's absence from home, they could have had no idea that the case was to develop, as the Judge remarked, into one 'almost unexampled in the annals of crime'. But very soon indeed the peculiar demeanour of the bereaved husband, the terrible nature of the injuries done to the victim, the paradoxical character of the supposed robbery, set their minds busily to work.

Detective-Inspector Gold had reached the scene in advance of Detective-Superintendent Hugh Moore; and Sergeant Breslin and P.C. Williams immediately called his attention to the mackintosh which they had been careful not to disturb. To discourage Wallace's curiosity they had shut the parlour door behind them, and Wallace, taking the hint, had retired to the living-room. Still leaving the garment undisturbed, Inspector Gold now went to the living-room and asked Wallace:

'What about the mackintosh, Mr Wallace?'

'It is mine,' he said.

Superintendent Moore upon his arrival at once went 'down on the floor' to examine very carefully the mackintosh's 'position in relation to the body'. It seemed to have been 'tucked in at the side; no part of the body rested upon it'. Getting to his feet he opened the door and called to Wallace.

'He came and stood on my left, slightly behind me,' testified the superintendent. 'I said to him: "Is this your mackintosh?" He stooped slightly and put his hand to his chin. I looked at him and he made no reply for probably half a minute or so. I said: "Had Mrs Wallace a mackintosh like this?" He remained in the same position and did not answer. Sergeant Bailey was standing in front of me, by the sideboard, and I said to him: "Take it up and let us have a look at it." '

The two officers held it up by the sleeves. They saw that it was considerably stained with blood on the inside as well as on the outside.

'It's a gent's mackintosh,' observed the superintendent.

Wallace, still maintaining silence, took hold of a portion of it as though he were seeing it for the first time. Then at last he said, continued the superintendent's statement:

' "If there are two patches on the inside, it is mine." By that time we had found the two patches and, almost in a continuing sentence he said: "It is mine!" '

Mr Hemmerde: 'Then did he say anything else?'

'He said: "I wore it this morning, but the day turning out fine I wore my fawn coat this afternoon." I asked him where he had left it. He said: "Hanging in the hall." '

In his cross-examination *Mr Oliver* asked the superintendent if he knew the accused had acknowledged ownership of the mackintosh to Mrs Johnston.

'I know that *now*,' he said.

'And to P.C. Williams?'

'That is right.'

'And to some tall officer who had come into the kitchen?'

'Yes.'

'Then,' declared Counsel, 'this is what happens: you, a Superintendent of Police, Mr Gold, an Inspector of Police, and a Sergeant, standing together, interrogate him as to whose mackintosh it is. Are you surprised that he was doubtful?'

'All the more reason why he should say at once: "It is mine." '

Mr Oliver's next question recoiled somewhat on his own head.

'What inference do you draw from his hesitation to acknowledge the mackintosh to you, when he had acknowledged it to four different people—three of them policemen?'

'That he was beginning to think that the mackintosh was dangerous, and that the police had formed a certain idea,' answered Superintendent Moore.

They had indeed 'formed a certain idea'—an idea which explained many of the paradoxes and puzzles which confronted them, and went a long way towards explaining others.

4

'Did Mr Wallace, while the police were examining the house, say anything?' *Counsel for the Crown* asked Mrs Johnston.

'Yes, he did say: "Julia would have gone mad if she had seen all this"—meaning the strangers knocking about the house.'

'Can you tell me what his attitude was the whole time?'

'At first he was quite collected.'

'What do you mean by "at first"?'

'Before my husband went for the police.'

'. . . And then?'

'Then twice he shewed emotion by putting his hands to his head, and he sobbed.'

'Where were you when he did that?'

'In the kitchen.'

'Was anybody else there?'

'No.'

'How long would it be that he was shewing this emotion by sobbing?'

'Just momentary.'

Mr Oliver (cross-examining): 'With regard to that, did he appear like a man who was suffering from a shock before your husband left?'

'Yes, to some extent.'

'It is very difficult, of course, to judge what is passing in other people's minds?'

'Manners are so different, aren't they?' she answered amiably if a trifle obliquely.

'Twice, you say, while you were with him some time later he broke down altogether?'

'Yes, he sobbed.'

'The two times you saw him break down were before the police arrived?'

'Yes.'

'During that time did he display emotion from time to time?'

'Yes; and then, if we were left in the kitchen alone, he appeared as if he would break down, and he seemed to pull himself together when a great many were knocking about.'

'You were with him a considerable time?'

'Yes.'

'Did you think there was anything suspicious about his manner from beginning to end?'

'No, I did not.'

Under Mr Oliver's skilful questioning Mrs Johnston had travelled quite a long way from her answer to Counsel for the Crown that Wallace's emotion had been 'just momentary'.

On the subject of Wallace's demeanour Inspector Gold had this to say in answer to *Mr Hemmerde*.

'He was cool and calm. I did not see anything of emotion in him at all at the death of his wife.'

'Was there anything in particular which drew your attention to that?'

'When I first went into the house he was sitting in the kitchen. He had the cat on his knees and was stroking it.'

As reported, Inspector Gold concluded his answer with the words: 'He did not look to me like a man who had just battered his wife to death', and this has sometimes been quoted as indicating that the inspector had his doubts about Wallace's guilt. But whatever his exact words may have been the meaning he obviously intended to convey was, 'He did not look to me like a man whose wife had just been battered to death'; and that this is the sense in which the Court understood him is clear from the fact that Mr Oliver made no allusion to this point in his cross-examination. Nor is there anything else in the inspector's evidence to suggest that he harboured any doubts as to Wallace's guilt.

Superintendent Moore described Wallace's demeanour thus:

'Quiet and collected; smoking cigarettes and talking generally.'

Both before and since the date of this case means have been used to decoy a householder away from his house in order that it may be entered and robbed; both before and since the date of this case men have entered premises which they knew to be occupied at the time by an unprotected female, and have used greater or less violence upon her person, for the purpose of robbery. In this case it is clear that the sender of the telephone message and the murderer of Julia Wallace was one and the same person; and if that person were Qualtrough, and his purpose was to rob the house, then he would know that its achievement would inevitably involve violence to Julia. It may therefore be assumed that he would come armed with some instrument of attack. He would obviously take precautions against leaving finger-prints, but it would not matter in the least to him if he left indistinguishable smears and smudges of blood all over the house; it would not matter in the least if traces of bloodstained water, and a wet and bloody towel, were discovered; but it would matter exceedingly if he ventured out into the lighted streets of Liverpool at the early hour of 8.45 p.m. with traces of the crime still upon him.

Both before and since this crime men have murdered their

wives, by violence or other means, but invariably motive has been discernible; in this case one might say that the total absence of motive was so conspicuous as to be in itself suspicious. One must ask oneself whether a man, so addicted to solving mathematical puzzles, so interested in the study of crime, as was Wallace, might not have employed his knowledge to plan a crime which would shew all the careful premeditation, the use of clues intended to mislead, and the carefully calculated time-factor as did the murder of Julia Wallace? Might not also the natural curiosity of such a man, with his scientific leanings, prompt him to watch with absorbed interest the work of the distinguished specialist as he examined the dead body, and would he not be fascinated in observing, at close quarters, the proceedings of the highly trained detectives? And is it not equally probable that when he is excluded from the contemplation of these engrossing spectacles, and finds himself alone in the company of a compassionate woman, that the tremendous strain which he has placed upon his nerves should find a vent in sudden outbursts of emotion? Finally, is it not again possible that a man soured by frustration and poisoned by a diseased organ might not have conceived some obscure motive of his own for killing his wife?

We must keep these possibilities in mind as we proceed.

10

The Case Takes Shape

'There is certainly no eye-witness, except the actual murderer,
besides the dead woman, and, therefore, the evidence in this case,
and the evidence that can be brought against anybody here, is
purely circumstantial. You know in many cases, especially of
murder, the only evidence that is available is circumstantial
evidence; but circumstantial evidence may vary in value almost
infinitely.'[1]

I

SUPERINTENDENT MOORE asked Wallace if either he or
his wife had any relations who ought to be informed of
the tragedy. Wallace replied that his wife had none; that
his brother was abroad, but his brother's wife was living at
83 Ullet Road. A car was therefore sent to fetch her. On her
arrival Mrs Amy Wallace shewed great distress, for, as she told
the police, she had spent some time with Julia that very afternoon, leaving her about half past four. She was informed that
she might be required to give evidence at the inquest and would
certainly be required formally to identify the body at the
mortuary. She was also asked if she would accommodate
Wallace himself at her house for the next few days, to which
she consented.

When Wallace was told of this arrangement he strongly
objected to leaving his 'little home' and all his possessions:
however he had little choice in the matter, as he was informed
that the plumbing was to be dismantled forthwith for the purpose of carring out various tests. He submitted without protest
to a search being made of the clothes he was wearing, and
undertook to make a statement at the Anfield Bridewell. When

[1] Mr Justice Wright in his address to the jury.

he returned from doing this last it was after midnight and, having packed a bag, both him and it were conveyed to Ullet Road by police car. Before leaving he was asked if any object, such as might have been used to kill his wife, were missing from the premises. He took the superintendent up to the laboratory where there were two or three hammers and some other tools on the work-bench, and, indicating these, said that nothing was missing; nor was he aware of anything missing anywhere else except a dogwhip which used to hang in the passage and which he had not seen for some months.

Professor MacFall and Professor Roberts did not take their departure until 1 a.m., by which time special lamps had been brought and the body photographed from every angle. Photographs were also taken of the bloodstains on the walls and elsewhere, the nature and character of which had greatly interested Professor MacFall, who had already made a rough diagram of them. An ambulance then carried Julia's body away to Prince's Mortuary.

Superintendent Moore remained behind for another two or three hours, and the police then removed a variety of objects which Professor Roberts required for microscopical examination and chemical analysis. These included the mackintosh, the hearthrug and the suit of clothes Wallace had been wearing. They also took Wallace's diary though most of its contents were inadmissible as evidence.

As in the case of Courvoisier the detectives quickly reached the conclusion that the indications of theft were unnatural—the work of someone attempting to imply that robbery had been committed. Nevertheless, the usual routine inquiries were begun: advertisements were issued requesting taxi-drivers and the operators of public vehicles to come forward with any information which might assist the police; laundries and dry-cleaners were warned to keep a careful watch for garments bearing suspicious marks or stains; visits were paid to lodging-houses, railway stations, night cafés and other places where a suspect might resort. None of these things produced any clue which seemed likely to lead to 'R. M. Qualtrough'.

While these inquiries were being pursued other investigations were taking place at Menlove Gardens and Wolverton

Street. At the latter plumbers were engaged from an early hour on the morning of the 21st. The basin in the bathroom and the sink in the scullery were removed and sent, with their waste-pipes, to be tested for traces of blood. The bath was similarly examined and seemed not to have been used since it was last cleaned. The drains were taken up in the hope of discovering the weapon, and the search for this was extended even to the main sewers. But although it was never found, on that Wednesday morning the police were given a description of an article, alleged to be missing from the house, which in weight and shape would certainly resemble closely the implement with which the deed must have been done.

This description emanated from Mrs Jane Draper, the charwoman employed by the Wallaces for four hours each Wednesday morning. For some reason she had not attended the previous Wednesday, 14th, so the last time she had done so was on the 7th. Inspector Gold, having fetched her to the house on the 21st, bade her 'take a good look round and see if anything was missing'. Having done so at her leisure she informed him that she could not find an iron bar which had always been kept in the parlour fireplace for scooping out spent matches, cigar-ette ends and other débris from under the gas-fire.[1] It was 'just a bit of iron', rather pitted with rust, she said; sometimes it stood up on end in a corner of the fireplace, at others it lay out of sight beneath the kerb. It had been in the latter position on 7th January; she particularly remembered that, because she had used it to retrieve a screw which had fallen off one of the gas-brackets while she was dusting and rolled under the grate.

In due course the police had a replica made to Mrs Draper's specification, and at the trial, after Professor MacFall had described the fatal wound on Julia's temple, he was handed this replica and asked if it, or something like it, could have in-flicted the injury. Weighing it in his hand he replied:

'Yes, just such a weapon. If a blow was made with this, it would produce the appearances I found.'

---

[1] She also stated that 'a small poker used in the kitchen fire' was likewise missing, but from her description of it, it seemed unlikely to have been the weapon used. Wallace denied all knowledge of the iron bar in the parlour, and declared that, if the kitchen poker could not be found, Mrs Draper 'must have thrown it out with the ashes'.

While these activities were in full spate at No. 29, Professor MacFall was engaged in conducting a post-mortem on Julia's body, and the inquest was being arranged for the following afternoon, Thursday, 22nd. On this being opened the only evidence taken was that of Amy Wallace as to identity. In reply to questions from the Coroner she said she did not know deceased's exact age, but believed her to be fifty-two. She repeated the statement she had made to the police, that she had visited Julia on the afternoon of Tuesday, 20th January, and said: 'When I left her at 4.30, my sister-in-law was then the only person remaining in the house. *She was then in her usual health except for a slight cold.*'

The Coroner adjourned the inquest until 5th February, 'by which date they might know what the position was'. But on that date the reopening was a mere formality in order to effect an adjournment for another ten days. Meanwhile the police had submitted their reports, and these having been studied by the Director of Public Prosecutions, it was decided to arrest Wallace and charge him with the murder. On the evening of 2nd February, therefore, Inspector Gold and two other officers presented themselves at 83 Ullet Road for this purpose. On their reading the warrant to him Wallace said: 'What can I say in answer to such a charge, of which I am absolutely innocent?' When cautioned and charged at the main Bridewell he made no reply.

At the reopening of the inquest on 25th February, Mr Hector Munro, of Messrs. Davis, Berthen and Munro, solicitors, appeared on behalf of Wallace, and the Coroner made another adjournment with the words: 'In view of the criminal proceedings in connection with this case I propose to adjourn it until such time as those proceedings are likely to be concluded.'

The police court proceedings lasted seven days. At the close of the case for the Prosecution, and on being required to plead, Wallace said:

'I plead not guilty of the charge against me, and I am

advised to reserve my defence. I would like to say that my wife and I lived together on the very happiest terms during the period of some eighteen years of our married life. Our relations were those of complete confidence and affection for each other.' Up to this point his voice had been firm and calm, but as he continued speaking it began to gather emotion. 'The suggestion that I murdered my wife is monstrous. That I should attack and kill her is, to all who knew us, unthinkable and un-believable—all the more so when it must be realized that I cannot gain one possible advantage by committing such a deed. Nor do the police suggest I gained any advantage. On the contrary, in actual fact I have lost a devoted and loving comrade; my home life is completely broken up, and everything that I held dear has been ruthlessly uprooted and torn from me.' He had wept openly in Court earlier that day; now again sobs choked him. 'I am now left to face the torture of this nerve-wracking ordeal. I protest once more than I am entirely inno-cent of this terrible crime.'

The magistrate, Mr R. J. Ward, then committed Wallace for trial.

3

The trial of William Herbert Wallace for the murder of his wife opened at St George's Hall, Liverpool, on Wednesday, 22nd April 1931. It is surprising and unfortunate that no account of this case has been included in that invaluable series, *Notable British Trials*, and there consequently exists no com-plete, *verbatim*, report of the proceedings available to the public.

The gist of the case for the Prosecution was that Mrs Wallace, in obedience to her husband's request, had got the parlour ready for a musical evening in the usual fashion. Wallace meanwhile went upstairs to 'clean himself up' after his day's work, taking the mackintosh and the iron bar with him. Having taken off his outer clothing and arranged it so that he could quickly don it again, he had returned downstairs wearing the mackintosh as a protective cover over his under garments. His wife was sitting on the armchair which she had drawn closer to the fire in order to warm herself while she awaited him.

Entering, he had struck her down before she had had time even to realize his intention. As she fell forward her long skirt had come in contact with the fire and had begun to smoulder. Grabbing her by the hair, he had dragged her clear, then had administered those ten further blows with great rapidity and violence upon her head. Slipping off the mackintosh, and wiping his feet, the weapon and his hands upon the hearthrug, he had then washed off what blood remained upon him, donned his outer clothes and set off for Menlove Gardens to create his alibi.

In his opening speech Mr Hemmerde suggested that the burns on the mackintosh were contracted in an attempt to destroy it; later he substituted the more probable theory that they had been caused by its catching alight when Wallace stooped to drag his wife away from the fire. In his opening speech Mr Hemmerde made the two following points:

1. 'The history of our criminal courts shews what elaborate precautions people can sometimes take. One of the most famous criminal trials was of a man who committed a crime when he was naked.'

2. 'A man might perfectly well commit a crime wearing a raincoat, as one might wear a dressing-gown, and come down, when he was going to do this, *with nothing on, on which blood could fasten.*[1]

In the first of these quotations Mr Hemmerde was referring to the case of Courvoisier; in the second he is not suggesting that Wallace himself was naked under the mackintosh, but that he had taken off all clothing, such as his suit, shoes and socks, 'on which blood could fasten'.[2]

[1] Author's italics.

[2] In a recent book, *More Criminal Files* (Arco Publications Ltd., 1958), Mr John Rowland writes:

'The case that Mr Hemmerde put forward can be expressed quite simply and shortly. It was that Wallace, having persuaded his wife to go and light the fire in the sitting-room (it was there that the piano stood; it was therefore there that they had their musical evenings) went upstairs and undressed completely. This explained the absence of bloodstains on his clothes. He then put on the mackintosh, which would, he thought, receive any blood which might be spilled, crept downstairs, armed with a poker or the iron bar or both, savagely killed his wife, who had been completely taken by surprise, and then attempted in a futile way to burn both the mackintosh and his wife's body, finishing by trying to fake a burglary.'

It is at least to be hoped that the quotations from Mr Hemmerde's speeches to

Proof that the mackintosh had been used in the manner which the Prosecution alleged depended mainly on the character of the bloodstains upon it, and for an interpretation of that point they relied on the expert evidence of Professor MacFall. Perhaps because his evidence, based on such demonstrable factors as photographs and diagrams, constituted a formidable argument in support of the Prosecution's theory, the Defence thought it necessary to produce an alternative theory of their own and to submit that of the Prosecution to the forces of ridicule, as in the following passage of Mr Oliver's closing speech to the jury.

'The prosecution have got to satisfy you,' he said, 'of the case they bring against the accused. What is their case? It varies from day to day. At the police court it was this: Wallace in a mackintosh killed his wife. No suggestion that he was naked. They come here, and some genius has observed that he was dressed; he must have blood upon his clothes . . . upon his trousers, too. . . . He could not have washed them. So we have the learned Recorder suggesting that he was naked. . . . Could you conceive the picture of the husband naked in a mackintosh coming in to play the violin?'

But though ridicule can be a potent weapon, on this occasion it missed fire because the 'learned Recorder' had suggested no such thing. What he did suggest is epitomized in his *own* closing speech which followed upon that of Mr Oliver:

'Now my learned friend has said that one has a theory: that I have suggested a theory that this man was playing the violin, or was down there playing music with his wife, naked and wearing a mackintosh. You know perfectly well I have suggested nothing of the sort. What I did say to you is: you must not attach too much importance to the fact that there was no blood found upon a man, because people have been known to commit crimes without anything on. In this case we know this: here is a man who was admittedly changing upstairs—*he has admitted he was changing*. It is clear that his mackintosh took some part in this matter. . . . You have heard evidence that suggests

the jury, which are given here, will correct the impression that he ever suggested anything so palpably absurd as that Wallace attempted to burn his wife's *body* at the gas-fire in the parlour of a suburban villa!

to you that this mackintosh, and the dress, were both burned by the gas-fire in that room. . . . Can you picture to yourself a man[1] coming into that room and taking up the nearest raincoat to put on to commit a murder? There are marks under the arms of blood, where a man might pull his hand through. . . .'

After calling the Court's attention to the fact that the prisoner had himself stated that his wife never wore his mackintosh, and commenting upon Professor MacFall's evidence concerning the distribution of the bloodstains, Mr Hemmerde demanded:

'Who was wearing that coat? . . . Is it not perfectly possible that he [Wallace] had interrupted his change of garments upstairs and, using that coat, had come downstairs—*not* with a view to playing the violin naked in a raincoat, but to come down there while she supposed he was getting himself ready—cleaning himself up—for the evening's music? That is the suggestion made. You may think there is something in it. You may think there is nothing in it. But you do not get rid of it by the humorous suggestion of my learned friend that a person does not play the violin naked in a raincoat.'

The basis of the case for the Defence was that robbery was the motive for the crime; that having lured Wallace away by means of the telephone call Qualtrough had rung the door-bell at 29 Wolverton Street, and that Julia, *suffering 'from a severe cold'*, had taken her husband's mackintosh down from its peg in the hall and thrown it about her shoulders before going to answer the door. She had led the visitor into the parlour, lighted the wall-bracket to the right of the mantel-piece, stooped, turned on the gas-tap and lighted the gas-fire, and, while rising from doing this, was struck down.

Against this argument there was, first of all, the evidence of Mrs Amy Wallace that at 4.30 that afternoon Julia was 'in her usual health except for a *slight* cold'. Secondly there was the evidence of Wallace himself, who had declared that his wife had put nothing round her shoulders when she had accompanied him down the backyard and into the alley at 6.50. Why then should she put so chilly a garment as a mackintosh 'over her shoulders' merely to answer the front

[1] i.e. an intruder.

door? But supposing she had done so, and had entered the parlour with it on, would it not have slipped off her shoulders when she raised her arms to light the gas-bracket? And how did it receive blood splashes *across the front* when it was hanging down her back? It is interesting to observe whence the Defence derived this theory that Julia had draped the mackintosh about her shoulders.

Mr Roland Oliver (cross-examining Mrs Johnston): 'Do you think it was possible from the position it was in[1] that it was thrown round her shoulders to go to the front door?'

The Judge (to Counsel): 'You mean she had thrown it on?'

Mr Oliver: 'Yes, to go and open and the door—that is my suggestion.'

Mrs Johnston: 'That was *my* idea.'

Mr Oliver: 'You had that idea too?'

Mrs Johnston: 'It just flashed across my mind, because it was a peculiar thing—a mackintosh—and I said to Mr Wallace that she might have thrown it over her shoulders to go to the front door.'

She had remembered Wallace's remark as they were crossing the backyard: 'She will not be out as she has such a bad cold.'

The Judge himself acknowledged that the case for the Prosecution was strong. Its weakness lay in the fact that they had put forward no motive. This does not necessarily mean that they could not suggest one, but rather that none which they could suggest would be admissible.

We have already seen that the theory of robbery put forward by the Defence as the motive, though it might have a superficial plausibility, was as full of holes as a sieve. And in this connection an interesting point arises. Asked by the police if he harboured suspicions against anyone Wallace emphatically declared in his first statement that he did not, and this he subsequently repeated. Yet a few days later, when he probably guessed that he was under suspicion himself, he came forward with the suggestion that the young man who had acted for him during the period he was in hospital would know that on a Tuesday the whole of the week's collection would be in

[1] i.e. 'bunched up' under right shoulder of the corpse.

the house, while if he called on some pretence of business and offered to await Wallace's return, Julia would have invited him into the parlour and lighted the gas-bracket and the fire.

Fortunately for himself the man—whose name Wallace gave the police—was able to satisfy them that he was nowhere in the Anfield neighbourhood on the night of the crime, and Wallace then suggested someone of the name of Harris who was equally able to establish his innocence. It was this attempt to divert suspicion from himself to a colleague, as much as anything else, which caused the office staff of the Prudential to ostracize Wallace when, after the quashing of his conviction, he was transferred to an indoor occupation.

The Time-Factor

'There is some circumstantial evidence which is as good and
conclusive as the evidence of actual eye-witnesses. In other cases
the only circumstantial evidence which anyone can present still
leaves loopholes and doubts.'[1]

I

THE police observed that Wallace possessed a long, loping
stride, and Inspector Gold, a man of similar height, conducted a number of tests in connection with the time-
factor—tests which were checked and counter-checked by
several other officers. He found that it took him four minutes
to reach the telephone kiosk from the door of 29 Wolverton
Street; therefore, supposing Wallace had left his house at 7.10
on the evening of Monday, 19th, and not at 7.15 as he stated,
then the complaint he made to the telephone operator could
have been recorded at 7.15, as was the case. Other tests also
proved that he would have had ample time to talk to Mr
Beattie over the line, and then reach the City Café by 7.35
or 7.40.

If he had left Margaret Martin at Clubmoor not later than
5.50 on the afternoon of Tuesday, 20th, he could, it was demonstrated, have been back in his house by 6 p.m. The time
Wallace himself gave was 6.5, and the time of his subsequent
departure for Menlove Gardens as 6.45. It will be remembered
that he was unobserved from the time he left Margaret Martin
until the time he spoke to Thomas Phillips, conductor of the
tram he boarded at the Lodge Lane junction—a time which
Phillips gave as '7.6 or 7.10'. Police tests as to the length of

[1] Mr Justice Wright in his address to the jury.

time it would take him to cover the distance from 29 Wolverton Street to the tram junction varied from a minimum of fifteen minutes to a maximum of nineteen. The minimum time, therefore, that Wallace had in which to take his tea, murder Julia, rid himself of traces of the crime and reach the tram junction was sixty-one minutes, and the maximum, seventy.

There was evidence to shew that Julia was alive at 6.30. The point upon which Wallace's fate hung was how much longer she remained alive after that time; for obviously the later she was last seen alive by an independent witness, the less likely was it that Wallace could have committed the crime. But it was a matter of surprise that the Prosecution produced only one witness to give evidence on the point.

Alan Close, aged fourteen, had, for the past two years, delivered milk at 29 Wolverton Street each evening from his father's small dairy just off Breck Road. Usually he did this by bicycle, but it so happened that on Tuesday, 20th, the bicycle was out of commission, so he set out with a crate of cans on each arm and his father's injunction in his ears to 'hurry up and get back' for the next load.

As he turned up the footway from Breck Road into Wolverton Street, he said he glanced up at the illuminated dial of the clock on Holy Trinity Church. From this point it was only 60 yards to the Wallaces' front door. Alan Close's technique was to put their half-pint can of milk on their doorstep, rap with the knocker, then step over the low intervening parapet and repeat the performance next door. On that evening of Tuesday, 20th, Julia Wallace opened the door promptly, took in the can, reappeared with it empty a moment or two later and handed it back to Alan Close with the remark that he 'should hurry home as he had a bad cough'.

'I remember the night Mrs Wallace was murdered,' he told the Court. 'I delivered the milk at half past six. I remember the time because when I passed Holy Trinity Church it was twenty-five minutes past six, and it takes me five minutes to get to Mrs Wallace's.'

Now, if Close were correct, that would mean that Wallace had from 20 to 25 minutes in which to kill Julia and do what he had to do before leaving to catch his tram. Naturally the Defence did their utmost to reduce this time-factor to an impossibly narrow margin by calling witnesses to contest the evidence of Alan Close. The first of these was *Allison Wildman*, a newspaper boy, aged sixteen, who stated that he had passed Holy Trinity Church at 6.35, and that it took him two minutes to get from there to Wolverton Street. Having thrust a newspaper in the letter-boxes of the four houses on the other side of the road, he crossed to No. 27.

Mr Oliver: 'No. 27 is next door to No. 29—Mr Wallace's house?'

'Yes.'

'When you delivered your paper at No. 27 that evening what was happening, if anything, at No. 29?'

'I saw a milk-boy standing on the step of No. 29?'

'Tell us, will you, what time that was?'

'. . . . It would be twenty-three minutes to seven when I got there.'

'When you went away where was the boy?'

'Still on the step.'

Mr Hemmerde (cross-examining): '. . . You said to your mother: "I saw another boy there about 6.35 last night." That was after you heard of the murder?'

'Yes.'

David Jones[1] testified that he had delivered the *Liverpool Echo* every evening for four or five years at 29 Wolverton Street. *On the evening of the murder he did so at 6.35, and he saw nobody about.*

The evidence of these two witnesses for the Defence certainly does not tally, because if Jones was on the doorstep of No. 29 at 6.35, and both his and Wildman's estimate of the time was correct, then he ought to have seen *both Wildman and Alan Close*. On the other hand, if Jones' estimate of the time was correct—and Wildman's wrong—then that does tally with the evidence of Alan Close, *who would have left No. 29 four or five minutes before Jones arrived.* The Judge, in the course of his summing-up, had this to say on the point:

---

[1] His age is not given, but he was an adult. The Defence called two other witnesses as well, but their evidence was purely hearsay, and since his lordship ignored it in his summing-up we can do the same.

'The Defence called two witnesses; one was the newspaper man, Jones. . . . He was not very precise as to his time, but the newspaper was afterwards found in the house, so it must have been collected.[1] Then there is the boy Wildman, who says he was delivering newspapers next door and saw the boy Close, and he puts the time at something like 6.37. I must say I do not agree with any attacks that were made upon the police in the conduct of this case.[2] I think they have done their duty with great enthusiasm and ability, but I cannot help thinking that they were guilty of an error of judgment in not calling the two witnesses Jones and Wildman in the course of the Prosecution. It is true that Jones' time may be a little uncertain, and Wildman, although he had mentioned it to his mother next day, had already associated—although I don't think that ought to affect the position—with the solicitor for the Defence. But that rather indicates in a case of this sort, where the ascertainment of the time within as narrow a limit as possible is so important, that they are witnesses who, I think, ought to have been put before the jury in the case by the Prosecution.'

His lordship then stressed the matter by saying that, owing to this error of judgment, the case, on this important point, depended 'entirely on the evidence of the boy Close'. The police had been swift in making contact with Close; Wallace's solicitor had been equally swift in making contact with Allison Wildman, having done so on the very morning after the crime. Thus was created one of those 'loopholes and doubts' to which his lordship referred in his address to the jury.

Mr Hemmerde, in his closing speech, did his best to mend the breach.

'The man who made his plans, whether the boy was seen at 6.30 or 6.35 . . . had between that time and 6.45—practically twenty minutes—and there is no reason to suppose that a man who had done a thing like that would go very slowly. . . . He was trying to create an alibi, and he would go as fast as he could. I say there is ample time for it.'

The Judge observed: 'It is perfectly true that if he planned

---

[1] i.e. picked up off the mat by Wallace or his wife.
[2] His lordship was alluding to certain accusations levelled at them by Mr Roland Oliver.

and executed this scheme he would have got everything ready, and everything would have gone in the way of its execution with the utmost precision and rapidity.' But, as his lordship reminded the jury, the accused might have had, at the narrowest margin, only ten minutes at his disposal, and that when he boarded the tram at Lodge Lane he was 'apparently completely dressed and, apparently, without any signs of discomposure. . . . It does not follow that he did not do it, but you have to be satisfied that he did do it.' His lordship also pointed out that 'nobody actually noticed him when he got on the tram at St Margaret's Church', close to Wolverton Street, where Wallace stated he had caught a tram to the junction at Lodge Lane; so nobody could be called to testify whether he had *then* shewn signs of haste or 'discomposure'.

The medical evidence, though copious, provided the jury with no help as to the time of death. The normal temperature of the living human body is 98.4° Fahrenheit. The usual formula for arriving at the time of death in such a case as this is to subtract the rectal temperature of the body from 98.4 and divide the difference by 1.5. The result is, *approximately*, the time, in hours, since death took place. But in making this calculation allowance has to be made for the age of the subject, their physical condition and muscular development, and the temperature of the surrounding atmosphere. This test was never carried out in the case of Julia Wallace, but even if it had been the result would have been too provisional to be of any help in deciding a question, not of hours, but minutes. Professor MacFall's evidence on the subject was based on the progress of *rigor mortis*; medical witnesses called by the Defence, not having seen the body, could only dispute his conclusions, and, as the Judge observed: 'You have nothing which will enable you to fix the time of death that evening.'

2

Professor MacFall was on rather firmer ground when it came to another aspect of the time-factor.

The Judge: 'If the head was struck, of course the woman would fall forward?'

'Yes, my lord.'

'And after that she was struck while on the ground?'

'Yes, I can prove that.'

Mr Hemmerde: 'Can you say how many blows were struck altogether?'

'Eleven. . . . I have put it definitely at eleven.'

'How long would it take to inflict those eleven blows?'

'I think they could all be inflicted—I have timed it—in less than half a minute.'

'Would the first blow be sufficient to cause death?'

'Yes, quite.'

One must also apply the time-factor to the egregious Qualtrough. Presumably, since he had no means of knowing whether Wallace intended to accept his invitation to visit him at Menlove Gardens 'East', he would watch him board a tram travelling in that direction before ringing the bell at 29 Wolverton Street. He could be confident that Wallace would be absent for at least an hour, for the trip there and back alone would consume that time. And an hour should be ample time for Qualtrough to achieve his purpose and get clear away.

But Wallace, in order to explain why the doors of his house were 'fastened against him', claimed that Qualtrough was still there on his return from Menlove Gardens *two hours later*, and then fled by the back, and this explanation was incorporated by the Defence in their theory of the crime.

Why should Qualtrough have lingered so long on the premises?

Wallace left his house at 6.45. St Margaret's Church, where he said he caught a tram to Lodge Lane, was only five minutes' walk from Wolverton Street. So Qualtrough would be ringing the bell of No. 29 at seven o'clock, or very soon after. The murder of Julia would be the action of a moment and Professor MacFall calculated that it would take 'less than half a minute' to deliver those ten superfluous blows. But let us give Qualtrough a quarter of an hour after his admittance before he struck his first blow.

At 7.20 at the latest, then, he is in the parlour with the

weapon in his hand and the dead woman at his feet, and this part of his night's activities accomplished so adroitly that she has made no sound nor put up the least defence. Not a single article in that room has been displaced; there is a sideboard near the door, with drawers and a cupboard, but apparently he does not consider it worth searching, so he thoughtfully *turns off the fire and puts out the light*, and leaves the room, pulling to the door behind him.

Two minutes later he is in the living-room; the light is on, for Julia was sitting there when he rang the bell. Her handbag is lying on a chair under his eyes, but he ignores it; instead he perceives a small cash-box practically out of sight on the top of a cupboard over seven feet high. Taking it down and removing its detachable lid he finds that it contains Treasury notes and silver to the value of £4, an American $1-note, a postal order for 4s. 6d. and a crossed cheque for some small amount. The crossed cheque will be useless to him, but he still takes it, along with all the rest, except, for some obscure reason, the $1-note. Some of the coins drop from his fingers as he pockets them and fall on the floor. He leaves them where they are, but carefully replaces the lid on the cash-box and tidily returns it whence it came. There is no clue to the impulse which makes him wrench the door off the trumpery and unlocked little cupboard, break it in half and fling it on the floor. If it is rage at finding so little, one would expect him to vent his feelings on the cash-box.

Let us be generous to Wallace and the Defence and give Qualtrough fifteen minutes in which to do what he has done in the living-room. The time, therefore, is now 7.35 or 7.40.

As he did not take the four Treasury notes from the ornament on the mantelpiece in Julia's bedroom, or the trinkets which she had left lying on her dressing-table, one must assume that, as Wallace suggested, he resisted the invitation of the light which Wallace had turned low after changing his clothes there to go to Menlove Gardens, and never entered that room at all. Nothing appeared to have been touched in the laboratory, and nothing was missing, so all that Qualtrough seems to have done upstairs is to disorder the bed in the front bedroom. If he took as much as ten minutes over that prank, he would have been downstairs once more by 7.50.

And what then? Why not go while the going is good—for he can hardly know that the absent husband will be so extraordinarily persistent in his search for 25 Menlove Gardens East? But he does not go. Having bolted both the doors against Wallace's return he remains where he is, bloodstained and unwashed, and only when he hears that 'gentle' rapping of the front-door knocker *an hour later* does it occur to him to leave the scene of his crime! But first of all he thriftily turns out the living-room light!

That cunningly devised plot to lure the householder away from home and obtain entrance to his house, that quick, deft kill, that miraculous care in leaving no finger-prints or smudges of blood on walls, or doors, or furniture, right to the very moment of his dark-enshrouded flight, when contrasted with his unsystematic search for what he came to get and all the inconsistencies surrounding it, and, finally, with his long-delayed departure, *simply do not make sense.*

If such a situation as this formed the basis of a crime story —and that story was fortunate enough to find a publisher—how justified the critics would be in turning it to ridicule. And how surprising it is that anyone so devoted to solving detective problems 'of the higher kind' as Mr Agate, should have overlooked so glaring an absurdity when considering this case.

12

The Bloodstains

'You have heard some description of the crime so far as it can be reconstructed. It was a crime which involved, apparently (and here we are going rather into the region of speculation), this woman going into the parlour, and, no doubt, turning on the light and lighting the stove. It must, no doubt, be coupled with the fact that they generally lived in the kitchen, but on occasion they went into the parlour when they wanted to have some music, and, on occasion, when visitors came.'[1]

I

I T WAS not until *Professor MacFall* entered the witness-box, on the second day, that the trial of William Herbert Wallace rose to any point of tension.

He was an experienced witness, and knew precisely what was, and what was not, admissible as evidence. The first questions put to him by *Mr Hemmerde* were concerned with the position of the body, the nature of the wounds and the progress of *rigor mortis*. Witness was then led on to describe the nature and direction of the bloodstains on the walls and furniture in the parlour, which were matters of paramount importance to the Prosecution's case.

Mr Hemmerde inquired whether this witness could form an opinion as to where the deceased was at the time the first blow was struck.

'Yes; if you take these [blood-marks] and concentrate them upon a central position, they concentrate fairly definitely in front of the chair.'

'The chair by the side of the fire?'

'The armchair on which is the violin-case.'

[1] Mr Justice Wright in his address to the jury.

234

'. . . She was standing somewhere near the fireplace?'

'I think it is a little too low for standing.'

'What do you deduce from that?'

'It is suggested to my mind that she had been sitting on that chair, with the head a little forward and turned slightly to the left as if talking to someone.'[1]

'What about the violin-case—would not that be in the way?'

'No, the violin-case would not be in the way if she sat in the chair. I sat in the chair and it did not interfere—if she was sitting on the front of the chair. . . . If you put the head in that position, and imagine it in that position as the source of the blood, the blood goes exactly in every direction and fits in with the appearances found.'

Presently Mr. Hemmerde asked the witness if he had seen the mackintosh. He replied in the affirmative and said that it was 'partly burned on the lower right front'. In answer to the Judge he added:

'The burning is upon the right side; the bloodstains are all over it . . . inside and outside.'

The Judge: 'There were bloodstains also on the right side?'

'Yes, my lord.'

To further questions from his lordship and Mr Hemmerde, witness said that the bloodstains on the left sleeve were very characteristic.

The Judge: 'The projected blood on the left sleeve was on the outside?'

'Yes, my lord, and in this direction too. That is rather important, I think.'

'What does that projection shew?'

'Either that there had been a spurting of blood, or a splashing of blood, in front, presumably when somebody had it on.'

Mr Hemmerde: 'Supposing that someone had been wearing it?'

'The source of the blood was from the front, and if anybody was wearing it, then the spurt of the blood from the front comes in this same direction.'[2]

'Looking at that, the suggestion has been made that the

---

[1] Or glancing towards the door at the sound of her husband's approach.

[2] i.e. in the same direction as had the blood on the walls and other objects.

deceased might have thrown it over her shoulders to go to the door, and then to have been, I suppose, struck down when she had it on?'

'. . . There was no suggestion from the appearance that that had been the case.'

In addition to this, there was, as the witness pointed out, a bloodstain on the *inside of the sleeve* such as might have been made by the withdrawal of the murderer's hand had he been wearing the mackintosh when he committed the crime and then taken it off.

Mr Oliver (cross-examining): 'You see the handle of the gas-fire is on the right-hand side, and just above is the gas-light: suppose a woman went into that room, lit the gas and then lit the fire, she would have to stoop down, would she not?'

'Presumably, yes.'

'If she did that with her back towards the doorway, and someone was on her right-hand side, he would be in a position to strike her as she rose?'

'He would.'

'And her head might well be in the very position in which you put it?'

'Exactly.'

Counsel went on to suggest that if the deceased had been sitting in the armchair, as witness had described, her body would have prevented the blood from falling on the violin-case. 'Would you tell me how the bloodstains got on the violin-case?' he asked.

'I have said she would be leaning forward. . . . There is a direct line open between her head and those blood patches. It can be seen to be falling.'

'She was struck in front?'

'Yes; the blood goes up.'

'. . . Whether clothed or naked, it would be necessary, would it not, in all commonsense, that many splashes of blood would fall upon the assailant? . . . When the blood vessels are broken, as in this case, the splashes fly out, do they not?'

'Yes.'

'Would you not agree that it is almost certain that the assailant would have blood upon his face and clothes?'

'On his left hand I think he would.'

'What about his right?'

'. . . You do not find the blood so much on the hand that holds the weapon.'

'Not when blow after blow is delivered?'

'No. It is done by the person's getting hold of the victim by the hair; there would be a great deal of blood upon the left hand and not upon the right.'

'The last blows being probably struck with the head on the ground, there would be blood upon his feet and the lower part of his legs for certain?'

'I should expect that.'

'So that the mackintosh would . . . leave the legs from the knees downwards exposed to the blood?'

'Yes.'

'. . . Would you agree that it would be almost certain the assailant would have blood under the finger-nails?'

'Not necessarily. Touching things, unless you scrape the things, you do not get blood under the nails.'

The absence of any signs that the assailant had washed any-where in the house and what deductions, if any, could be drawn from the progress of *rigor mortis* were gone into at con-siderable length. Asked how he would describe the victim's state of health, Professor MacFall replied that she was 'a weak woman; a feeble woman'.

Mr Oliver had opened his cross-examination of the Pro-fessor by taking up the question of the accused's 'abnormal behaviour' with which Mr Hemmerde had completed his ex-amination in chief.[1] We quote it here, however, as the con-cluding portion of Professor MacFall's evidence on account of its outstanding importance with regard to our question: '*Why was Julia Wallace killed?*'

Mr Oliver: 'I want to begin with the last bit of your evidence.'

Professor MacFall (producing a diagram) : 'May I put in this before that? You have not had the position of these blows put in, and I have a note I made at the post-mortem shewing the position.'

The Judge: 'You have a sketch?'

[1] *See* pages 209–10.

'Yes, my lord. . . . It shews the position after the hair is removed and the head shaved. It shews the nature of the cuts.'

Mr Oliver: '. . . How can these indicate who did it?'

'I have a great reason for this myself.'

'Can you give me, quite shortly, what your reason is?'

'I can. *I formed an idea of the mental condition of the person who committed this crime. I have seen crimes, many of them of this kind, and know what the mental condition is. I know this was not an ordinary case of assault or serious injury. It was a case of frenzy.*'

The Judge: 'We may have already formed that opinion. When blows are struck by anyone, that probably does produce frenzy, but that is a matter for the jury.'

Mr Oliver: 'With reference to the last matter, you have noticed that my client has been under medical observation as to his mental condition ever since his arrest?'

'I know that he will have been.'

'If there is anything to be said about his mental condition, there are people competent to say so who have lived with him?'

'Yes—I do not wish to express any opinion.'

One of the great arts of advocacy is to know precisely when to *stop* putting questions to a witness.[1] Professor MacFall's answer to the last question was exceedingly cautious, and Mr Oliver would probably have been wise to pursue the matter no further. But he failed to exercise this restraint and the answers he received to his next questions were by no means helpful to his case; in fact they probably influenced the jury in arriving at their verdict more than any other single factor in the evidence.

Mr Oliver: '*If this is the work of a maniac, and he is a sane man, he did not do it—is that right?*'

'*He may be sane now.*'

'*If he has been sane all his life, and is sane now, it would be some momentary frenzy?*'

'*The mind is very peculiar.*'

'*It is a rash suggestion, is it not?*'

'*Not in the slightest. I have seen this sort of thing before—exactly the same thing.*'

[1] 'The danger which seems to have an irresistible fascination for most cross-examiners is that of the one question too many.'—Mr Justice Hilbery.

'*Rash to suggest in a murder case, I suggest to you?*'

'*I do not suggest who did it at all.*'

'*The fact that a man has been sane for fifty-two years, and has been sane while in custody for the last three months, would rather tend to prove that he has always been sane, would it not?*'

'*No, not necessarily.*'

'*Not necessarily?*'

'*No; we know very little about the private lives of people or their thoughts.*'

'*Let us go back; you have told the jury that you were much struck with his demeanour. You noticed it at the time, and were very much struck with his callous demeanour?*'

'*I was.*'

'*Why did you not say so at the police court?*'

'*Because I was not asked.*'

At last Counsel desisted; but there could be only one impression left on the minds of the jury: that Professor MacFall, a figure of great renown in the realm of medicine, of vast experience of criminal cases and of human nature, knew that a man who had been sane all his life could murder like a maniac without being aroused to any flaming passion, and could plan such a crime as this one without the incentive of pecuniary, or any other obvious form of, gain.

2

Professor Roberts, the Liverpool City Analyst, in reply to *Mr Hemmerde* stated that the mackintosh was 'extensively and heavily bloodstained, both inside and outside'. He did not think an assailant wearing it when striking those blows would contract much blood upon his hands, legs or other parts of his person. There were stains in the centre of the hearthrug such as could have been made by the assailant wiping his feet and hands upon it. There were fragments of burned mackintosh near the fire, and nowhere else in the house. The burns on the side of the skirt had been made by contact with that fire.

Mr Oliver (cross-examining): 'A man who was not anxious

239

to leave his boot-prints in blood about the house might have wiped his boots on the hearthrug might he not?'

'Yes.'

'Your suggestion is not confined to naked feet?'

'No.'

Professor Roberts had found no bloodstains on the suit of clothes which Wallace had been wearing when he left the house for Menlove Gardens, none on the cash-box or on an American $1-bill found in it. The smudge of blood across the inmost of the four folded £1-notes in Julia's bedroom had, he believed, been made by her assassin.

Mr Hemmerde: 'The blood extended over the note?'

'Yes; it extended right the way up to the top. It is a smear which might be caused if you had blood on your thumb and you opened them like that.' Witness went through the motions of opening and counting the bundle.

'The suggestion has been today that somebody by picking them up, might have put blood on them—anybody who had blood on their hands, picking them up from the jar on the mantelpiece; you heard that?'

'Yes, but they did not put this blood on them.'

Under cross-examination, however, witness admitted that the mark might have been made 'by a man with a bloody finger', but added that, if so, 'he ought to have seen it'.

The police denied having touched the notes, but Wallace had stated that he had felt his wife's pulse when he discovered her lying dead, and P.C. Williams said that he had seen him extract the notes from the receptacle. So the blood *might* have got there by that means.

Professor MacFall was at first equally positive that the blood-clot on the lavatory pan must have been dropped there by the murderer, but he, too, under cross-examination by Mr Oliver, was compelled to admit that it might just as easily have been dropped there by one of the investigators. So here were further 'loopholes and doubts'.

In his closing speech for the Crown, therefore, *Mr Hemmerde* said: 'Never mind about the clot of blood upstairs. Never mind about any fine points about the notes. Can you believe that anyone would have ever committed such a crime merely for gain—the small gains in a Prudential agent's house?'

Mr Oliver sought to shew, quoting the evidence of Mr Crewe, that 'there might be expected to be anything between £20 and £30, or, if it was a monthly collection, £80 to £100 in cash,' adding that the Prosecution 'tries to escape that by saying that Mr Crewe is a friend of Wallace. . . . What was to prevent them calling the Prudential, with their books, to prove this thing properly? They have got the power. Instead of that he calls a witness[1] who gives you the figures; I call Wallace who corroborates them.'

It is unlikely that the company's books would have provided information very different from the evidence of Mr Crewe, and this, though corroborated by Wallace himself, was not entirely favourable to his cause. Mr Crewe told the Court that Wallace paid in his collections to the district office every Wednesday or Thursday—usually Wednesday—and 'that anyone who knew him, or knew about his habits or employment, might expect him to have the bulk of his cash by Tuesday night'. But anyone who knew Wallace, and his habits or employment, might also be presumed to know that his collections *in the middle of the month* were slight and that *his principal collection was made in the last week*. For instance in the week culminating in the murder Wallace's collection amounted to £14 out of which he had paid £10 in Sick Benefits, thus leaving him with only £4 in hand—the sum which, he alleged, was missing from the cash-box.[2]

3

An incident which had first emerged during the police court proceedings received further publicity at the trial through the evidence of *Mr Beattie* and *Mr Caird*. It told against the accused.

At about 10.20 p.m. on 22nd January these two members had left the chess club and were awaiting their homeward tram

[1] Mr Crewe.
[2] And, incidentally, the amount found in the ornament upstairs. Asked if he usually kept money there, Wallace said he did, for current expenses, and of course there was no means of disproving this assertion.

and apparently discussing the crime. Suddenly Mr Caird uttered the warning: 'Mr Beattie, he is here.' And, stated Mr Beattie in his evidence, 'I saw the accused standing there.'

The Judge: 'You went to him, I suppose?'

'We recognized one another, and then he said: "Oh, that telephone message—can you remember definitely what time you actually received it?" I said: "Well, seven or shortly after." His reply was: "Can't you get it a bit nearer than that?" I said: "I'm sorry, but I can't." He said: "Well, it is important to me, and I should like to know if you can get nearer to it than that." I said: "I'm sorry, I can't." '

Mr Hemmerde: 'After you said you could not help him there, what did he say next? Did he say where he had come from?'

'Yes; he said: "I have just left the police; they have cleared me." '

'What did you say to that?'

'I said: "I am very pleased to hear it, very pleased." '

Detective-Superintendent Moore, on the subject of this same incident, stated in evidence that on the following day—23rd January—he had seen the accused at the Bridewell. 'I asked him: "You saw Mr Beattie of the chess club last night?" The accused agreed that he had. When I asked the accused why he had told Mr Beattie that the police had cleared him, and why he had remarked to Mr Beattie that the time of the receipt of the telephone message was important to him, he replied: "I had an idea—we all have ideas. It was indiscreet of me." He said he could not explain any further.'

4

If the Defence have reason to believe that local opinion may be prejudiced against an accused person, a submission can be made to have the case tried before another Court. Similarly, at the close of the case for the Prosecution, the Defence can submit that there is no case for it to answer. In the Wallace case it is significant that neither of these submissions was made.

Mr Hemmerde was scrupulously fair in his handling of the

case for the Crown. As Recorder of Liverpool he himself presided over a criminal court and had had ample experience of judging the guilt or innocence of accused persons. There was never any doubt that in this case the opinion he formed was adverse to the prisoner. That opinion may to some extent have been based on material supplied by the police which was inadmissible as evidence. What that material may have been will presently be considered.

It was not Professor MacFall's function to do more than tender his evidence in accordance with the facts. It was only the injudicious questions put to him by Counsel for the Defence which drew forth replies that indicated he possessed medical knowledge which convinced him of the prisoner's guilt.

Perhaps the most difficult decision the Defence has to take is whether or not to place the accused person in the witness-box. If they do not, it may provoke an adverse comment from the Judge and an assumption by the jury that there is something to conceal; if they do, the result may be even more detrimental to his cause. Everyone knows that juries are sworn to find their verdicts on the evidence before them, and many conclude that this is limited to the spoken word. But demeanour may convey as much as utterance. So long as the prisoner stays silent and immobile in the dock his personality remains hidden from the Court, but the moment he enters the witness-box it is revealed.

Ronald Light, of the Green Bicycle mystery, and Mrs Alma Rattenbury, of the Villa Madeira murder, were both under the gravest suspicion, and both had to face rigorous cross-examinations; yet the demeanour of both expressed candour and truth, and they were acquitted. On the other hand the demeanour of another insurance agent on trial for murder, F. H. Seddon, although his evidence reads well—as does Wallace's—was such that it gave the lie to all his utterances.[1] The same criterion must be applied to Wallace himself. Whether the verdict would have been any different had he not gone into the witness-box is a moot point, but, having done so, there can be no doubt that he created an unfavourable impression with the jury.

It has been claimed by some that Mr Justice Wright

[1] See *The Trial of Frederick Henry Seddon* in the *Notable British Trials* series.

summed up in favour of Wallace. The Lords of Appeal, however, decided that he had done so 'with complete fairness and
accuracy'.

'You have had very forcible speeches from Counsel on both
sides,' he told the jury, 'and they have put before you in very
great detail their view of the evidence in the case. . . . The
considerations have been very fully laid before you. *You* are the
judges of the facts. *I* am not the judge of the facts at all. But it is
regular and usual, especially in these cases, for the Judge to
make some survey of the evidence which has been laid before
the jury, because that may help the jury, although they are the
judges of the facts. . . . If I omit or overstress any matter contrary to your view it is your view which is the dominant view
in this case.'

His lordship's speech lasted seven hours. At the end of one
hour those ten men and two women whom he had been
addressing returned a verdict of *Guilty*.

The day of Wallace's conviction was 25th April 1931, and
on that date a year later he wrote:

'I seemed to see myself standing erect in the dock. I was
all ready to step out into the street the instant, as I expected,
the verdict Not Guilty was given. . . . I recall it all—the grin
on the face of the prison officer who led me to the dock as
he noticed me hat in hand. And his remark: "Optimistic,
eh?" . . . Again I saw myself looking for the exit from the
dock into the well of the Court, and thinking that I would
take a taxi from the rank outside the building. I felt once
more the hush that descends on the Court as the Clerk of
Assize rose to ask the foreman of the jury for the verdict. . . .'

That little picture, etched by his own pen, illustrates his
bearing in the dock throughout the proceedings: his self-
confidence; his faint, but unmistakable, air of condescension
and superciliousness.

13

The Accused

'The fault, dear Brutus, lies not in our stars,
But in ourselves, that we are underlings.'[1]

I

THE lives of men who have achieved fame from small beginnings remind us, whatever their sphere, how various were the reasons, impulses and influences which impelled and sustained them along the arduous and hazardous roads they trod; how wide their range and how, often, conflicting: some worthy, others unworthy—for the element of vanity is never absent in human affairs.

When the man's environment and his chances of success are reasonably good, the flame of his genius burns the more brightly as he surmounts each impediment in his path. But when his environment hampers his genius, as do chains a prisoner's limbs, when he is harassed by frustrations, he may resort to any expedient to attain his ends. Much depends upon the character of that man; and much of a man's character depends upon his physical condition and spiritual inspiration.

Wallace's lack of education and of an established background certainly impeded the development of such genius as he possessed. Scrutinizing such records as there are of his life from his fourteenth to his thirty-third year, it strikes one that, although all were spent in commercial employment he never remained in the service of any one firm for any length of time. We do not know whether he went from one situation to another because he grew dissatisfied with each in turn, or because each of his employers in turn grew dissatisfied with him. We have

[1] *Julius Caesar*, Act I, Scene 2.

only his word for it that illness was the cause of his leaving India, although we do know that it was illness—and very grave illness—which brought him back to England from Shanghai in 1907.

Mr Rowland takes the view that Wallace's mind was 'rather untidy and undisciplined', and reaches the conclusion that the range of his interests was 'wide but superficial'. Mr Veale, on the other hand, considers that Wallace was 'industrious, methodical, studious and enterprising'. Is it not possible that he possessed a curious ambivalence which manifested itself in complex and diversified impulses at various periods in his career; that his intellectual capacity fluctuated with the fluctuations of his disease? It certainly seems to have been his misfortune to emanate something which repelled those whose good opinion he sought to win, and he could not forgive them their recoil from him. In the pages of *John Bull* he uses the phrase, 'my ill-starred life'. It would seem to be apposite.

One is not in a position to make any authoritative statement as to why he lost his post at Harrogate, but the evidence now unearthed points to the probability that he lost it because he had lost the confidence of his employers, and it is suggested that this was the result of financial embarrassment. If so, he certainly learned a sharp lesson; never again did he incur debts; on the contrary, he grew parsimonious to a degree, except for certain personal indulgences.

Counsel for the Crown (to Detective-Sergeant Bailey): 'Could you say, was Mrs Wallace very well dressed?'

'I should say she was very poorly dressed.' . . .

Counsel for the Defence: 'You have been asked whether this woman was poorly dressed, and you said she was?'

'Yes.'

'Did you know that this man had a banking account?'

Counsel for the Crown: 'We do not dispute that he had one.'

The Judge (to Counsel for the Crown): 'Will you tell the jury that it was in credit to the extent of £152?'

'Yes, my lord, we agree to that.'

The jury could see that the quality of the accused's own clothes was good, and they were aware that his earnings averaged some £6 a week—a sum equivalent to thrice that amount today—and he had no one to support except Julia and himself. The Prosecution—and also the Defence—knew that throughout the seventeen years of her life in Liverpool Julia Wallace had worn the garments she had bought before her marriage had taken place; they knew that the people of Anfield used to comment upon her 'old-fashioned and untidy appearance', and had noticed her increasing lethargy and look of exhaustion. They knew that the laboratory at 29 Wolverton Street contained a microscope—a most expensive article of equipment. They knew that Wallace had bought a violin for his own diversion, and that, too, had not been cheap. They knew that he would walk miles to save a tram fare and that he rarely, if ever, offered so much as a cup of coffee to his fellow-members of the chess club; that he gave the impression of being very abstemious, yet, though 'he did not drink to excess', he was by no means impartial to whisky consumed in the seclusion of his own house.

2

Of the many who have written about the Wallace case, it is possible to discover only three or four who seem to have had any inkling as to why Wallace referred to his life as 'ill-starred'. One of these is Mr Veale, who says:

'It may be recalled that he left India, and later Shanghai, owing to ill-health. Did he continue to suffer from ill-health? He died two years after the trial. *His medical history might be illuminating.*'[1]

Mr Veale is guarded; Miss L. Dorothy Sayers, one of the earliest writers on the case, is more positive.

'On February 26th, 1933 [*she says*],[2] Wallace died of cancer of the kidneys. It is, of course, well known that diseases affecting these organs produces very remarkable

[1] Author's italics.
[2] *The Anatomy of Murder* (Published 1936).

and deleterious[1] changes in a person's character, but whether the trouble had already begun in 1931,[2] and if so whether it could have resulted in so strange a madness, with such a combination of cunning and bestial ferocity as the murderer of Julia Wallace displayed, is a matter for physicians to judge. So far as can be seen Wallace shewed no signs of mental or spiritual deterioration either before or after the crime.'

Had Miss Sayers forgotten Professor MacFall's evidence?—
'*I have formed an idea of the mental condition of the person who committed this crime. I have seen crimes, many of them of this kind, and know what the mental condition is. I know it was not a case of ordinary assault or serious injury. It was a case of frenzy. . . . He may be sane now. . . . The mind is very peculiar.*'

Of more recent writers on the case Mr Rowland also asserts that Wallace 'was suffering from cancer of the kidneys, and from this he died on February 26th, 1933', but he evidently senses that there is something else to be discovered for he goes on to say:

'The very absence of apparent motive is, in fact, one of the points which make me doubt whether any of those who have written about the case have altogether hit off the psychological make-up of the people concerned. That there must be some matters which have hitherto escaped detection seems to be quite beyond doubt.'[3]

Since Mr Rowland devoted a whole book to the case it is surprising that he made no effort to detect what those matters were. This is something which Mr Nigel Morland claims to have done, and he writes:

'My own investigations reveal that far from death being caused by cancer of the kidneys, he actually died of cancer

---

[1] The effects are not necessarily deleterious. Sometimes they alter the individual's character for the better, sweetening it to a submissiveness which borders on saintliness.

[2] As we have seen, Wallace began to suffer from kidney trouble before 1907, a fact of which Miss Sayers would seem to have been unaware.

[3] *Op. cit.*

of the throat. This cancerous condition had also affected the lung (more correctly, the condition is called cancer of the *bronchus*). There is no pain in the early stages, and there was little evidence of disease, except for shortness of breath and other manifestations.'[1]

One wonders what sort of investigations Mr Morland can have made, for the truth is that William Herbert Wallace did not die of cancer of the throat, or of the *bronchus*, or even of the kidneys. His death took place at the Clatterbridge Hospital, Bebington, Cheshire, on 26th February 1933, and the column, *Cause of Death*, in his Death Certificate contains the following entry:

> 1 *a.* Uraemia
>   *b.* Pyelonephritis.
>   *c.* Left kidney removed 30 years ago.
> *Post-mortem* Certified by Elizabeth Lansdown, M.R.C.S.

Commenting on this at the request of the present writer a prominent Harley Street surgeon observes:

> 'Pyelonephritis is inflammation of the kidney and pelvis of the kidney. . . . It is quite possible for a man to have a low grade type of fever with infected kidneys which would produce emaciation and mental changes. The incessant pyrexia from which he must have been suffering . . . *might quite easily increase his mental alertness and make him a pervert or a genius.*[2]
> 'Wallace certainly did not die of cancer, because the manifestations of cancer would have been widespread in his particular case and would have been noticed *post-mortem*.'

3

When Wallace left hospital in 1928 he knew that the disease had attacked his remaining kidney and that he had, at

---

[1] *Op. cit.* On December 16th, 1958, Lord Birkett, in his *Postscript* to a B.B.C. reconstruction of the case in the Home Service, also stated that the cause of Wallace's death was cancer.

[2] Author's italics.

most, only a very few years to live. It was then that the need to marshal his thoughts prompted him to begin his diary. He was always concerned with facts, and from then until the eve of the telephone message—18th January 1931—he entered into it notes as to his physical symptoms, Julia's state of health, his movements, and sometimes his thoughts and reflections. No self-pity flowed into its pages; he analysed himself with the same detachment as he analysed all else.

His mental and physical energy had always been considerable. It now grew feverish. Where he had previously walked to save a tram fare, now he walked because he must keep moving. His mind attained an abnormal vigour and perceptiveness; never before had he craved so intensely to do something impressive, and that craving culminated in his determination to master the violin. It was an astonishing achievement that, at the age of fifty-one, in a matter of a few months, and with no more than some half-dozen lessons from an amateur, he was able to play sonatas by Mozart and Beethoven.

He, who had previously invited no one to his house at Wolverton Street, now invited Mr Crewe and Mr Caird—separately—during that winter of 1929–30 to come and hear him play the violin. Both were suitably impressed, and both within their respective orbits commented on the remarkable nature of such an accomplishment in a man of fifty-one who had never before touched any musical instrument. At the office, as at the chess club, Wallace found himself regarded with a new respect which could not fail to afford him secret elation and stimulate his starved ego.

The religious instinct which had supported and consoled his wife through all her trials and tribulations had probably been for long a subject of academic interest to him. As a doomed man it is not surprising that the question of an after-life, in which Julia so implicitly believed, should have attained a new significance for him, and on *13th February 1929* we find him noting in his diary:

'On the way home with ——[1] had a discussion on religion. I find he is, like myself, indifferent to the dogmas and

[1] The name is omitted in published versions of the diary.

rituals of the churches and chapels, and agrees that, if there is a hereafter, the man without any so-called religious beliefs, and a non-church attender, but who lives a decent life, and who abstains from telling lies, or cheating, or acts of meanness, and who honestly tries to do good, has as much chance of getting there as the professed Christian who attends his place of worship regularly.'

Little more than a month later he listened to Ibsen's play *The Master Builder* over the radio. As many know, this great drama was based upon Ibsen's own life, and was classified by James Agate as a play 'with a groundfloor of realism and a symbolist upper storey'. It is the story of a builder of soaring genius and ambition, but lacking both the architectural qualifications and the capital to satisfy either. He married a devoted wife and connives at the destruction by fire of her family home, which constitutes her spiritual habitation here on earth. Cutting up its beautiful grounds into building plots he converts it into a residential estate, thereby laying the foundations of his fame and fortune as a Master Builder. In the process he repudiates both God and his conscience. But eventually he becomes tormented by the knowledge that his triumph has been barren because it has been achieved by the destruction of all his wife held most dear, and by the stifling of her love. As a form of recompense he throws all his genius into building her a new house, but in an agony of despair realizes that this can never form a real home or compensate and console her for all she has lost, or repair the injury he has done her. With a mind distraught he exposes himself to the ordeal he most dreads, his terror of heights, and climbing to the top of the tower which crowns the house, he falls from it to his death.

This intense drama made an extraordinary impression upon Wallace, who perhaps heard in the passionate desperation of the Master Builder's words, and the haunting resignation in those of Mrs Solness, his wife, the echo of his own and Julia's story; for had he not, like Solness, riven the home which Julia loved from her, and all that she possessed, in order to further his own ends? Had he not stifled her life and made it the void it was—and to what purpose? Only to meet with failure.

He thus recorded the occasion in his diary:

'*20th March 1929*. Listened in to *The Master Builder* by Ibsen. This is a fine thing, and shews clearly how a man may build up a fine career, and, as the world has it, be a great success, and yet in his own mind feel that he has been an utter failure, and how ghastly a mistake he has made to sacrifice love and the deeper comforts of life in order to achieve success. *Curious that Julia did not appreciate this play! I am sure she did not grasp the inner significance or real meaning of the play.*[1]

One wonders if, perhaps, Julia *did* grasp its significance, and gallantly concealed the fact from him.

Less than three months after he had made that entry he was again in hospital. Now he knew that the fatal disease was rapidly gaining ground; now he knew that, although the end might not come for another year or two, his life hung by a thread which at any moment might snap. His feverish energy had greatly abated and given place to a state of abstraction. He shewed indifference towards his former interests, except his violin-playing. He spent a considerable portion of his leisure reading in the public library in Breck Road, and although his attendance at the chess club had grown irregular, he would sit at the table in the living-room of 29 Wolverton Street absorbed in some chess problem while Julia did her mending. Three months and six days before her murder he made the following entry in his diary:

'*26th October 1930*. No one has ever had any knowledge of a previous existence. If I previously existed as a thinking organism I probably argued much as I do now, and now that I am here I recognize clearly that immortality means absolutely nothing to me. Any individuality I possessed formerly has gone. So, too, when I pass out of this existence, individual immortality is meaningless unless I am able to retain something of my present; and the fact that my previous existence is now meaningless argues that the next

[1] Author's italics.

existence has also no meaning for me. So why worry about a life hereafter which for me has no meaning?'[1]

There is another entry in the diary for that year which possesses some interest:

'*6th November 1930*. The tournaments [chess] are now up, and I see I am in Class Three. I suppose I could play better, but I feel it is too much like hard work to go in for chess wholeheartedly: hence my lack of practice keeps me in a state of mediocrity—good enough for a nice game, but not good enough for really first class play.'

We have no clue to Wallace's state of mind as Christmas came and went, and the bells of Holy Trinity Church rang in the New Year, 1931, but most certainly 'the wheel of fate was turning, turning. . . .' Then come the two final entries before the tragedy.

'*Saturday, 17th January 1931*. Had a slight attack of 'flu all day and did not do my usual collection. Prevention is better than cure. Steeped my feet in mustard and hot water, followed by a cupful of whisky and hot water.'

If he committed the crime, its design must have already been worked out in his mind when he wrote those words, and only forty-eight hours later he would put through that fateful telephone call. He was to tell the Court that he had given his wife a full account of that mysterious message; that he had discussed with her as to whether or not he should keep the appoint-

[1] Wallace is evidently confusing the doctrine of immortality with that of reincarnation—which forms no part of the Christian faith. It is curious that the diary contains no reference to Stoicism, since after the quashing of his conviction he was to create the illusion that he was a disciple of that philosophy, and to claim that he had modelled his conduct on the *Meditations of Marcus Aurelius*, in the teachings of which he had 'steeped himself since boyhood'. 'To me,' he wrote, 'it is the Golden Book among all books . . . I craved for it in my condemned cell—more than for food. By an unfortunate series of circumstances it was the only book I wanted that I was unable to obtain during the month I lay under sentence of death.' The self-pity, however, which is the most distinguishing feature of his *Life Story* is hardly consistent with the doctrine of the Stoics, and it is here suggested that he only adopted this profession of Stoicism after his trial in order to erase the impression which the evidence as to his callousness had created during it.

ment vicariously made with the unknown Qualtrough; he even suggested that she had encouraged him to do so.

If that were so, Mr Hemmerde asked him, how did it come about that the parlour had been prepared for an evening's music? Wallace replied that it often remained in that state from one musical evening to the next.

'With the piano open?' asked Counsel incredulously.

Julia had been a musical woman; Wallace himself was a musical man; the piano was an excellent instrument—perhaps the one which Julia had had in her house at Harrogate—and it was well cared for. Yet Wallace expected the Court to believe that in the depth of winter, and in an unheated room, it was quite normal for them to leave the piano open day and night for, perhaps, several days—as had been done apparently over that week-end, with the music on the music-rest, and his violin ready to hand across the arms of the chair.

His diary lay in front of Mr Hemmerde, with that final entry made before the crime.

'*Sunday, 18th January 1931*. Mustard worked wonderfully. . . . It is unusual to let Sunday go by without some practice on my violin.'

On the Saturday and Sunday, then, there had been no music; on Monday, 19th, Wallace had left home soon after tea and by 7.45 was seated opposite his opponent at the chess tournament—so there had been no music on that evening either. Next night, when the police examined that parlour with specially powerful lamps and other equipment, they could discover nothing to suggest that the piano had stood open, with the two music-scores in place, and the violin across the arms of the chair, for four full days; on the contrary, the whole room had the aspect of having been got ready very recently indeed.

When they looked at the crockery, stacked unwashed on the draining-board of the scullery sink, at the sugar-bowl and plate left behind in the living-room, at the work-basket beside Julia's chair with the threaded needle piercing the mending protruding from it and the thimble lying on top, they could not escape the conclusion, which these so forcibly suggested, that Julia had been darning beside the fire when her husband returned from Clubmoor that evening; that she put aside her work to get ready the tea; that, when this was over, he bade her prepare the parlour for music; that while she went to do his bidding he betook himself upstairs to do what he had to do; that after hearing the door close behind the milk-boy he had softly descended, and soundlessly entered the parlour on his naked feet. As soon as she was conscious of his presence she had instinctively turned her head to the left—'as though speaking to someone'—and then, before she had time to move or exclaim, he had struck her down with the iron bar he was carrying in his hand.

14

Why was Julia Wallace Killed?

'This man's metallic: at a sudden blow
His soul rings hard. I cannot lay my palm,
Trembling with life, upon that jointed brass.
I shudder at the cold, unanswering touch.'[1]

I

CAN one see absolutely eye to eye with James Agate that
the murder of Julia Wallace was 'planned with extreme
care and extraordinary imagination'? There was certainly 'extreme care', and the time-factor was concocted with
mathematical exactitude: but 'imagination' was either singularly lacking, or singularly over-elaborated when the plan was
put into effect.

The Menlove Gardens alibi would have been far more
convincing had Wallace been less persistent in his inquiries.
And as the police went from room to room at 29 Wolverton
Street, Liverpool, viewing the absurd smashing of the cupboard
door in the living-room and similar incongruities, such as
Julia's undisturbed bedroom with the light burning invitingly in
it, the bits of jewellery on the dressing-table and the money in the
ornament on the mantelpiece, and then observed how the bed
had been tumbled in the otherwise undisordered spare-room,
they saw in it all not the work of a robber who had intruded,
but of someone who was trying to create that impression.

Precisely the same impression had been gained by the
police as they went from room to room of 14 Norfolk Street,
London, in 1840. And that impression had proved correct.
In both cases there had been a curious absence of bloodstains
anywhere except in the immediate proximity of the victim, and

[1] *Middlemarch*—George Eliot.

256

Barrall's Photo Press News

WILLIAM HERBERT WALLACE

Leaving the court of Criminal Appeal after the quashing of his
conviction. Joseph Edwin Wallace is on the left.

in neither had there been any indication as to where the assassin had washed or what he had used to dry himself. In both a single, well-directed and powerful assault had caused instant death. In the first case the murderer had been a vigorous young man who had killed his victim with one slash of a knife and turned his back upon him; in the second a brain and hand no less cool and steady had killed the victim with a single blow on the temple, and then had delivered ten subsequent blows with all the ferocity of sudden frenzy.

Inquiry into Wallace's medical history revealed that he was in the final stages of a disease which might render him liable to just such sudden frenzy, but this could not be used in evidence against him. All that did emerge in Court came from the lips of Professor Macfall under cross-examination by Counsel for the Defence.

At the gallows' foot Courvoisier confessed how he had committed his crime and afterwards washed at the sink. Professor Roberts told the Court that Julia's murderer had evidently wiped the bloodstains from his feet, legs and hands, and from the weapon, on the hearthrug. But this would not be enough: he would have to *wash* as well. For this purpose all he had to do was to run some cold water into the enamel basin in the scullery and empty it afterwards in the backyard; then sluice out the basin and do the same. If he had read the case of Lizzie Borden he would know that there was evidence to suggest that the murderer had used *paper* with which to dry. It was thick paper, and its remains were discovered in the kitchen stove. If Julia's assassin improved on this by using tissue or toilet paper, all traces of it would have been destroyed in the living-room fire.

2

Mr John van Druten, playwright and student of criminal psychology, poses the questions:

'Who killed Julia Wallace so brutally and senselessly? Who was the mysterious stranger, using the name of

Qualtrough, who made the telephone call that took Wallace from his home that night? Was it, as argued, Wallace himself, carefully planning an alibi?

'If it was, what is the explanation of the items in Wallace's diary after he had been acquitted [*sic*], items in which he protested love and affection for his dead wife? Could these, if they were not genuine, have been the ultimate extreme of hypocrisy?

'To what degree will the power of rationalization extend? Could Wallace be guilty, yet manage to deny the knowledge or admission of his guilt even to himself? It seems improbable, impossible, but so do the fantasies, the heaping inventions, of psychopathic liars.'[1]

The workings of the mind are always mysterious and often unaccountable—and what mental abnormalities may not possess a man of ingenuity and ambition, whose ego has been starved, whose hopes have been thwarted, whose career has ended in failure, whose system is poisoned with disease, and who knows that death is round the corner?

We know that all the money Wallace possessed at the time of his wife's death—apart from his salary—was £152 in the bank; and so completely had Julia's property vanished that he told the Court he was unaware that she had £90 in a savings' bank.

It is sometimes easier to forgive those who injure us than those we have injured. Did Wallace, therefore, *hate* Julia because of the injury he had done her in dragging her down with him in his fall from the Olympus of Harrogate? And as her 'energy and vivaciousness' wilted and died, and she became a sick and feeble shadow of her former self, did she exist as a torturing reminder of what might have been?

On the other hand she had no relatives, no friends, and had become so weak and helpless that for the past nine months it had been necessary to engage Mrs Draper to clean the house once a week. Did Wallace, then, perhaps *love* Julia and kill her because he decided that death by one swift blow, before she ever knew what was happening, was better than the

[1] *The Widening Circle*—John van Druten (Heinemann, 1957).

indigent existence which must inevitably be hers as soon as the tenuous thread of his own life snapped?

We know so little of the thoughts of others. As Professor Theodore Lessing has written: 'We do not even know if, when animals tear each other to pieces, they do not experience a certain sensual pleasure, so that when the wolf strangles the lamb one can say equally well, "he loves lambs" as that "he hates lambs".'

3

'The fantasies, the heaping inventions, of psychopathic liars'—do we not perhaps catch an echo of them in some of Wallace's writings?

While still living at 29 Wolverton Street he entered in his diary, which he resumed:

'6th October 1931. I cannot disguise from myself that I am dreadfully nervous about entering the house after dark. I suppose it is because my nerves are all so shattered after this ordeal, and this, together with the recurring fits of grief and anguish over my dear Julia's end, makes me horribly depressed and apprehensive. . . . Left to myself I am for ever trying to visualize what really happened. Although I am convinced ——[1] killed her, yet it is difficult to get proof. It would be a great relief if he could only be caught and the foul murder brought home to him. . . .'

Can the process of rationalization be extended to such a degree that the perpetrator of a crime can even attribute his guilt to somebody else? It is a phenomenon not unknown to psychiatrists.

The hostile attitude of Wallace's former clients in Clubmoor led the Prudential to give him a compassionate post in their main office, but the ostracism to which he was subjected by his colleagues compelled him to resign and seek refuge outside Liverpool. He took a cottage at Bromborough, on the

[1] Name suppressed in the published edition.

Cheshire side of the Mersey, and here he existed shunned and boycotted by his former acquaintances, whom he had the bitterness of observing crossing roads to avoid him, or staring intently into shop windows as soon as he appeared. And all the time he knew that the sands of his life were running out.

4

In one of his effusions for the Press Wallace wrote the following:

'Now let me say this:
'*I know the murderer!*
'In the porch of the front door of this lonely house of mine I have fitted an electric switch and lamp. They are not there for the convenience of friendly visitors. . . . These things have been placed there to safeguard my life. . . .

'The position of the switch is known only to myself, and before I open my door I touch it, so that the house, outside and inside, and every recess where an assailant may be lurking, are lit up.

'The figure which one day I fully expect to see crouching and ready to strike will be that of the man who murdered my wife.

'He killed Mrs Wallace with such savagery as he was capable of, and has reason for attempting to remove me before I complete the only mission I have left in life—to place him in the condemned cell I occupied. . . .

'Today report reaches me that his appearance suggests mental disturbance and deterioration.'

Needless to say this 'mission' was as imaginary as all else. And thus he goes on:

'Chess was one of the passions of my life. Liverpool was a great chess-playing centre, and I was well known in the circle. I have no one to play chess with now. But some evenings I get out my board, put the pieces on the squares, and settle down to working out difficult problems.

'A minute or two passes. Then I, who in the past have matched my brains against some of the greatest players in the world,[1] realize that I am not concentrating on the board, though I sit staring at it. Some shadow seems to rise between me and my beloved game.

'I suddenly draw back. I know what it is. Chess is mixed up now with the terrible drama of my life. Even my proficiency in my hobby was used as a weapon against me. . . .

'Can you wonder, then, that when I sit alone in the evenings with my chess-board in front of me, the shadow of the dock, the shadow of the Judge in the black cap—yes, even the shadow of the scaffold itself—rise up before my eyes? I push away the chess-board, as I have already pushed away the microscope.'

At length he could no longer endure his isolation. He obtained the services of an elderly woman named Annie Mason to be his housekeeper. Then, as the last stages of his disease ravaged him, he was removed to Clatterbridge Hospital, where, on 9th February 1933, he made his Will, leaving £100 to Annie Mason, and the residue of his estate to his brother. And on 26th February he died.

At the time of his wife's murder he had, as we know, possessed £152. Two years later probate was granted on a sum of £1196.

His pen had served him well.

---

[1] He was never more than a third-rate player (*see* page 253) in an obscure little club. This gives the clue to all the rest of his pretensions.

Index

A

Adolphus, John, Q.C., 64 and *fn*, 65, 66, 67, 69, 70–4, 84, 85, 87, 93, 100, 102–3, 120
Agate, James, 133, 148, 176, 233, 251, 256
Albert of Saxe-Coburg-Gotha, H.R.H. Prince, 12, 84–5
Alloway, Thomas Henry, 106
Atlay, J. B., 77*fn*, 87*fn*, 121, 125, 126

B

Bailey, Lady Janet, 82–3, 84
Bailey, — (Detective-Sergeant), 211, 246
Baldwin, John (Parish Constable), 28, 29, 30, 33, 40–1, 54, 55, 77–8, 79, 102, 103
Ballantine, William (Serjeant-at-Law), 44 and *fn*, 63, 66, 67, 88, 89–90, 99
Banks, Lydia, 98
Baup, Rev. —, 60, 111, 118
Beattie, —, 167, 170–3, 174, 175, 241–2
Bedford, 5th Duke of, 13 and *fn*
Bedford, 6th Duke of, 13
Bedford, 11th Duke of, 73*fn*
Breslin, — (Police Sergeant), 208, 210

Brock, Alan, 121
Burton, Lady, 122–3
Burton, Sir Richard, 122–3

C

Caird, —, 172, 173–4, 176, 241–2, 250
Carr, Henry, 19, 37, 41, 47, 98
Carver, Rev. —, 106
Clarkson, — (Barrister), 90, 91
Close, Alan, 178, 227–9
Collier, — (Police Sergeant), 82
Cope, W. W., 106, 109, 111, 112, 117
Courvoisier, François Benjamin, 14–128 *passim*, 217, 221
Crewe, Joseph, 165, 166, 177, 184, 187, 188, 189, 190, 250
Cumming, Richard, 86, 87, 95, 97

D

Davis, Thomas, 98
Dawson, G. R., 38
Defoe, Daniel, 28*fn*
Denman, Lord, 125
Dennis, William George, 151
Deyes, —, 172, 177
Draper, Mrs Ruth, 218
Duke, Winifred, 182*fn*, 206*fn*

D3